Global Entertainment Media

Global Entertainment Media

A Critical Introduction

Lee Artz

WILEY Blackwell

This edition first published 2015
© 2015 John Wiley & Sons, Inc

Registered Office
John Wiley & Sons, Ltd, The Atrium, Southern Gate, Chichester, West Sussex, PO19 8SQ, UK

Editorial Offices
350 Main Street, Malden, MA 02148-5020, USA
9600 Garsington Road, Oxford, OX4 2DQ, UK
The Atrium, Southern Gate, Chichester, West Sussex, PO19 8SQ, UK

For details of our global editorial offices, for customer services, and for information about how to apply for permission to reuse the copyright material in this book please see our website at www.wiley.com/wiley-blackwell.

The right of Lee Artz to be identified as the author of this work has been asserted in accordance with the UK Copyright, Designs and Patents Act 1988.

Wiley also publishes its books in a variety of electronic formats. Some content that appears in print may not be available in electronic books.

Designations used by companies to distinguish their products are often claimed as trademarks. All brand names and product names used in this book are trade names, service marks, trademarks or registered trademarks of their respective owners. The publisher is not associated with any product or vendor mentioned in this book.

Limit of Liability/Disclaimer of Warranty: While the publisher and author have used their best efforts in preparing this book, they make no representations or warranties with respect to the accuracy or completeness of the contents of this book and specifically disclaim any implied warranties of merchantability or fitness for a particular purpose. It is sold on the understanding that the publisher is not engaged in rendering professional services and neither the publisher nor the author shall be liable for damages arising herefrom. If professional advice or other expert assistance is required, the services of a competent professional should be sought.

Library of Congress Cataloging-in-Publication data applied for

9781118955444 (paperback)
9781118955437 (hardback)

A catalogue record for this book is available from the British Library.

Cover image: © Danil Melekhin / iStockphoto

Set in 10.5/13pt Minion by SPi Publisher Services, Pondicherry, India

Printed in Singapore by C.O.S. Printers Pte Ltd

1   2015

Contents

Introduction

Entertainment, Television, and Cultural Hegemony

Tell me a story. Make me laugh. Entertain me. From childhood on, humans share stories to inform, educate, and entertain. In every joke and pastime, lessons about social norms, values, and morals are shared. We have laws, but stories express why we have laws and what happens to those who disobey. Entertaining stories from Aesop's fables, fairytales, and the latest Disney animation express and evaluate good and evil.

In the twenty-first century the primary storytellers are global media, and "like stories told around the campfire, they promote and criticize some identities and kinds of social organization and celebrate others. In doing so they reflect the interests of the storyteller" (Machin & Van Leeuwen, 2007, p. 39). The stories circulated most widely are those created by consolidated international media: children's stories in cartoons, telenovelas, game shows, action-adventures, situation comedies, mysteries, anime, factual entertainment, sports, music, movies, and news. All of them are entertainment.

Global entertainment crosses national and cultural boundaries, promoting consumerism in theme and format, adjusting to local cultural norms and affecting the social order in many identifiable ways, some of which will be discussed in this book.

From the earliest media studies to contemporary concerns, media have been understood as central to society but not all have agreed on media's political or cultural effect, nor has there been agreement on the relationships between media and the rest of the social order. This book finds media

Global Entertainment Media: A Critical Introduction, First Edition. Lee Artz.
© 2015 John Wiley & Sons, Inc. Published 2015 by John Wiley & Sons, Inc.

to be part of our larger social order that has recognizable social class divisions. Such an approach challenges the accepted knowledge broadcast by contemporary media and protected by their academic admirers. I follow the Chilean novelist and social critic Ariel Dorfman (1983) in that I do not pretend to infallibility, but "feel it is my duty to profane the secular cathedral and wonder out loud, in the middle of the service that gathers the priests of knowledge, and the faithful to be enlightened" (p. 136) how do the architecture and icons of popular media become so worshipped and to what values and beliefs are we converted?

This is not an American phenomenon. Technological progress and growing competition push media corporations to expand their businesses nationally and internationally. Around the world, in Britain, Germany, India, Japan, Brazil, and everywhere commercial media predominate, media express cultural values, social norms, and even commonsense universal beliefs.

New global structures of production and distribution are altering daily life and cultures. Just as new social relations of production appear in leading capitalist enterprises, the economic operations and cultural contributions of global media have been transformed as well. For the average man and woman, consumption and consumer goods become means for expressing identity and lifestyle, particularly when occupational and economic roles lose their significance as sources of values in the face of popular culture and ubiquitous media presence and power.

Entertainment

With the advent of media deregulation, privatization, and commercialization, nations around the world have opened their media operations to transnational mergers, joint ventures and foreign direct investment (FDI). As part of the neoliberal drive to privatize everything, commercial enterprise dominates media in most countries. Privatized, commercialized media turn to advertising and subscription for profits, looking to reduce production costs at the same time. Not surprisingly, entertainment media is now the most prevalent media form in every country. Following deregulation, entertainment media in Europe took a quantum leap – from 93 to some 1,500 entertainment channels (according to *Screen Digest*, as cited in Thussu, 2009, p. 38). In Africa, francophone transnational media broadcast mostly movies, sports, music, and children's programs (Mytton,

Teer-Tomaselli, & Tudesq, 2005). In India, News Corp's Star TV is indicative of television formats: of its 10 trans-Indian channels, nine are dedicated to entertainment, music, and sport (Thussu, 2005, p. 165). East Asian television, especially Japanese and Taiwanese, is wedded to entertainment, advertising, and "idols" who appear on talk, music, and even fictional series to titillate and stimulate fans and consumers (Karlin, 2012; Galbraith, 2012). Drama, sport, music, games shows, and variety shows comprise the bulk of television broadcasting in Latin America. With the appearance of commercial broadcasting in Russia since the 1990s, entertainment dominates television schedules (Endaltseva, 2011; Vartanova, 2008). "Commercial TV and print media in Turkey promote this culture of entertainment" (Algan, 2003, p. 185). Even accepting the news value of various television magazine shows, the US television schedule is primarily entertainment: dramas, soaps, situation comedies, children's shows, game shows, reality contests, sports, and lifestyle/hobby stations predominate. Global entertainment media reached $2.2 trillion in revenue in 2012, with entertainment media "rapidly embracing new and emerging technologies" and television remaining the primary source of programming for all media platforms (MarketingCharts, 2008). Former Disney CEO Michael Eisner notes that "the entertainment industry is not so much Americanizing the world as planetizing entertainment" (Miller et al., 2008, p. 176).

Entertainment rules television, radio, and mass market periodicals, from sport, fashion, and recreation, to lifestyle, home improvement, and good housekeeping. This is now a global condition. Even factual entertainment as produced by National Geographic, Discovery, and on occasion BBC, retreats from political and historical documentaries encompassing social contexts to make slick presentations concerned with human interest, celebrity, and non-controversial subjects (Mjos, 2009).

One might even classify much of the news as entertainment. It is often difficult to separate "hard" news of political, social, and scientific consequence from entertaining "soft" news about celebrity or human spectacle. In their drive for audiences, network programmers curb investigations about the state of the world and offer up "happy" news and all kinds of entertaining, titillating news about crime, disaster, and danger. Networks and publishers offer circus-like spectacles to attract viewers. The US war on Iraq gets airtime, but appears as entertainment: in brilliant images of explosions, dramatic shots of "terrorist" leaders in dark garb, or melodramatic stories about heroes and their families. STAR News in India has an "obsessive interest in glamour, crime, and celebrity culture. At the heart of this agenda is the popularization of news by making it accessible and entertaining, thus expanding the audience base for advertisers" (Thussu, 2007, p. 599). In Britain, as programmers chase ratings for advertising revenue, the news agenda gives way to an "emphasis on celebrity, crime, and consumer journalism" (Thussu, 2009, p. 34). In other words, news has become infotainment as the logical progression of commercial media's emphasis on consumer entertainment.

On first glance, entertainment may seem to be less political, less pedagogic, than news, but a closer look reveals that all entertainment carries kernels of cultural values, social norms, and political ideology. There is no such thing as "just" entertainment. All stories and images express worldviews, conceptions of humor, beliefs about gender, beauty, success, and right and wrong. Entertainment provides a perfect vehicle for transporting advertising and consumerist ideology. "Entertainment offers the image of something better to escape into, or something we want deeply that our day-to-day lives don't provide" (Dyer, 1992, p. 18).

Entertainment media are part of a larger culture industry, organized and operated according to the same profit motives that inform other industries. Global media entertainment as it is now structured represents the temporary triumph of transnational capitalism, produced and distributed through joint ventures with local and national firms.

Media do not stand apart from society and its capitalist social relations; commercial media reflect and reproduce the social relations and cultural practices necessary for the smooth functioning of the global capitalist system. This book intends to spotlight some of the characteristics and trends of transnational capitalism and the transnational media environment, hoping to overcome the reluctance by many to recognize social class relations as central to understanding global media.

Transnational Media and Democracy

What is sorely missing from much contemporary media studies is an analysis of media as capitalist institutions, institutions with corporate structures, corporate practices, and corporate goals. It's as if Western media scholars have yet to have their rude awakening to the "true nature of the capitalist system" (Jakubowicz, 2007, p. 370).

In the twenty-first century, there is no "our" media. Transnational media corporations (TNMCs) do not belong to or represent the interests of the average citizen of any nation. Media are part of a transnational system of production for profit. Media aid and abet – indeed, they are crucial to – promotion of transnational capitalism and consumerism on a world scale. Advertisers stimulate. They want happy images, quick fixes, non-reflective viewers and readers; advertisers don't want citizens thinking about the world. They want consumers focused on the next best thing for sale. And media want advertisers.

Jan Nederveen Pieterse (2009) imagines that the non-Western world has "turned the tables" on the formerly dominant nations (p. 57). Pieterse's metaphor is useful but misapplied, as are similar contentions about the rise of the Asian tigers or BRIC (Brazil, Russia, India, China) countries and the economic or cultural displacement of the United States or Britain and Europe. No tables have been turned. In fact, the integration of capitalist production across national boundaries may be understood as the production of more tables laden with a capitalist bounty of commodities. However, unlike a community potluck of sharing, these tables are for the display of plenty that can only be bought and sold by a global elite.

Chapters 1 and 2 narrate the development of transnational capitalism and how it has altered the production of commodities for national markets, how social relations among corporate owners cross-national borders, and how the production and distribution of goods and services involve workers, managers, and contractors from around the world in a unified, integrated, but transnationally dispersed process of accumulating wealth for corporate shareholders. Pieterse blames media for "dozing at the wheel" and lacking "civic vigilance" (2009, p. 59). Here Pieterse's evocative metaphor once again is poorly employed: media owned, organized, and directed by transnational capitalists and their managers are at the wheel of information and communication, but they are not dozing. As Chapters 3 and 4 illustrate, media are driving the news, entertainment, and culture down the road of market values, immediate gratification, and consumerism.

Transnational media, owned cooperatively by media firms from multiple nations, actively work for deregulation, privatization, commercialization, and advertising-driven mass entertainment. Transnational media do not want public service broadcasting, political diversity, and least of all democratic civic vigilance. As this book will demonstrate, Pieterse and others perceiving the displacement of dominant nations or dominant media by China, Brazil, India, or localized community media need to look over the table, over the wheel, down the road, and over the horizon. The economic and political drivers of globalization have won allies and partners from every nation and every culture, forming a new, energetic, and politically powerful transnational capitalist class. Even members of the Chinese state bureaucracy have become millionaire capitalists aligned with GM, Ford, Disney, Sony, News Corp, and Bertelsmann.

American and European dominance has not been defeated, it has crystallized outside of any national identity or interest. Even as they continue to jockey for individual advantage, diverse national capitalists have united in transnational mergers, joint ventures, partnerships, and other collaborations. The economic, political, and cultural leadership (including the media) has been reorganized. The promotion of consumerism, the market, and transnational capital is expressed in the diversity of images, stories, and ideas disseminated and repeated through transnational media: images, stories, and ideas that leave little for democratic imagination or application.

Media and Audience

Of all media, television and film have the widest global distribution. Television is ubiquitous; in some developed countries close to 100% of the population has receivers. TV is a center pillar in the Japanese movie industry, financially and organizationally (Davis & Yeh, 2008, p. 70). China has 400 million television sets, the United States 220 million, and Japan 86 million (Media Statistics, 2013). Worldwide more than 1.2 billion households have at least one television (IDATE, 2010).

The television industry organized transnationally is well-positioned to dominate the Internet and mobile content services (ITVE, 2010) with an abundance of entertainment available for mobile distribution expanding the reach and repetition of television programming. Orchestrated fandoms and interactive participation via text "voting" further enhance the integration of television and film content into daily life. Thus, film and television industries remain primary producers of entertainment worldwide, which gives the owners of movie studios and television networks tremendous power as purveyors of media representations of our world and our lives.

Television and movies circulate images and stories from which we learn of society's preferred values, norms, and behaviors. Television and film narratives flood everyday life, saturating culture with spectacles of fantasy. We become more spectator than participant. Our lives are filled with gratifying texts, videos, and images. Such pervasive communication provides the symbolic material for how we actively construct our own lives and the world in which we live. Television and blockbuster movies pleasantly distract us from more serious, more consequential issues like the environment, mass unemployment, unhealthy products and lifestyles. Much media entertainment further dehumanizes with insult comedy, violent drama, and cage fighting sports, despoiling even the modest pleasures available.

In the last few decades, corporate media in every country have developed more global strategies, turning to transnational arrangements. Transnational capitalist media lead through FDI, joint ventures, and mergers as they search for cultural diversity for their content. Importantly, transnational entertainment media also advance advertising and consumerism, practices crucial to transnational capitalism. As media become transnationalized, a "vast entertainment-driven economy has formed for the purpose of expanding audiences and maximizing profits" (Galbraith & Karlin, 2012, p. 12). Given the prominence of media entertainment within and across nations, entertainment media function as the primary means for extending "the reach of the prevailing political terrain, bringing into one orbit zones of society that seldom encountered the same ideas simultaneously" (Rajagopal, 2001, p. 151).

The chronic and urgent economic question facing commercial media is how to capture audiences for their programs and how to deliver audiences to advertisers. Past practices relied on direct export of the product (e.g., Hollywood and network offerings dubbed into the language of the "foreign" audiences with the little regard for cultural variations). The global dissemination of content – mistakenly called "cultural imperialism" – nurtures a homogenous middle class culture of pop music, fast food, action movies, animated features, and other McDonaldized, Disneyfied, Hollywood fare that appear to be part of local cultures.

Diversity without Democracy

Claims about the "democratization of content" by privatized media reduce democracy to consumer choice and practices that conveniently lead to "populations being better integrated into the global market" (Srebreny, 2009, p. 51). Diversity in genres does nothing to further democratic decision-making and the equitable sharing of scientific and technological advances. Afghanistan now has 15 television channels – each warlord has his own – while the "diversity" of channels advances democracy not one bit.

Content diversity tailored with local icons, scenes, language, and actors is part of the global strategy of transnational media, a strategy interfering with an authentic plurality of voices having open, non-commercial, democratic access to the media. Diversity in entertainment content helps transnational entertainment media reach larger and more diverse audiences, provides audiences to advertisers, and expands the reach of consumerism with homogenized themes and formats filled with cultural variety.

For years, *Who Wants to Be a Millionaire?* was a top show from Latin America to Japan, from Europe to India, because the hosts, the questions, the languages were all repurposed for diverse national and cultural audiences. The show, of course, unabashedly promotes individual competition, the desirability of personal wealth, and consumerism – not cooperation, democratic access to resources, or production for human needs.

The dominant economic forces in the world have temporarily succeeded in becoming the dominant cultural and social forces in society, reorganizing work and daily life, while advancing market relations through entertainment and consumerism. Transnational capital leads. Unfortunately, these clear class interests have been neglected in most contemporary analyses. This book aims to apply the profound findings of international political economy to the developing transnational media institutions and their practices. This book reviews the changing social relations that organize the world, summarizes the processes of global capitalist leadership, including the role of entertainment media in promoting consumerism and market values, and identifies the links between transnational capitalism and its transnational media.

To aid in this journey, the concept of cultural hegemony resting on political economy will be advanced in Chapter 5 as an aid for understanding the appeal of transnational media content. Cultural hegemony expresses the consent that citizens give to the cultural and political leadership of transnational capitalism because we perceive some benefit and no alternative.

Hegemony and Consent

For now, commercial media practices and values prosper because TNMC leadership and investment are welcomed, even invited. Indeed, TNMC global predominance is not based on control or coerced domination, but hegemony – their social and cultural leadership has widespread international consent.

Hegemony occurs when participants in a social relationship *consent* to the policies and leadership of a dominant group. Consent is assured only to the extent that the leadership sufficiently meets the needs of allied and subordinate groups (Gramsci, 1971; Artz & Murphy, 2000). For the cultural hegemony of transnational media corporations, leadership and power stems from its collaborative effectiveness – local and national capitalist media owners, protected and bolstered by their own governments, solicit and join transnational media partnerships. The corporate consent demonstrated in cooperative media productions parallels the audience consent given to the practices of consumerism. Local TNMC partners willingly contribute culturally familiar local representations for TNMC entertainment content. Whatever the specific local variant or hybrid, the dominance of the hegemonic commercial model and values are apparent: atomized, individualized, and consumerist entertainment become the new global norm.

While cultural dominance cannot be denied (too many examples of forced takeovers and media monopoly belie as much), *predominance* is more accurate as leading global media have found hegemonic attraction and persuasion more cost-efficient and politically effective. Throughout the world, deregulated, privatized media have accompanied the parallel political reform of governments, reflecting the intimate connections between civil society and the state. Of course, liberalization of media does not guarantee an open, democratic society; Guatemala, El Salvador, and Qatar have private media but few civil liberties. In fact, many governments continue to mete out punishment and repression, but they do so with more legitimacy when they have the cover of non-unionized, temporary labor, two-candidate demonstration elections, and privatized media. In most cases, transnational and local media defend the newly reformed states. In all cases, privatized media legalized by the newly reformed states promote *complementary* cultural forms (entertainment) and practices (individualism, consumerism) that advance and reinforce global market relations at the expense of public interest.

Occasionally, resistance by sections of the working class and other politically disenfranchised groups spill over into public discourse and media coverage, opening the door to some limited working class and indigenous participation, as in Mexico following Chiapas, or in Ecuador, Greece, Spain, and Egypt over the last few years. Yet, no matter how deep the social crisis, private media seldom balk from staunch support of their national capitalist class (Fox, 1988). Corporate media may vary in size, stature, temperament, and format, but never in allegiance to their class.

Consent to capitalism is established through social relations organizing work and through images and narratives that explain those relations in an entertaining fashion. And, entertainment dominates media content everywhere. Public access to news, policy, and discussions about local, national, and world issues "cede their place to the pleasure taken in electronic media spectacles where narration or the simple accumulation of anecdotes prevails over reasoned solutions to problems" (García Canclini, 1993, p. 24). News Corp, Disney, Bertelsmann, Sony, Ghibli, Reliance, and other transnational media firms contribute to a global entertainment universe, leading most other smaller media along the same path of spectacle, infotainment, and a diversity of mass entertainment, driving out democratic public media access and even public service media.

Cultural hegemony

Given the prevalence of entertainment media, the expression of how things are and how things ought to be is dominated by stories written by corporate media producers from Disney and Bertlesmann to Canal + and Viacom with images and messages that "create and reinforce their audiences' attachments to the way things are" (Schiller, 1976, p. 30). These stories and themes are not a one-time deal: they appear in show after show, station after station, and mass market magazine after newspaper lifestyle section.

Capitalist cultural hegemony indicates broad consent and participation in the transnational free market project pressuring labor for more work and lower pay while providing reinforcing narratives and ideologies in media content. The most effective content includes challenges and creative adaptations that appeal to diverse cultures while demonstrating a preference for existing capitalist social relations. Allegiance to this hegemonic class perspective is apparent in transnational media's commitment to a commercialized global culture, a culture that has several remarkable characteristics (revised from Artz, 2003):

1. Consolidated control tightens. Ownership of the production and distribution of the global culture has geographically "de-centered" with more local and national sites of production, while consolidation continues, supported by regional co-aspirants and domestic media subcontractors. Transnationally, about 10 companies dominate, but hundreds provide essential complementary support.

2. Entertainment formats predominate. From Ghana to Brazil to Singapore and the West, broadcasting genres, music, and movies are entertainment. Public media access, investigative journalism, and political documentaries have declined.
3. Consumerism rules. Marked by individualism, immediate gratification, and unfettered acquisitiveness, consumerism is expressed in hierarchical fictional and nonfictional narratives in privatized mass communication.
4. Cultural hybrids flourish. Variations draw from rich and diverse traditions, as in Brazilian telenovelas and rap, Nigerian juju videos, and Islamic and green pop in Turkey. Yet, when controlled and represented by corporate media, most advance and none challenge the basic individualist, consumerist tenets of the capitalist market.
5. Media variety promotes cultural homogeneity. Hybrid forms provide diversity in local content for uniform global themes apropos of global capitalism. The global culture of transnational capitalist media features two complementary yet distinct representations: hybrid content packaged in standardized forms and hegemonic themes.

Localizing the Global

Chapter 6 considers cultural hybridity and other perspectives, addressing how local and national media often appear to construct alternatives to global capitalism and consumerism. Hybridity in particular is a characteristic of all communication, including media entertainment from any source. Hybridity reflects the creative contributions and resistances to intercultural exchanges by domestic media producers, cultural artists, and active audiences, either as accommodating or resisting responses. Yet, most hybrid content reflects an intercultural homogeneity wrapped within a capitalist consumerist model. The international success of *Ugly Betty*, MTV, network game shows, pop music, and other homogeneous cultural products indicates that subordinate, yet aspiring, classes around the world find pleasure, comfort, and assurance in the cultural similarity of consumption in all countries. TNMC television produce localized entertainment formats like quiz shows, telenovelas, and competitive reality TV as cost-efficient commercial strategies for maximizing audiences (Keane, Fung, & Moran, 2007). In signing on to the cultural hegemony of transnational capital, local media collaborate with TNMCs to creatively hybridize commodified cultural products and models to fit local cultural or political sensibilities. "Globalized" cultural practices represent local interests and meanings, occasionally allowing subversion of global media messages with more politically conscious interpretations and uses (Kraidy, 1999, 2002; Robertson, 1992) but just as frequently, power remains intact except for the local particulars. If the local market is still a commercial enterprise, not a community hall, it provides no real alternative to the supermarket chain. At any rate, transnational media have adjusted quickly, realizing that hybrid alterations are largely non-threatening, potentially very profitable, and politically preferable as evidence of dominant media's cultural diversity and sensitivity. In addition to the locally generated hybrid culture, TNMCs now produce their own commodified hybrids gleaned from cultures around the world. Homogeneous or hybrid, the structure of power remains.

Chapter 6 reminds us that the consumption of media commodities is a social practice, open to interpretations and use beyond the intent of the producer. The cultural meaning and consequence of any text have as much to do with the social and political context of reception as they do with the sender–receiver dynamic. In Managua, Nicaragua, Brazilian soap operas are viewed by entire neighborhoods at the homes of those few with televisions, permitting much more democratic communication and meaning construction than that done by the single viewer passively atomized in a North living room. Still, interpretations by readers and viewers are neither autonomous nor necessarily superior to the meanings proposed by writers and producers. Without access to mass communication resources, audiences everywhere are handicapped if their constructions of meanings remain creative personal reactions to the mass productions of others, primarily the corporate few.

What is progressive about cordoning off human subjects as active receivers who are relegated to reconstructing meanings produced by others? Why not have a society and media that allow citizens to produce their own texts for mass distribution? The "reader-as-producer" perspective expresses little concern regarding globalization or power, despite the fact that most intercultural communication and dialogue are filters – simultaneously pasteurizing cultural activity and bolstering capitalist media hegemony. Constraining audiences as receivers retards the communication process. There is no democracy if the majority cannot speak in their own terms with full access to media production and dissemination.

Entertainment media present images and narratives that *represent* diverse voices as a substitute for actual communication by the diverse majority speaking in its own voice. In other words, TNMC cultural hegemony thrives because (in very practical terms) it not only presents the most popular versions of commercial culture – the representative epitome of success – it also appears to be the best promoter of indigenous culture and cultural diversity.

Chapter 7 looks at action movies that share a thematic and ideological consistency across cultures – movies that employ challenges to authority and social norms only to reinvigorate the status quo before the final credits roll on screen.

In addition to action movies, other entertainment content drawn from independent, indigenous, or hybrid mixes are widely distributed by corporate media. However, in hegemonic terms, any music, movie, art, political discourse, or social commentary that passes through corporate media filters must meet the prerequisites of mass entertainment and profit, thereby weakening and undermining any political edge, class independence, or democratic potential. For now, transnational capitalist media and their cultural leadership mute and lead the working class and other diverse subordinate groups because mass culture provides favorable and rewarding representations and images. From *Big Bang Theory* and *American Idol* in the United States, to *Rebelde* in Mexico and the popular radio show *Our New Home* on Afghan radio, life is good!

Thanks to TNMCs, we can laugh, work, play, and shop in our own little worlds without regard, concern, or even awareness of any unpleasantness. Individually consumed mass pleasure makes for a solid consumerist hegemony. Indeed, a central tenet of capitalist media hegemony worldwide is to promote an interclass culture of pleasure based on continuous consumption. In image and narrative, this interclass culture is strictly affluent middle class in outlook: professional, managerial, or entrepreneurial and aspiring to move closer to the corporate center. Yet, to the extent that the global media set agendas and popularize models of entertainment, mass culture closes down public discourse.

Only when cultural practices reject commercialization will public discourse open up possibilities for a truly new world order. Chapter 8 highlights developments in democratic media access in Venezuela as part of its Bolivarian revolution.

Diversity with Democracy

As noted, cultural diversity per se is not the issue. TNMCs will happily emphasize the cross-cultural character of the elite or moderate intercultural contributions that might jilt the blander middle class palette into hybrid cross-overs (e.g., African music via Paul Simon, de-Latinizing Ricky Martin, Korean K-pop hybrids). More importantly, advertising and commercialized entertainment "undermines people's will to understand" their own social conditions and individual potential, while hegemonic middle class lifestyles are emulated and even internalized (Mattelart & Mattelart, 1992, p. 153). Furthermore, a media focus on celebrity, spectacle, and dancing cats undercuts attention to history and the future, while a focus on individual consumption and desire denies collective, democratic, and more creative possibilities for humanity.

The problem with the TNMC culture industry is not only in the stories they tell of hyper individualism, but also in how they occupy the collective consciousness with celebrity, trivia, and self-aggrandizement. Pleasure is marketed as the goal, but it is always just beyond our reach, requiring another consumer purchase, then another. Of course, pleasure is not the same as happiness, satisfaction, or human fulfillment.

This book offers a "conjunctural" analysis of the historical moment that is marked by the maturation of transnational capitalism and its social relations. Claims, illustrations, evidence, and arguments presented here speak to conditions we collectively face around the world. This offering is not intended to be a final statement on the way forward, but does make an appeal for a clearer materialist analysis and resolute action based on what we know.

What we do know and what the pages of this book confirm is that the spread of transnational media based on market imperatives debases labor, feeds individual desire, legitimizes mass consumption, mass production, and privatization – obstructing humanity's fulfillment in the process.

Hybrid variations that do not challenge atomized pleasure, mass hedonism, or the commercial model may surely represent subordinate classes and cultures, but they do so as unwitting servants for capitalist cultural hegemony. For instance, by independently producing his own hybrid blend of Ghanian "highlife" music with American pop and reggae, Kojo Antwi may have revived his country's classic sound, but he cannot stem the multinational "flooding of Sub-Saharan Africa with flimsy pop," especially after impresario Quincy Jones takes over Antwi's productions, softening them for the world music market (Zachary, 2001). In other words, the economic goals of transnational media ultimately conflict with the social and cultural needs of communities, nations, and working classes worldwide. As local media solicit TNMCs and become commercialized, they are subjected to the laws of market more than the needs of the community. Privatized media subvert the local even if they remain local because they emulate the commercial global media and the model they value.

Consumerism (local or global) is created, planned, and organized according to a value system obeisant to corporate goals. Likewise, media and cultural practices adhering to privatization and commercialization are created, planned, and organized for similar corporate ends. Global capitalism, in other words, creates a transnational consumer market and cultivates a consumerist ideology.

TNMCs measure value in terms of sales of audiences to advertisers and sales of media merchandise to audiences. Yet, an increase in the quantity of goods does not systematically improve the well-being of humanity. Not surprisingly, consumerism and advertising appear as the legitimate forbearers of capitalist-defined democratic freedom: the free flow of information and free consumer choice impersonate the ultimate "free" society. Global capitalism will not willingly advance either democratic practices or democratic cultural exchanges. To paraphrase the abolitionist Frederick Douglas, capitalist globalization concedes nothing without demand. This book argues that we would be better off to break with the atomized consumer model of global entertainment media and turn to more democratic media with citizen creativity and participation whose goal is improving the quality and joy of human life.

References

Algan, E. (2003). Privatization of radio and media hegemony in Turkey. In L. Artz & Y Kamalipour (Eds.), *The globalization of corporate media hegemony* (pp. 169–192). Albany, NY: New York University Press.

Artz, L. (2003). Globalization, media hegemony, and social class. In L. Artz & Y. Kamalipour (Eds.), *The globalization of corporate media hegemony* (pp. 3–33). Albany, NY: State University of New York Press.

Artz, L., & Murphy, B. O. (2000). *Cultural hegemony in the United States.* Thousand Oaks, CA: Sage.

Davis, D. W., & Yeh, E. Y. (2008). *East Asian screen industries.* London: British Film Institute.

Dorfman, A. (1983). *The empire's old clothes: What the Lone Ranger, Babar, and other innocent heroes do to our minds.* New York: Pantheon.

Dyer, R. (1992). *Only entertainment.* New York: Routledge.

Endaltseva, A. (2011, November). Russian popular television in the 21st century. Paper presented at National Communication Association Convention. San Francisco, CA.

Fox, E. (1988). *Media and politics in Latin America: The struggle for democracy. Communication and human values.* Beverly Hills, CA: Sage.

Galbraith, P. W. (2012). Idols: The image of desire in Japanese consumer capitalism. In P. W. Galbraith & J. G. Karlin (Eds.), *Idols and celebrity in Japanese media culture* (pp. 185–206). New York: Palgrave Macmillan.

Galbraith, P. W., & Karlin, J. G. (2012). Introduction: The mirror of idols and celebrity. In P. W. Galbraith & J. G. Karling (Eds.), *Idols and celebrity in Japanese media culture* (pp. 1–32). New York: Palgrave Macmillan.

García Canclini, N. (1993). *Transforming modernity: Popular culture in Mexico.* Austin: University of Texas Press.

Gramsci, A. (1971). *Selections from the prison notebooks.* Q. Hoare & G. N. Smith, Trans. New York: International Publishers.

IDATE. (2010). *TV 2010: Markets & trends, facts & figures.* IDATE: Cedex, France. Retrievedfromhttp://www.international-television.org/tv_market_data/world-tv-market-2010.html

ITVE. (2010). TV market data: World television market (2008–2013). International Television Expert Group. Retrieved June 19, 2013, from http://www.international-television.org/tv_market_data/world-tv-market-2010.html

Jakubowicz, K. (2007). *Rude awakening: Social and media change in Central and Eastern Europe.* Cresskill, NJ: Hampton Press.

Karlin, J. G. (2012). Through a looking glass darkly: Television advertising, idols, and the making of fan audiences. In P. W. Galbraith & J. G. Karlin (Eds.), *Idols and celebrity in Japanese media culture* (pp. 72–93). New York: Palgrave Macmillan.

Keane, M., Fung, A. Y. H., & Moran, A. (2007). *New television, globalization, and the East Asian cultural imagination.* Hong Kong: Hong Kong University Press.

Kraidy, M. M. (1999). The global, the local, the hybrid: A native ethnography of globalization. *Critical Studies in Mass Communication,* 16, 456–476.

Kraidy, M. M. (2002). Hybridity in cultural globalization. *Communication Theory,* *12*(3), 316–339.

Machin, D., & Van Leeuwen, T. (2007). *Global media discourse: A critical introduction.* New York: Routledge.

MarketingCharts. (2008, June 20). Global entertainment & media to reach $2.2T in 2012, driven by digital, mobile. *Marketing Charts.* Retrieved from http://www.marketingcharts.com/television/global-entertainment-media-to-reach-22t-in-2012-driven-by-digital-mobile-5012/

Mattelart, A., & Mattelart, M. (1992). *Rethinking media theory: Signposts and new directions.* J. A. Cohen, Trans. Minneapolis: University of Minnesota Press.

Media Statistics. (2013). Televisions (most recent) by country. *Nationmaster.com.* Retrieved from http://www.nationmaster.com/graph/med_tel-media-televisions

Miller, T., Govil, N., McMurria, J., Wang, T., & Maxwell, R. (2008). *Global Hollywood 2.* 2nd edn. London: British Film Institute.

Mjos, O. J. (2009). *Media globalization and the Discovery Channel networks.* New York: Taylor & Francis.

Mytton, G., Teer-Tomaselli, R., & Tudesq, A. (2005). Transnational television in sub-Saharan Africa. In J. Chalaby (Ed.), *Transnational television worldwide: Towards a new media order* (pp. 96–127). London: I.B. Tauris.

Pieterse, J. N. (2009). Representing the rise of the rest as threat: Media and global divides. *Nordicom Review, 30,* 57–72.

Rajagopal, A. (2001). *Politics after television: Hindu nationalism and the reshaping of the public in India.* Cambridge, UK: Cambridge University Press.

Robertson, R. (1992). *Globalization: Social theory and global culture.* Thousand Oaks, CA: Sage.

Schiller, H. (1976). *Communication and cultural domination.* White Plains, NY: International Arts and Sciences Press.

Srebreny, A. (2009). Maps and mandalas, division and multiplication: Media and global divides. *Nordicom Review, 30,* 39–56.

Thussu, D. K. (2005). The transnationalization of television: The Indian experience. In J. Chalaby (Ed.), *Transnational television worldwide: Towards a new media order* (pp. 156–172). London: I.B. Tauris.

Thussu, D. K. (2007). The 'Murdochization' of news? The case of Star TV in India. *Media, Culture & Society, 29*(4), 593–611.

Thussu, D. (2009). *News as entertainment: The rise of global infotainment.* Thousand Oaks, CA: Sage.

Vartanova, E. (2008). Russian media: Market and technology as driving forces of change. In E. Vartanova, H. Nieminen, & M. Salminen (Eds.), *Russian media 2007: Convergence and competition* (pp. 20–31). Helsinki: Communication Research Center, University of Helsinki. Retrieved from http://www.hssaatio.fi/images/stories/tiedostot/RUSSIAN%20MEDIA%202008%20-%20EXTRACTS%2020%20NOVEMBER%202008.pdf

Zachary, G. P. (2001, April 16). Loving the highlife. *In These Times,* pp. 30–32.

Further Reading

Artz, L. (Ed.) (2007a). *The media globe: Trends in international mass media.* Lanham, MD: Rowman & Littlefield.

Thussu, D. K. (2006). *International communication: Continuity and change.* 2nd ed. London: Arnold.

1

Twenty-First Century Capitalism and Transnational Relations

In a world of entertainment media filled with consumer advertising, who does not know about iPhones, Coca-Cola, Budweiser, or the World of Warcraft and Guitar Hero? At the front end of the twenty-first century, media broadcasting and wireless messages relentlessly promote these and other must-have consumer goods. Yet, how many happy consumers know that Apple uses poisonous chemicals in its Chinese manufacturing plants (Walters, 2012)? Know that Coke depletes ground water aquifers in Rajasthan, India, threatening agriculture and the lives of thousands of farmers (Indian farmers, 2008)? Which coffee drinker is aware that a German equity firm bought Caribou Coffee to close down 80 stores in the Midwest? Do beer drinkers taste the added water in their Budweiser, put there as part of a profit strategy by the Brazilian CEO of the company's Dutch owners? Do gamers linked on-line in the World of Warcraft or Call of Duty find irony in a French firm producing and marketing those military games even as French citizens protest real military action in the Mideast? Most likely, few consumers are aware of the investment, production, and marketing campaigns of the corporations responsible for the personal goods and services of daily life.

Even fewer know that making possible the slick advertisements and the immediate gratification of these and similar consumer products are thousands of workers around the world, some making as little as 21 cents an hour. Women and children work 12 hour days in firetraps for Disney, Sears, WalMart, and Sean Combs in Bangladesh (Hart, 2012). Likewise, workers for Apple's iPhone and iPad Chinese supplier are

Global Entertainment Media: A Critical Introduction, First Edition. Lee Artz.
© 2015 John Wiley & Sons, Inc. Published 2015 by John Wiley & Sons, Inc.

forced to work in unsafe factories under inhumane conditions (Qiang, 2013). While major media tout competitive free market globalization as the way to improve the quality of life for all, major transnational corporations (TNCs) pursue an eternal fight for greater profits as global poverty and inequality worsen (Chossudovsky, 1997). Worldwide viewers have seen *Yo soy Betty, la fea* (*Ugly Betty*), the telenovela by Fernando Gaitan, that has been translated into 13 languages and broadcast in 74 countries (Kraul, 2006). Few know that Colombian media success is partly driven by the low-cost, non-union labor of creators, producers, and technicians working under repressive anti-labor laws. We watch. We enjoy. We buy.

Knowledge of and attraction to consumer goods result from global entertainment media that extol the "myth of consumer agency to convince consumers that they are empowered by what they consume" (Galbraith & Karlin, 2012, p. 25). These are the same transnational media corporations (TNMCs) that do not inform us about the conditions of production or the social and environmental consequences of our consumerist lifestyles. Entertainment for profit, the norm for all capitalist media, does not encourage news and information for the common good. Advertising-driven entertainment wed to codes and conventions of mundane formats does not even meet elementary levels of artistic creativity. This is not a question of high or low culture, but a recognition of the structural constraints on access to cultural production and creativity by all. In the interests of democracy and an informed global citizenry that deserves access to the creative use of media, this book investigates how entertainment media contribute to the globalization of capitalism and the creation of a global consumer culture.

The world is undergoing dramatic changes in the organization of production, trade, communication, and culture. Because these changes seem to be occurring everywhere, globalization has become the catchword to describe various dimensions of a dynamic, complex process. In popular and academic literature, globalization has been used to explain "a process, a condition, a system, a force, and an age" (Steger, 2005, p. 7). In fact, enough has been written about globalization to fill a small library (see Ritzer, 2009). This book will not attempt to review or unearth the lineages or contours of the ongoing conversations on globalization. However, the many competing and sometimes contradictory versions of what globalization involves should not obscure its existence or its consequence.

Capitalism and Social Class

Scholars in International Political Economy and world systems theory have identified and documented the development of transnational corporations (TNCs) led by an emerging transnational capitalist class (TNCC) (van der Pijl, 1998; Sklair, 2001; Robinson, 2004; Carroll et al., 2010). To make sense of these discoveries and put them into meaningful context for understanding global entertainment media, which also is an industry mass producing standardized cultural goods (Horkheimer & Adorno, 2007), this chapter reflects on capitalism, social class, and class formation. Entertainment media are integral to almost all social, cultural, and political activities of society (Golding & Murdock, 1991, pp. 17–22; Artz, 2006, pp. 14–23).

Capitalism is a social system in which resources and the means of production are privately owned. Capitalism, as a social system based on the creation of private profit from production by wage labor, requires the constant expansion of production and consumption. Capitalism's ceaseless drive for profits leads to a never-ending search for resources and markets. In the late nineteenth century, many advanced industries, having reached the limits of expansion within their own national boundaries, turned to other regions for resources and markets. Competition and conflict led to two world wars among emerging imperialist powers. The industrial expansion of capitalism following WWII was complemented by a renewed search for more resources and markets in the developing world. Still, capitalism has not escaped the recurring contradiction of overproduction – more goods and services are produced than the working and middle classes can purchase, even with extended credit. Consequently, capitalists continue their quest for more consumer markets, even as they continue the onslaught on wages and social welfare. Since the 1970s, leading sections of the capitalist class found the international integration of national production to be appealing and ultimately more profitable: outsourcing, off-shore production, subcontracting, and decentralization of production for local markets brought increased profits by decreasing labor and transportation costs. In the United States, employment declined, job security and wages went down, while work hours increased and production became more regimented. This new global system of production and distribution has led to new social relations and a global capitalist class.

Production and Class Formations

All societies have used natural resources like wood, metal, water, and agricultural products from nature and developed by humans, but as long as the raw materials remain in the ground or standing in the forest, as long as the fruits and vegetables remain on the trees or vines or in the ground, they are useless. It takes human labor to transform natural resources into usable goods (a fact obscured by advertising and the consumer culture, from Nike and Budweiser to Honda, Disney, and McDonald's). A variety of techniques and practices to sustain human life have been used over the thousands of years of our existence. In expropriating nature and the production of goods and services, men and women have entered into social relations reflecting the organization of productive activities. All productive practices include and reproduce particular social relations – practices and relations, even when contradictory, are organically interconnected. Societies have arisen through this combination of production and social relations in a multitude of ways, from primitive communism, feudalism, chattel slavery, capitalism, colonialism, and socialism to name the more well-known. In the twenty-first century, transnational corporations have instituted new productive activities from joint venture investment relations to integrated decentralized production chains and standardized distribution methods. Transnational corporations comprise new social class formations (integrating capital classes across national borders) and new global social relations (the de-industrialization of developed countries and the rapid industrialization and consumerization of developing nations), including the remarkable transformation of social classes – peasant and farmers have become repositioned as agricultural and industrial workers at the rate of 50 million per year (Kalb, 2011, p. 2), although many will become casual or unemployed workers. In 2012, as corporate media rhapsodized about the economic recovery, more than 200 million were out of work.

Capitalism is a social system in which resources and the means of production are privately owned and operated for individual profit, not necessarily for social use or the common good. Capitalism requires labor power to obtain the natural resources and put the machinery in motion for production. Wageworkers are paid for their labor time and skill, but not the total value of their work. The commodities produced are sold on the market, but workers are paid less than the value of what they produce. Capitalist profits come from this sleight of hand. Capitalists keep the difference between the value of the commodity and the price of labor, including the labor necessary for manufacturing machines and transporting materials. The value of labor appears in Wall Street business reports as labor productivity – expressed as the value produced by one hour of work. After factoring in the costs of material, machinery, and transportation – all costs dependent on labor, as well – the difference between the hourly wage and labor productivity is the hourly profit appropriated by the corporate owners. Workers are paid for their labor time and skill, but not their productivity. This understanding makes abundantly clear why corporations would strategically become transnational: by moving production to low-wage countries, the value of the commodities remains about the same in the international market, but the cost of labor is significantly lower, providing increased profits on all goods sold (International Labor Organization, 2013; Bureau of Labor Statistics, 2012).

Transnational corporate relations are necessary if firms hope to maximize local economic, political, and cultural benefits. Thus, international and multinational corporations "merge" with national or other multinational firms, increasing access to local labor and markets, and usually defeating national competitors in the process. Machinery, technology, and skill embodied in machines and technology, through science, invention, and innovation improve the efficient use of labor power. National firms often willingly integrate into transnational firms to have access to capital and the latest technology and technique – or face failure given superior capitalist operations. Modern capitalism organizes the immense productive capacity of international wage labor with the latest technology and machinery available. In striving for increased labor productivity, businesses now even use technology to monitor employee behavior, enforcing a work regime of stricter productivity (Semuels, 2013). Not technology for democracy. Technology to improve profit. Technology to extract more from labor.

The social relations of production of capitalism are not as advanced, progressive, or socially egalitarian as the productive capacity and the means of production would allow. Production is highly socialized: the labor process is collectively organized with an extensive division of labor, increasingly on a global scale. For the most part, individuals do not sew their own clothing, grow their own food, or build their own furniture. Instead, to meet the needs and desires of society, clothes, cereal, sofas, music, and most other socially useful goods are mass produced by tens of thousands of working people – albeit contained in privately owned enterprises. Individuals with many different skills perform many different tasks: discovery, design, extraction, transport, manual labor, skilled machining, assembly, packaging, quality control inspection, and machinery maintenance. This is a social process. Producers are "not simply individual workers, side-by-side, in a given enterprise," but workers who "have been made into a real 'collective' worker by the division and organization of labor" (Jalée, 1977, p. 12) and by the production of commodities to be sold for profit. Commodities are produced for exchange, for profit; their use or social need is incidental although complex social interactions are needed to produce even the most incidental commodity.

In the globalized capitalist system component operations occur in multiple sites of production, such that even the smallest item destined for mass consumption requires a highly socialized, coordinated collective effort. A typical cell phone, for example, is manufactured from diverse natural resources and synthetic materials, including oil, metal, plastic, silicone, quartz, copper, gold, coltan, and other materials – each having complex extractive, refining, manufacturing, and development processes, as well as a number of levels of design, development, and transportation. The little 2"×4" media device represents the combined creative and productive efforts of millions.

The Contradictions of Capitalist Social Relations

In contrast to the highly socialized and collective activity of production, neither the actual producers of goods nor citizens as a whole direct or decide the goals and practices of production. Instead the means of production – from raw materials to machinery and technology, from factories to ships and railroads, from oil and oil rigs to tankers – are privately owned, operated, and managed for individual private profit. Tens of thousands of workers participate in the actual transformation of nature and production of material goods, but the decisions on when and how to use those resources, the costs (including environmental and human consequences), and profits resulting from the collective human effort are all siphoned off by a very few. In other words, production is socialized, but decisions and profits are privatized under corporate control. As capitalism becomes increasingly transnational, the capitalist class improves its coordination and communication, while initially the growing transnational working class remains divided geographically, linguistically, culturally, and politically. Consequently, the benefits from the collective knowledge and efforts of humanity are even more unevenly distributed among social groups and individuals – even in advanced capitalist countries. The income gap in the United States is the highest since the Great Depression. According to a 2013 Associated Press survey, "four out of five U.S. adults struggle with jobless-ness, near-poverty or reliance on welfare" (Yen, 2013). As pensions are reduced and other social services slashed, shoplifting by senior citizens in Japan has doubled since 2002 (Nohara & Sharp, 2013). Yet, the world's top 240 billionaires have four times enough wealth to end global poverty for all of humanity (Oxfam, 2013). There's a concept for a children's story about morals! Two hundred hoard wealth, while millions have no food. As transnational activity gathers steam, poverty and inequality continue to set new historic proportions.

The combination of advanced productive forces and private ownership of the means of production contributes to social relations that require millions of workers and managers, who own no productive resources beyond their own labor, to sell their labor power to capitalist owners in order to live. On one side, with some 90% of the world's population, we have workers (including laborers, machine operators, technicians, engineers, clerks, and more) without whom no production would be possible, strug-gling to maximize their wages and salaries, often by working more hours or more jobs. On the other side, there are capitalists – in Occupied Wall Street terms, "the 1%" who own the means of production – seeking maximum profits from their machinery and property by increasing the productivity of the labor power they employ, either by lowering wages or increasing efficient production practices. These contradictory relations are not relations between individuals per se, but are social relations between classes of individuals linked to each other by an insurmountable contradiction between private ownership of the means of production and the highly collective, social nature of production.

These two disparate social classes appear as separate groups defined by their relation to the means of production. The capitalist class owns the means of production but does not use the machinery or technologies. The working class does not own the means of production, but does all the work. Labor gives material expression to production by physically using tools, machinery, and mental and manual labor on raw materials and technology. In terms of production, the working class owns only its labor power, which must be sold to the capitalist for a wage, whereas the capitalist depends on the worker to create goods at a wage below its value, so goods may be sold for profit. Other classes can be identified according to their relationship to the means of production. Middle class managers are excluded from ownership of the means of production and as administrators are generally excluded from actually using the means of production; instead their social position is one of organizing the production process, including directing workers, solely to maximize the profits for the capitalists. In return, managers receive salaries (drawn from the profits generated by labor productivity).

These broad categories are crude outlines. More specific class groupings can be identified in each larger social structure (Wright, 1985). There are obviously multiple and complex differences within and between classes and sections of classes and in different conjunctural moments in different capitalist countries. Nonetheless, defining social class according to its relation to the means of production and its position in the productive process provides an analytical lens for understanding the character and significance of transnational capitalism and global entertainment media and helps make sense of contemporary economic, social, political, and cultural conditions.

Let's be as radical as reality: capitalism causes hunger. Although there are currently 1 billion hungry people in the world, there has long been enough global food production to feed everyone (Sadik, 1991). There are enough resources to feed everyone in the world, but shareholders refuse: corporate profits would dramatically shrink. Shareholder rights trump human rights. The technology for solar, wind, and geothermal power and increased public transportation are readily available, but corporate profits from fossil fuel production would decline. The structures of modern capitalism, including its state formation, preclude many rational, democratic decisions and practices. Of course, structurally situated classes do not completely explain or predict all social relations or social upheavals. Structures don't act; people do.

Transnational production also brings together a powerful, consolidated transnational capitalist class and a numerically immense, but (for now) politically disoriented, transnational working class. By 2018, developed countries' production will account for less than half of the world's production (Chance, 2013). Transnational production structurally undermines the economic power of the working class in the developed world – deindustrialization reduces the economic weight and political power of the working class in the United States and Europe. Cross-border production and control over resources permits the transnational capitalist classes to short-circuit working class activity, as labor everywhere is subjected to competitive "best practices," anti-labor laws, and privatized for-profit social services. Resistance by labor in one region can be muted by moving production elsewhere – avoiding confrontation while effectively undermining working class economic and political demands within each single nation. In some countries, national chauvinism, fostered by domestic conservative politicians, politically interferes with working class cross-border coordination (Kalb & Halmai, 2011). Meanwhile, new centers of industrial production, particularly in East Asia, are quickly forming new working classes. By 2002, China had twice as many industrial employees as all the G7 developed countries combined (Banister, 2005).

From this brief account we can draw three conclusions useful for understanding the development of transnational capitalist activity. First, the social organization of the means of production provides a useful approach for identifying the formation of social classes. Secondly, based on their relationship to the means of production and to other classes, social classes have varying degrees and kinds of power. Finally, the political power and socio-cultural impact of each class depend on the outcome of its interactions (battles, alliances, negotiations) with other classes and its ability to articulate and popularize an ideological-cultural project that appeals to other important social forces and classes. Each conclusion helps explain the appearance and impact of transnational capitalism and the formation of a transnational capitalist class, including its transnational media.

Transnational Capitalism

Corporations have long sought access to valuable natural resources and consumer markets around the world, while Western media have exported entertainment promoting Western cultural norms (Schiller, 1976), but transnational corporations are new phenomena. Transnational corporations are distinguished from international or multinational corporations by their relations of production. An *international* corporation does business across national borders by selling products produced in one nation to consumers in another (e.g., Warner Bros. exports Hollywood productions to Europe). *Multinational* corporations are owned and based in one nation, but a multinational also owns subsidiaries in another nation. The subsidiary produces commodities in and for the other national market. Ownership, control, and profits of the subsidiary, however, remain with the national parent corporation (e.g., CNN-Europe produces news in several countries, but production decisions and profits remit to Time Warner in the United States). In both instances, the capitalist class structure provides more material and political resources to the dominant national capitalist class than to subordinate working classes. The relative benefit that international and multinational corporations hold compared to the productivity of their own domestic working classes ultimately proves insufficient for increasing profits. Sales cannot keep pace with costs; prevailing wages cannot sustain consumer-driven demand. Even where labor activism secured improved working class benefits in wages and working conditions, global overproduction plagued multinational operations. Because capitalism needs unending growth, corporations seek increased labor productivity with decreased labor benefits at home (through Reagan- and Thatcher-era attacks on labor) and an increased expansion of markets for an overabundance of commodities.

By the end of the twentieth century, globally active companies were developing new systems and relations of production to increase profits by increasing consumption and exerting additional downward pressure on wages. Distinct from nationally based firms, these transnational corporations and industries operate across borders as part of internationally integrated production regimes. *Transnational* corporations are owned by multiple companies from two or more nations producing and distributing products as "local" commodities in each nation and sharing profits among the multiple national owners (e.g., Reliance India buys 50% of DreamWorks and enters into a joint venture with Chinese filmmakers to produce movies for all three markets; Szalai, 2012). Transnationals declare, "We are not multi-national, we are multi-local" (as cited in Iwabuchi, 2002, p. 90). Mergers and acquisitions, joint ventures, and foreign direct investments (FDI – investments by one company in a company based in another country) have blurred the national identity of many transnational firms that enlist local labor to make local products. The tally by the United Nation's Conference on Trade and Development reports over 78,000 transnational companies (UNCTAD, 2008).

Transnational corporations have no national home per se and certainly no national allegiance. Their only allegiance is to capitalist shareholders from the two or more nations seeking profits from commodities produced and sold in multiple nations. Philosophically and amorally, corporations have no obligation to make art, history, or any social contribution; "to make money is our only objective," according to former Disney CEO Michael Eisner (as quoted in Sun, 2001). As Thomas Middelhoff, chairman of Bertlesmann, remarked when his German company took over US-based Random House in 1998, "There are no German and American companies.

There are only successful and unsuccessful companies" (as cited in Robinson & Harris, 2000, p. 35). Transnational firms do not override national or cultural boundaries; they depend on and exploit national characteristics of the appropriate national class for operation in that country. The transnational capitalist class "seeks to accumulate profit on a global scale and ... has no particular interest in destroying or sustaining local cultures apart from the drive for increased profitability" (Sklair, 2001, p. 256).

In the twenty-first century, capitalism has become the first truly world system: capitalism has not only finally displaced all precapitalist formations, it has also completed the commodification of every meaningful instance of social life, replacing nation-state public institutions and responsibilities with privatized, for-profit operations across the board – from natural resources such as land and water to social necessities such as education and health care (Robinson, 2004). By the 1990s, the volume of off-shore production by TNCs exceeded the amount of trade between states (Miller et al., 2008, p. 113). A key ingredient and outcome – not the cause – of this restructuring of capitalism has been the transnationalization of corporate media and its commercial-entertainment-consumerist model of communication (Artz, 2003, 2007; Rantanen, 2005).

The Transnational Corporate World

Transnational production is not some new "Western" business tactic, some neo-imperialist strategy of US companies. Rather, transnationalism results from the logic of national capitalist expansions that have reached global dimensions. Social contradictions are inherent to capitalist social relations; crises provide factual proof. But contradictions and crises may also lead to change (Fuchs, 2013, p. 295) and frequently class struggles over resources. In the midst of each crisis which impacts countries, industries, and individual corporations unequally, all corporations desperately seek out new, more efficient means for securing profits, methods, and relations that could lower wages and increase profits, while still trying to maintain some social equilibrium between classes. The impulse towards a pan-Asian film industry "is not just good business, but simple survival ... [I]ntegration with and assimilation into the Asian and mainland Chinese market is unavoidable" if any national filmmaker expects to remain viable (Davis & Yeh, 2008, p. 93). Hong Kong-based Applause Pictures, for example, invests in films in Korea, China, Japan, Thailand, and other countries with co-productions using location shooting, multinational talent, and low-budget crews. In general, capitalists can fracture social relations within their national territories by entering production and distribution markets abroad, simultaneously creating profits from lower costs and enforcing lower social expectations at home. Consequently, by the 1980s, forward-thinking capitalists began moving capital and production across national borders as a means to expand their markets and improve their profits, handicapping working classes at home. National interests restrict their operations; globalizing capitalists become cosmopolitan transnationalists.

For capitalism, "every limit appears as a barrier to overcome" (Marx, 1973, p. 408), including ecological limits, national welfare systems, public services, and national boundaries. Transnationals from the North and South pool their capital around the world in enterprises that are connected with "a myriad of other firms: transnational and domestic, large and small, public and private ... a bewildering variety of interorganizational collaborative relationships" (Dicken, 2003, p. 223). In fact, "it is increasingly difficult to separate local circuits of production and distribution from the globalized circuits that dictate the terms and patterns of accumulation worldwide, even when surface appearance gives the (misleading) impression that local capitals retain their autonomy. There are of course still local and national capitals, and there will be for a long time to come. But they must 'de-localize' and link to hegemonic transnational capital if they are to survive" (Robinson & Harris, 2000, p. 38). Some corporations merge across borders, combining two national companies into one transnational enterprise. In other cases, one national company or TNC acquires another national company, bringing local social forces into the transnational process while circumventing regulations on foreign ownership.

Transnational capitalism engulfs the world through a wide variety of economic practices now quite familiar: subcontracting, outsourcing, licensing, co-productions, along with increased joint ventures, mergers, acquisitions, and FDI, including through private equity firms – all indicating the increased linkage of national capital into transnational operations. In their study of 37 million companies and investors worldwide, Andy Coghlan and Debora MacKenzie (2011) mapped which companies "interlock" with others through shared investments and directors. The web of ownership revealed a core of 1, 318 companies that owned roughly 80% of global revenues of the TNCs. "Often, cooperation between [TNC] corporations allow them to ... collectively dominate the entire market" (Marshall, 2012), through their multiple national brands and multiple transnational operations.

Rob Van Tulder and Alex van der Zwart (2005) note that most industries have become concentrated globally among a handful of TNCs. In telecommunications, the top 10 companies control 86% of the global market, while just three global news agencies (Reuters, Associated Press, and Agence France-Presse) dominate global information.

Consider American icons Heinz and Burger King, both now owned by Brazilian private equity firm, 3G Capital Management. Heinz still owns food manufacturer Glaxo India and has joint ventures with Getz foods in the Philippines and Sanguan Foods in China to sell Heinz ketchup and other products. IBM ThinkPad? That's owned by Chinese-led transnational Lenovo. The AMC Entertainment cinema chain? Chinese, again. Smithfield, the largest pork producer in the world? Chinese. Sara Lee? Now a subsidiary of Mexico's transnational food giant, Grupo Bimbo. Tata Motors of India owns Jaguar and Land Rover.

European-led transnationals already share ownership in many "American" name brands: Gerber, Holiday Inn, Alka-Seltzer, Ray-Ban, LensCrafters, Lysol, Woolite, Motel 6, Trader Joe's, and many more. Even *American Idol* is owned by Bertelsmann, a German transnational media company. Bertlesmann's RTL division, Fremantle Media, also distributes Colombia's Radio Cadena Nacional (RCN) telenovela Y*o soy Betty, la fea* across Europe, while Chinese networks purchase Televisa's Mexican version, *La fea mas bella*, which includes marketing guidelines (McCabe, 2013). Lufthansa looks to an alliance with Turkish Airlines as an option to compete with Qatar Airways and Emirates Airlines for long-distance travelers to Asia.

In media and culture, accelerated transnational production and distribution flows "have made it difficult, and possibly insignificant, to specify the original source of transnationally circulated cultural products" (Iwabuchi, 2002, p. 19). Baseball is indigenous to the Dominican Republic; *Donald Duck and Friends* is considered a national television tradition in Sweden; Tokyo youth believe KFC is Japanese. National and local cultures are inundated with transnational production. Unless one investigates closely, the relations are often unrecognized and unrecognizable.

Pockets of Micro Transnationalism

Pockets of secondary activity may at first glance appear to be outside of transnational circuits or be idealistically conceived as alternatives to TNC relations, but on further review indicate their connections to the transnational order. Bangladeshi small-business women renting cell phones for income, Moroccan women using websites to market their carpets and pottery, and diasporic media selling commodities to their dispersed cultural communities appear as examples of creativity and diversity available to small-scale media projects (Srebreny, 2009, p. 51). Yet, each of these practices work within and support the market universe, less as alternative media and much more as micro-instances of market values and capitalist norms. These micro-entrepreneurs willingly accept the tenets of capitalism and class inequality. As if only other poor women were more entrepreneurial, poverty could be averted and the market would solve all individual problems!

Nollywood and Transnational Alliances

Several scholars (Miller, 2012; Larkin, 2008; Marston, Woodward, & Jones, 2007) have argued that Nollywood, the Nigerian video film industry, represents an alternative global network of production, now the second largest film industry in the world after India in terms of number of films. Because ethnically diverse productions are made quickly, at low cost, and informally with distribution primarily pirated and unlicensed, Nigerian video is seen as an alternative to transnational production. For $15,000 a typical Nigerian video can be filmed on location and then sold in small markets or appear on two UK television channels (Orgeret, 2009).

Nigerian videomakers and sales people illustrate the attraction of the global capitalist system that has been invited to a remote corner of global media entertainment. Nollywood "thrives" as a low-cost, low-profit, pirate capitalism in those "markets" that have little purchasing power, yet it is governed by the same industrial logic: actors and writers are low-wage workers creating commodities that bring profits to producers and marketers operating in a low-income environment. A warren of small business owners create their inventory (second- and third-hand) from reproductions and create their own markets from those unable to afford first-hand merchandise, not unlike the pirate export markets of India's Bollywood in "the niche markets of South Asian migrants ...

too small to be of interest to mainstream distributors" (Athique, 2008, p. 705).

Nollywood, pirated Bollywood, and other "alternative" market endeavors are essentially "low value scraps from the main banquet" of capitalism (Keane, 2006, p. 844). As these micro-markets are exposed to a diet of pirate videos, they emulate the larger mass market. As they raise global awareness of their creativity, they attract transnational finance and partners. Piracy, marginalism, and alternative niche practices have never been an impediment to capitalism. Piracy and local practices are not even truly alternatives to transnationalism; they assist and legitimize capitalist practices (O'Regan, 1991). In India, video reproduction had a similar cachet to Nollywood's rough-and-tumble entrepreneurism, but eventually followed a trajectory from piracy to regulated legitimacy as pirates, producers, and businesses collaborated whenever markets and profits warranted. Disney invested in Yash Raj Films in India, once the market (built by piracy) proved sizable enough to generate profits.

Today, in Lagos, Nigeria, "in the heart of these alternative networks, there seems to be a general sense … that the international" model is preferred (Miller, 2012, pp. 121–122). They may yet be linked to transnational media, but they want to be. This "alternative" business model is one step up from resale thrift shops, pawnshops, and yard sales seen in low-income communities across most developed countries.

Nollywood and other networked local productions and alternative distributors (from fair trade coffee coops to Angie's List and Napster) do not stand apart from transnational capital – they prosper (relatively speaking) on the margins of capitalist exchange, serving up commodities to those unable to partake in the richer consumer culture. Creatively, Nollywood labors on the edges of larger media markets, much like independent record labels and garage bands do; most flounder, many fail, a few find critical acclaim (e.g., Facets Cinematheque African Diaspora Film Festival in Chicago) and corporate suitors who offer contracts.

Since 2003, the transnational media firm Naspers has been broadcasting Nigerian films to 47 African countries over AfricaMagic, a continent-wide satellite station. Naspers has added AfricaMagic Yoruba and AfricaMagic Hausa to broadcast in those languages to Nigeria and neighboring countries (Adejunmobi, 2011). Nollywood's manufacture of thousands of films each year contributes to the transnational media system by nurturing the culture of movie watching to wider audiences, making it affordable to African working class diasporas, and bearing all of the risks and costs. If Nollywood films raise a sizable and desirable demographic, regional and transnational media selectively appropriate any creativity diversity that can turn a profit. As Naspers or other TNMCs find local co-producers and lower subscription costs, they will "have successfully placed [themselves] in a position to dictate trends for television programming in some Nigerian languages as well as determining the acceptable format for films in these languages and in English" (Adejunmobi, 2011, p. 76). Why would Nollywood producers refuse? They are, after all, small capitalist operators. By 2010 more profits came from selling videos to AfricaMagic than from selling DVDs in any "alternative" market (Nwachukwa & Njoku, 2010).

Even economic crises do not deter transnational corporate expansion. On the contrary, each shock from Mexico to Asia, from Greece to Spain to Cyprus has accelerated transnational integration of surviving local capitalists in affected countries into the ranks of TNCs. In 1998, following the East Asian economic crisis, the International Monetary Fund (IMF) required South Korea to "liberalize" its economy in return for a $58 billion loan. More than half the largest *chaebols* (traditional family-run and state-supported monopolies) were privatized and Korea now allows TNC investment and majority ownership, bringing sections of the Korean capitalist class into the transnational circuit. In Europe, although national networks persist, "the tendency is towards interlocking at the transnational European level" (Carroll et al., 2010, p. 175). The transnational consolidation of corporate Europe followed the 1980 recession, advanced in East Asia with the 1997 crisis, and in the United States after the dot-com bubble of 2001 (Carroll, 2010, p. 176) and continues apace globally since the 2008 world financial crisis. In the midst of that recession, transnational investors acquired $38 billion in electricity, telecommunications, and other formerly public utilities (Kikeri & Perault, 2010).

Quantifying Transnational Production

Transnational production is not some analytical or ideological concoction; it can be quantified. In 2003, UNCTAD began reporting a "transnational" index or TNI, which expresses the ratio of the value of corporate foreign to total assets, annual sales, and number of employees. The TNI gives a good indication of the extent to which an enterprise accumulates profits and capital transnationally as opposed to "home" market (UNCTAD, 2011). General Electric, a "US-based" corporation, holds more assets abroad than any non-financial firm in the world – over $500 billion in 2010 – with a TNI of 59.7% – meaning that over half of GE's wealth is held and created globally. Other 2011 examples from the 100 TNCs with sizable TNIs include: Vodafone (90.2%); Honda (70.7%); BP (83.8%); Nestlé (96.9%); Philips Electronics (87.7%). In 2004, only a very few of the top 100 TNCs had low TNIs. Chrysler (29%), Wal-Mart (24%), and Verizon (6%) made profits primarily in their domestic market. By 2011, Verizon was off the list, reflecting its almost exclusively national operation, but Wal-Mart expanded globally (35.1% TNI) and after Fiat purchased more than 60% of Chrysler, Chrysler-Fiat became a major TNC operating in multiple countries (76.4% TNI). By 2012, transnational production was even more prominent in world business: some 80,000 TNCs (compared with 40,000 in 1995) made $1.5 trillion in FDI, while holding more than $12.3 trillion in assets, and $28 million in sales. TNCs are now responsible for 40% of world GDP (UNCTAD, 2012), compared to less than 33% in 1995. By 2000, Viacom's Paramount studio had close to 50% of its sales in international markets (Havens, 2006, p. 48), a ratio not uncommon for other leading film producers, even without considering their extensive co-productions and joint ventures with other media firms.

Empirical evidence of FDI, cross-national mergers, strategic alliances, joint ventures, and interlocking directorships confirms the continued spread of TNCs. UNCTAD (2012) reported an increase in FDI to a record $684 billion in developing countries alone – more than twice the world FDI in 1995. TNCs employed more than 69 million workers, generating over $28 trillion in sales. In 2012, transnational mergers increased 53% to $526 billion. Capitalist production is continually being transformed from national capital to transnational capital. Meanwhile, existing TNCs are becoming even more transnational. Of the top 100 transnational companies, 17 have more than 90% of their assets in multiple countries. Sixty-two of the top 100 TNCs have a transnational index over 50%, compared to only 42 with 50% TNI in 1995.

Grupo Planeta

Even a little-known company like Grupo Planeta, headquartered in Spain's Catalan region, is transnational. Grupo Planeta, through its aggressive merger and joint venture strategies, has become the seventh largest firm in global publishing. Grupo Planeta has more than 70 worldwide newspaper and print subsidies/mergers, including in Argentina, Brazil, Chile, and the United States. The group owns Editis (the second largest publisher in France), has joint ventures in film, documentary, and children's programming in Europe, including an alliance with EM.TV AG in Germany, and has diversified into non-media partnerships such as Vueling Airlines, which offers cheap European flights (Szalvai, 2012).

Consolidation and Competition

While transnational capitalism consolidates, national and transnational competition remains. National capitalists compete within one nation, while transnational capitalists compete for resources and markets within many nations against national capitalists and against other transnational capitalists. Chrysler-Fiat, for example, competes with Ford and Fiat for customers in the United States. GM, in a 50-50 joint venture with Shanghai Auto Industry Group (SAIC) of China, competes for customers with Wuling (34% GM owned) in China, while Wuling also exports cars to Europe competing for customers against Chrysler-Fiat, Fiat, GM, Peugeot (7% GM), and other automakers. In 2011, GM/SAIC sold more cars in China (2,547,000), than GM sold in the United States (2, 504,000). Meanwhile, Chrysler-Fiat entered a joint venture with Tata motors in India and Chery Motors in China … Even if we believe corporations are individuals, where exactly is the national home of Chrysler, Fiat, GM, Wuling, SAIC? Similar structures and transnational production and distribution patterns mark other industries, from mining, oil, and machinery, to financial, chemical, pharmaceutical, electronics, and telecommunications (Phillips & Soeiro, 2012). Transnational production occurs in multiple nations, distribution and sales occur within the nation of production competing with "foreign" imports, while ownership is held among multiple capitalist financial interests and profits are shared among transnational owners, investors, and shareholders.

Different approaches by national regulators require a continuous churning of transnational negotiations across borders: Hyundai Motors maintains subsidiaries in Brazil, the United States, and India (from where it also exports), but to establish local production and sales in Turkey (Kibar), Egypt (Ghabbar), China (Beijing Auto), and elsewhere, Hyundai co-produces, co-owns, and shares profits. In other words, globalization of finance and trade does not specify each transnational relation: micro-economic integration of capitalist classes across national borders determines the configuration of new social relations of production.

The key process is the globalization of production – the decentralization of production chains and the worldwide dispersal of different productive segments of these chains as a coordinated, integrated capitalist practice. Flexible, part-time, and temporary labor result from transnationals traversing borders for low wages and limited benefits, pitting workers against unknown and unseen others, gutting the solidarity that arises from social interaction over time among collaborative, stable workforces. In the process, transnational capitalism has molded a disjoint global working class having fewer national distinctions and more social class similarities in their lived experience in a transnational environment – what Folker Fröbel, Jürgen Heinrichs, and Otto Kreye (2004) call a new international division of labor. Thus, globalization of capitalism has not ended center-periphery inequalities; it has spread those inequalities across borders. The wealthy in Beijing or Rio are arguably part of the developed "Global North" nations, while the unemployed working class in Gary, Indiana or Youngstown, Ohio have been pushed into a lifestyle formerly considered part of the developing "Global South" world.

> The vast majority of U.S. workers, however devoted and skilled at their jobs, have missed out on the windfalls of this winner-take-most economy – or worse, found their savings, employers, or professions ravaged by the same [transnational] forces that have enriched the plutocratic elite ... 65 percent of income growth in the United States went to the top one percent of the population. (Freeland, 2011)

The United Nations' *Human Development Report* places the United States at the bottom of the human poverty index for the leading 17 industrialized countries (Kirby, 2004, p. 212). It seems the new mantra of entrepreneurism, creative work, and freedom for flexible labor is actually a chant of crass disregard for the majority of working class families in the *überland* of capitalism.

The Transnational Capitalist Class

The global restructuring of production has led to new social class formations, including an emerging transnational capitalist class. The transnational capitalist class (TNCC) is that group of people who share a common
relationship to the process of social production and reproduction that is
structured and practiced across national borders. The TNCC has "identifiable actors working through institutions they own and/or control" (Sklair,
2001, p. 1). Transnational capitalists share ownership of the dominant
means of production in the world, integrated cross-border ownership,
production, and profit-sharing, consolidated in major corporations. These
corporations include: General Electric, Royal Dutch Shell, BP, Exxon Mobil,
Toyota, Total, Vodafone, ArcelorMittal, Nestlé, Volkswagen, Honda,
Anheuser-Busch, Deutsche Telekom, Ford, Siemens, BMW, Vivendi,
Nissan, Mitsubishi, Unilever, Proctor & Gamble, McDonald's, and other
familiar transnational firms, as well as some perhaps less familiar, including
Samsung, Aventis, E.on, Suez, Hutchinson Whampoa, ENI, Roche, Carrefour,
Mitsui, Glaxo Smith Kline, Petronas, Metro AG, CITIC, and dozens more
(UNCTAD, 2011). These TNCs are headquartered in Britain, Japan, United
States, France, Germany, Switzerland, as well as Spain, Italy, Netherlands,
Malaysia, Canada, Singapore, Korea, Ireland, and Australia and China.

The TNCC can be found in the leadership of the economic and political
structures of the world economy, apparent in ownership, investment, and
interlocking directorships. The TNCC is not simply a collection of individual
corporate owners who have embarked on a campaign of accumulation
and production. In most instances the world's top billionaires control
corporations and investments that are fundamentally transnational in
production and distribution (Forbes, 2014). The formation of a TNCC has
occurred because individual corporate owners have entered cooperative
relationships with others – sharing strategic plans, organizational control,
investments, costs, production protocols, and profit or loss. This structural
integration means that sections of national capitalist classes are moving
into transnational capitalist formations, not yet global in scope or syn-
chronicity, but transnational, often within but always beyond national
operations, identities, and interests. Because this class exists in material
institutions and social relations, they share "conduct, thought, feelings, and
judgments" (Bourdieu, 1992, p. 18).

A transnational capitalist class, comprising a segment of capitalist class
in almost every nation, has formed in and around these systems of

production and distribution. The TNCC is now "the dominant, hegemonic, fraction of capital on a world scale" (Robinson, 2004, p. 21), because transnational capital now "constitutes the 'commanding heights' of the global economy, and that fraction of capital imposes the general direction and character on production worldwide and conditions the social, political, and cultural character of capitalist society worldwide" (Robinson & Harris, 2000, p. 22). This predominant TNCC can be identified in other structural manifestations, as well.

The new TNCC has consciously and collectively forged transnational institutions to plan the development of the material relations of production, advancing market globalization as the practice and free market consumerism as the ideology for transnational capitalism. Within this crust of interlocking elites are some 6,000–7,000 capitalists who help set the agendas for TNCC political, economic, and social institutions such as the World Bank, World Trade Organization, Trilateral Commission, World Economic Forum, the G8, G20, NATO, the European Union, and other transnational organizations (Rothkopf, 2008).

Interlocking Directors for the TNCC

Leslie Sklair (2001) and Kees van der Pijl (1998) empirically establish that globalization is driven by identifiable actors working through corporations they own and institutions they control. Most importantly, transnational capitalists coordinate production and policy across companies and regions through interlocking cross-company management structures that facilitate capitalist interaction and planning.

Corporations are managed by boards of directors, including representatives of major shareholders and corporate bureaucrats with appropriate industrial, technical, or financial expertise. When directors sit on two or more boards, they are said to "interlock," indicating that the companies necessarily share information, direction, and decision-making interests through the physical presence of directors from different companies. According to William Domhoff (2006), through interlocking directorships, corporate owners and directors form an elite, cohesive community with common worldviews and understandings – essentially a formation of the capitalist class. For example, transnational class formation accompanied the changes in the ownership and production of Chrysler: US corporate members sat on Daimler's board during the late 1990s. In 2009, Chrysler was partly purchased by Fiat, which now has three of the nine directors on the board. As the *national* production and accumulation of profits shrink due to *transnational* ownership and production, the new class formation erodes the national corporate community's competitive position within the world system. Chrysler's capitalist shareholders become transnational – its owners and directors become part of a transnational capitalist formation seeking profits (to be shared transnationally) from production in multiple countries.

In very clear terms, director interlocks between transnational corporations reveal TNCC formation assembled in networks of cross-border connections. Transnational interlocks of directors of corporate boards establish class connections across national borders. Transnational interlocking assures shared capitalist class planning and decision-making across nation-states.

All TNCs have interlocking directorships and interlocking structures of governance (see muckety.com and ketupa.net). It is now regular corporate practice to maintain directorate interlocks across borders, clearly indicating a broadening of transnational class formation. For instance, China-based Lenovo, which bought IBM's PC business in 2005 and is now the world's largest PC firm, has nine members from six nations on its board of directors, as it moves into Brazil, India, and Russia (Kirkland & Orr, 2013). It is obvious that "globalizing firms are increasingly dominant" in national networks and a vibrant transnational capitalist class is "increasingly integrated" within nations and globally leaving national capitalists at a disadvantage in national markets overwhelmed by TNC production and distribution (Klassen & Carroll, 2011, p. 399).

While viewers and readers of popular media in Central Europe and across the globe share entertaining populist fare (from game shows and reality TV to sports and melodrama), sharing what amounts to a highly materialistic localized version of more polished European and US originals, transnational owners share a more cosmopolitan ethos emerging from their integrated business operations. Transnational capitalists travel in exclusive elite social circles nurturing a global business culture. "Global elites in each country increasingly tend to share similar lifestyles, including patterns of higher education (e.g., attendance at world-class business schools) and consumption of luxury goods and services" (Robinson, 2004, p. 31). Nationality does not interfere with the shared "cultural capital," which reinforces class identity, formation, and behavior (Bourdieu, 1987). TNCC members, whatever their national identity, exist in the same social class and political milieu.

Central European Media

The Central European Media Enterprises group (CME) produces programming and owns the largest broadcast stations across Central Europe, including in Bulgaria, Croatia, Slovenia, Czech Republic, Slovakia, and Romania. CME was founded in 1994 by Robert Lauder, director of cosmetic giant Estée Lauder. Time Warner owns 49.9% of CME. The company's board includes Caryn Becker, CEO of CLEAR wireless; Herbert Granath, an ABC vice-president, director of Crown Media, and partner in Eurosport TV; Alfred Langer, CFO of Celanese chemical company; Fred Langhammer, director of insurance giant AIG, Disney, and Japanese bank Shinsei. CME is majority owner of 1 + 1, a Ukrainian station, partners with Alexander Rodnyansky, CEO of Russian TV network CTC. These interlocks link CME to Axel Springer, Viacom, News Corp, AOL, Omnicom, Verizon, ATT, La Opinion, Bertelsmann, and Reliance Media in India. CME directors sit on transnational planning boards, including the Trilateral Commission, the IMF, and the Council on Foreign Relations, as well as Blackstone Group and Sunoco Carlyle (with over 1,500 joint ventures in 75 countries). Who owns CME? Names of directors can be found at muckety.com, but corporate shareholders and directors cross borders and industries, making CME a transnational exemplar. Axel Springer, a German-led transnational publisher, has similar joint venture relations throughout the region. In short, local media in Central Europe are already part of the transnational entertainment network.

The circles that capitalist elites move in are defined by interests and activities, not geography. Private equity manager Glenn Hutchins says, "You see the same people, you eat in the same restaurants, you stay in the same hotels. But most important, we are engaged as global citizens in cross-cutting commercial, political, and social matters of common concern" to transnational capital (Freeland, 2011). Complementing their interlocking corporate board meetings, elites gather in transnational policy groups and networks. In 2006, 45.5% of transnational capitalists sat together in elite class organizations (Carroll et al., 2010), including the Trilateral Commission, the World Economic Forum, and the World Business Council for Sustainable

Development. Such policy-planning groups further cement the organizational and cultural cohesion for the formation of collective transnational capitalist interests and action.

The next chapter opens with a brief overview of transnational capitalist policy planning and then turns to a larger discussion on transnational class leadership.

References

Adejunmobi, M. (2011). Nollywood, globalization, and regional media corporations in Africa. *Popular Communication, 9*(2), 67–78.

Artz, L. (2003). Globalization, media hegemony, and social class. In L. Artz & Y. Kamalipour (Eds.), *The globalization of corporate media hegemony* (pp. 3–33). Albany, NY: State University of New York Press.

Artz, L. (2006). On the material and the dialectic: Toward a class analysis of communication. In L. Artz, S. Macek, & D. Cloud (Eds.), *Marxism and communication studies: The point is to change it* (pp. 5–52). New York: Peter Lang.

Athique, A. (2008). The global dynamics of Indian media piracy: Export markets, playback media and the informal economy. *Media, Culture and Society, 30*(5), 699–717.

Banister, J. (2005, July). Manufacturing employment in China. *Monthly Labor Review*, p. 11.

Bourdieu, P. (1987). What makes a social class? On the theoretical and practical existence of groups. *Berkeley Journal of Sociology, 32*, 1–117.

Bourdieu, P. (1992). *An invitation to reflexive sociology*. Chicago: University of Chicago.

Bureau of Labor Statistics. (2012). International labor comparisons. Retrieved from http://www.bls.gov/fls/

Carroll, W. K., Carson, C., Fennema, M., Heemskerk, E., & Sapinski, J. P. (2010). *The making of a transnational capitalist class: Corporate power in the twenty-first century*. London: Zed Books.

Chance, G. (2013, January 22). Global governance in a changing world. *China Daily*. http://usa.chinadaily.com.cn/opinion/2013-01/22/content_16151239.htm

Chossudovsky, M. (1997). *The globalization of poverty: Impacts of IMF and World Bank reform*. London: Zed Books.

Coghlan, A., & MacKenzie, D. (2011, October 24). Revealed – the capitalist network that runs the world. *New Scientist*, 2835. Retrieved from http://www.newscientist.com/article/mg21228354.500-revealed--the-capitalistnetwork-that-runs-the-world.html

Davis, D. W., & Yeh, E. Y. (2008). *East Asian screen industries*. London: BFI.

Dicken, P. (2003). *Global shift: Reshaping the global economic map.* 4th edn. New York: Guilford.

Domhoff, G. W. (2006). *Who rules America? Power, politics and social change.* 5th edn. New York: McGraw-Hill.

Forbes. (2014). The world's billionaires. *Forbes.* Retrieved from http://www.forbes.com/billionaires/list/

Freeland, C. (2011, January/February). The rise of the new global elite. *Atlantic Magazine.* Retrieved from http://www.theatlantic.com/magazine/archive/2011/01/the-rise-of-the-new-global-elite/308343/

Fröbel, F., Heinrichs, J., & Kreye, O. (2004). *The new international division of labour.* Cambridge, UK: Cambridge University Press.

Fuchs, C. (2013). Why and how to read Marx's "Capital"? Reflections on Johan Fornäs' book "Capitalism. A companion to Marx's economy critique. *Triple C: Communication, Capitalism, & Critique, 11*(2), 294–309.

Galbraith, P. W., & Karlin, J. G. (2012). Introduction: The mirror of idols and celebrity. In P. W. Galbraith & J. G. Karling (Eds.), *Idols and celebrity in Japanese media culture* (pp. 1–32). New York: Palgrave Macmillan.

Golding, P., & Murdock, G. (1991). Culture, communications, and political economy. In J. Curran & M. Gurevitch, (Eds.), *Mass media and society* (pp. 15–32). London: Edward Arnold.

Hart, P. (2012, November 28). Reporting on sweatshops when your boss is in the sweatshop business. FAIR Blog. Retrieved April 8, 2013, from http://www.fair.org/blog/2012/11/28/reporting-on-sweatshops-when-your-boss-is-in-the-sweatshop-business/

Havens, T. (2006). *Global television marketplace.* London: Palgrave Macmillan.

Horkheimer, M., & Adorno, T. (2007). *Dialectic of enlightenment (cultural memory in the present.* Trans. E. Jephcott. (Originally published 1944). Palo Alto, CA: Stanford University Press.

Indian farmers, Coca-Cola vie for scarce water supply. (2008, November 17). PBS Newshour. Retrieved April 8, 2013, from http://www.pbs.org/newshour/bb/asia/july-dec08/waterwars_11-17.html

International Labour Organization. (2013). *Global wage report 2012/2013: Wages and equitable growth.* Geneva: International Labour Office. Retrieved from http://www.ilo.org/global/research/global-reports/global-wage-report/2012/WCMS_194843/lang--de/index.htm

Iwabuchi, K. (2002). *Recentering globalization: Popular culture and Japanese transnationalism.* Durham, NC: Duke University Press.

Jalée, P. (1977). *How capitalism works.* New York: Monthly Review Press.

Kalb, D. (2011). Introduction. Headlines of nation, subtexts of class. In D. Kalb & G. Halmai (Eds.), *Headlines of nation, subtexts of class: Working-class populism and the return of the repressed in neoliberal Europe* (pp. 1–36). New York: Berghahn Books.

Kalb, D., & Halmai, G. (Eds.). (2011). *Headlines of nation, subtexts of class: Working-class populism and the return of the repressed in neoliberal Europe.* New York: Berghahn Books.

Keane, M. (2006). Once were peripheral: Creating media capacity in East Asia. *Media, Culture & Society, 28*(6), 835–855.

Kikeri, S., & Perault, M. (2010, May). Privatization trends. *Viewpoint, 322,* 1–4. Retrieved from http://siteresources.worldbank.org/EXTFINANCIALSECTOR/Resources/322Kikeri_Perault.pdf?resourceurlname=322Kikeri_Perault.pdf

Kirby, P. (2004). Globalization, the Celtic Tiger and social outcomes: Is Ireland a model or a mirage? *Globalizations, 1*(2), 205–222.

Kirkland, R., & Orr, G. (2013, June). Thriving in a "PC-plus" world: An interview with Lenovo CEO Yang Yuanqing. *McKinsey Quarterly.* Retrieved from http://www.mckinsey.com/insights/high_tech_telecoms_internet/thriving_in_a_pc-plus_world

Klassen, J., & Carroll, W. K. (2011). Transnational class formation? Globalization and the Canadian corporate network. *Journal of World Systems Research, 17*(2), 379–402.

Kraul, C. (2006, September 16). Ugly never looked so good. *Los Angeles Times.* Retrieved from http://articles.latimes.com/2006/sep/16/business/fi-betty16

Larkin, B. (2008). *Signal and noise: Media, infrastructure, and urban culture in Nigeria.* Durham, NC: Duke University Press.

Marshall, A. G. (2012). No conspiracy theory – A small group of companies have enormous power over the world. *Alternet.* Retrieved from http://www.alternet.org/world/no-conspiracy-theory-small-group-companies-have-enormous-power-over-world

Marston, S. A., Woodward, K., & Jones, J.P. III. (2007). Flattening ontologies of globalization: The Nollywood case. *Globalizations, 4*(1), 45–63.

Marx, K. (1973). *Grundrisse: Foundations of the critique of political economy.* Trans. M. Nicholaus. New York: Penguin.

McCabe, J. (2013). Introduction: "Oh, Betty, you really are beautiful." In J. McCabe & K. Akass (Eds), *TV's Betty goes global: From telenovela to international brand* (pp. 1–25). New York: I.B. Taurus.

Miller, J. (2012). Global Nollywood: The Nigerian movie industry and alternative global networks in production and distribution. *Global Media and Communication, 8*(2), 117–133.

Miller, T., Govil, N., McMurria, J., Wang, T., & Maxwell, R. (2008). *Global Hollywood 2.* 2nd edn. London: British Film Institute.

Nohara, Y., & Sharp, A. (2013, July 26). Japan's elders turn to shoplifting. *Chicago Tribune,* p. A19.

Nwachukwa, M., & Njoku, B. (2010, May 9). Africa Magic provides platform for the African story – Segun Fayose. *Vanguard.* Retrieved from http://www.vanguardngr.com/2010/05/africa-magic-provides-platform-for-the-african-story-segun-fayose/

O'Regan, T. (1991). From piracy to sovereignty: International video cassette recorder trends. *Continuum, 4*(2). Retrieved from http://wwwmcc.murdoch. edu.au/ReadingRoom/4.2/oregan.html

Orgeret, K. S. (2009). Films out of Africa. *Journal of African Media Studies, 1*(3), 505–509.

Oxfam. (2013, January 13). Annual income of richest 100 people enough to end poverty four times over. *Oxfam International.* Retrieved from http://www. oxfam.org/en/pressroom/pressrelease/2013-01-19/annual-income-richest-100-people-enough-end-global-poverty-four-times

Qiang, L. (2013). Beyond Foxconn: Deplorable working conditions characterize Apple's entire supply line. *China Labor Watch.* Retrieved from http://www. chinalaborwatch.org/report/62

Phillips, P., & Soeiro, K. (2012, August). The global 1%: Exposing the transnational ruling class. *Censored Notebook: Investigative Research.* Retrieved January 15, 2013, from http://www.projectcensored.org/top-stories/articles/the-global-1-exposing-thetransnational-ruling-class/

Rantanen, T. (2005). *The media and globalization.* Thousand Oaks, CA: Sage.

Ritzer, G. (2009). *Globalization: A basic text.* Oxford: Wiley-Blackwell.

Robinson, W. I. (2004). *A theory of global capitalism: Production, class, and state in a transnational world.* Baltimore, MD: Johns Hopkins University Press.

Robinson, W. I., & Harris, J. (2000). Towards a global ruling class? Globalization and the transnational capitalist class. *Science & Society, 64*(1), 11–54.

Rothkopf, D. (2008). *Superclass: The global power elite and the world they are making.* New York: Farrar, Straus, & Giroux.

Sadik, N. (1991). Population growth and the food crisis. *Food, Nutrition and Agriculture.* Retrieved September 30, 2014, from http://www.fao.org/docrep/ u3550t/u3550t02.htm

Schiller, H. (1976). *Communication and cultural domination.* White Plains, NY: International Arts and Sciences Press.

Semuels, A. (2013, April 8). Monitoring every move. *Chicago Tribune,* p. 3B.

Sklair, L. (2001). *The transnational capitalist class.* New York: Wiley.

Srebreny, A. (2009) Maps and mandalas, division and multiplication: Media and global divides. *Nordicom Review, 30,* 39–56.

Steger, M. B. (2005). *Globalism: Market ideology meets terrorism.* Lanham, MD: Rowman & Littlefield.

Sun, F. S. (Producer). (2001). *Mickey Mouse monopoly: Disney, childhood & corporate power* (Motion picture). United States: ArtMedia Production.

Szalvai, E. (2012). Power and culture in media internationalization: The unusual case of a minority media conglomerate. *Revista de Negocios Internacionales, 4*(1), 28–56.

UNCTAD. (2008). *Development and globalization: Facts and figures 2008.* Geneva: United Nations.

UNCTAD. (2011). The world's top 100 non-financial TNCs, ranked by foreign assets, 2010. Bern, Switzerland: United Nations. Retrieved from http://unctad. org/Sections/dite_dir/docs/WIR11_web%20tab%2029.pdf

UNCTAD. (2012). *World investment report: Towards a new generation of investment policies*. Bern, Switzerland: United Nations. Retrieved March 21, 2013, from http://www.unctad-docs.org/files/UNCTAD-WIR2012-Full-en.pdf

van der Pijl, K. (1998a). *Transnational classes and international relations*. New York: Routledge.

van Tulder, R., & van der Zwart, A. (2005). *International business-society management: Leading corporate responsibility and globalization*. New York: Routledge.

Walters, S. (2012, February 4). Apple still shamed by China's iPod sweatshops six years after Mail on Sunday exposé. *Mail Online*. Retrieved from http://www. dailymail.co.uk/news/article-2096551/Apple-shamed-Chinas-iPod-sweatshops-SIX-YEARS-expos.html

Wright, E. O. (1985). *Classes*. London: Verso.

Yen, H. (2013, July 28). 80 percent of US adults face near-poverty, unemployment: Survey. *Huffington Post*. Retrieved from http://www.huffingtonpost.com/2013/07/28poverty-unemployment-rates_n_3666594.html

Further Reading

Robinson, W. I. (2004). *A theory of global capitalism: Production, class, and state in a transnational world*. Baltimore, MD: Johns Hopkins University Press.

Sklair, L. (2001). *The transnational capitalist class*. New York: Wiley.

2
Leading the Charge
Transnational Planning

Things don't just happen. To coordinate shared economic and political interests, corporate structure and practice is not enough. Globalization is planned. Transformation of global production from national to cross-border operations requires the coming together of sectors of national capitalist classes around a shared ethos, world vision, and the planning of agendas and projects (Miller, 2010). To craft a coherent perspective depends on a conscious organization of this emerging social class, through their own networks and social and political institutions. Leslie Sklair (2001) writes, "capitalism on a world scale, does not just happen. It is thought out, organized, managed, promoted, and defended against its opponents by identifiable groups of people working in identifiable organizations" (p. x). Transnational organizations have become abundant since the 1970s; however, a few stand out as both dominant sites of influence and representative of the form, including the Bilderberg Group, the Trilateral Commission, the World Economic Forum (WEF), the World Business Council for Sustainable Development, and the Organization for Economic Cooperation and Development.

These leading transnational policy groups are supplemented with national and regional associations of like-minded transnational capitalists and hundreds of "think tanks" comprised of selected management and technical experts, including, among others, the Atlantic Council, the Urban Institute, Center for Strategic International Studies, Brookings, the Aspen Institute, International Institute for Strategic Studies, Center for Economic Policy Research, the East Asia Institute, and many more (McGann, 2012). The Council on Foreign Relations, for example, which now has affiliate

Global Entertainment Media: A Critical Introduction, First Edition. Lee Artz.
© 2015 John Wiley & Sons, Inc. Published 2015 by John Wiley & Sons, Inc.

councils around the world, serves as "a testing ground for alternative policy recommendations, interlocking with other transnational policy groups" (van der Pijl, 1998, p. 114). In short, the transnational capitalist class is not a passive collection of capitalists with diverse nationalities; the TNCC is an active social formation seeking to establish its authority and leadership around the globe.

Trilateral Commission

One of the first and most prominent transnational policy groups is the Trilateral Commission (TC). Organized in 1973 by David Rockefeller, Zbigniew Brzezinski, and other Bilderberg members, the TC became an international planning group that included directors of the largest 100 global companies, including corporations that belonged to rival financial and national groups (Gill, 1992) and leading media firms. The TC sought to control and contain challenges to capitalism. The 1975 TC report, *The Crisis of Democracy*, bemoaned the "excess of democracy" and loss of authority for government and economic experts (Crozier, Huntington, & Watanuki, 1975, pp. 113–115). The TC intends to restore legitimate authority for a universalist, global political and economic order, beginning with restrictions on social welfare and labor rights.

World Economic Forum

Since 1987, the World Economic Forum (WEF) has assembled the "Davos men" who "have little need for national loyalty, view national boundaries as obstacles that thankfully are vanishing, and see national governments as residues from the past whose only useful function is to facilitate the elite's global operations" (Ash, 2005). WEF meetings include thousands of business and industry leaders, and hundreds of academics and major media representatives. Van der Pijl (1998) considers the WEF "the most comprehensive transnational planning body … a true International of capital, the first identifiable forum in which concepts of control" are discussed and implemented on a world scale (pp. 132–133). The WEF brings together leading sections of "transnational capital to construct a unifying vision, and presents to the rest of the world the interests of global capital in the guise of a universal vision" (Rupert, 2000, p. 15). The Forum launched the Uruguay round of the General Agreement on Trade and Tariffs which culminated in the creation of both the World Trade Organization and the World Bank (Miller, 2010). Media and telecom members of the World Economic Forum include: Bertelsmann, América Movil, Deutsche Telekom, Dogan Media, Facebook, Google, HAVAS, Interpublic, Omnicom, Pearson, Qualcomm, Samsung, Saudi Telecom, Telefónica, Vodafone, WPP, Yahoo!, as well as many other Media and Entertainment Industry members such as Univisión, Naspers, Aegis, CNBC/Comcast, and others.

All Together Now

In general, the influence of transnational clubs on this and other national or international policy "hinges" on their "loose and informal power" (Graz, 2003, p. 322) that is nonetheless class conscious. According to Will Hutton, editor of the *London Observer*, and a delegate to Bilderberg 1998, these transnational groups are part of "a global conversation that takes place each year at a string of conferences … the World Economic Forum in Davos in February, the Bilderberg and G8 meetings in April–May, and the IMF/World Bank annual conference in September. A kind of international consensus emerges and is carried over from one meeting to the next. This consensus becomes the background for the G8 economic communiqués. It becomes what informs the IMF when it imposes an adjustment programme on Indonesia, and it becomes what the presidents propose to Congress" (cited in Armstrong & McConnachie, 1998). These transnational "clubs" are not shadow governments of plutocrats manipulating international relations but a "strategic element" of social class "consciousness-raising forums where individuals representing elements of the state and civil society in affiliated countries can come to know and influence each other … part of a much wider international process of elite familiarization and fraternization, mutual education and, broadly speaking, networking" (Gill, 1992, p. 122).

Officially sanctioned institutions from the United Nations and its agencies, to the European Union, NATO, the African Union, the Arab League, and other regional political bodies coordinate discussions and multilateral economic and social policies for transnational development. Smaller gatherings like the Boao Forum in Asia, the TED conferences (Technology, Entertainment, Design), Aspen Institute's Ideas Festival, and Herb Allen's Sun Valley media conference contribute to the general transnational dialogue. Less well-known forums, like the European private banking and insurance forum, European Financial Services Roundtable; the Southern Africa Development Community (SADC); the Media Institute of Southern Africa; Latin America's Mercosur (the Common Market of the South); and similar regional bodies complement the larger transnationals with their own projects encouraging transnational policies for national governments and regional institutions "to commit to a truly single market for wholesale and retail financial services" working to "promote free and open markets throughout the world" (van der Pijl, 1998, p. 172).

The TNCC has emerged as the leading social force in the world, drawing national and regional economies and cultures into the orbit of transnational capitalism. This fundamental change in production and social relations has not just affected the capitalist classes, it has profoundly altered social relations among all classes, in every region and nation. The transnational capitalist class seeks to globalize all of social life: production, distribution, and consumption through deregulated non-national trade. The strategy of the TNCC is to bring all into capitalist production relations massaged by consumer ideology. As capital transnationalizes, global society has devolved into a multi-tiered order: (1) transnational and sub-transnational corporate owners and shareholders; (2) national capitalists; (3) the professional middle class of managers, technocrats, political elites, and academic experts; (4) the growing working classes in manufacture, transport, and service, including "middle-class" salaried employees; (5) casual and part-time labor; and (6) the vast legions of the unemployed poor, including small farmers and peasants. National capitalists drawn into the transnational bloc benefit from entry into successful circuits of production and profit. The TNCC has recruited and trained a secondary layer of support – managers and technicians who run the corporations and the agencies of the TNCC, such as the IMF, World Bank, and transnational forums, including the United Nations and various trade regimes. Politicians, university and think-tank experts, and media provide ideological legitimacy and technical solutions for privatization and economic deregulation – known more popularly as "neoliberalism." Below this transnational elite is "a small and shrinking layer of middle classes who exercise very little real power but who – pacified with mass consumption – form a fragile buffer between the transnational elite and the world's poor majority" (Robinson & Harris, 2000, p. 40). "Middle class consumption also has the great advantage of accommodating the privileges of the rich while supplying a quiescent horizon of aspiration to the popular classes" (Therborn, 2012). TNCC hegemony – leadership by consent – depends on mass consumerism, passive citizens, and a modicum of individual personal gratification among the middle classes.

Consumerism worldwide has been severely constricted by the combined problems of global overproduction, the declining spending power of "middle-class" consumers, and imposed national austerity programs. Meanwhile, for the world's majority inequality has exploded. It turns out that the world is not "flat" (Friedman, 2005): India's miracle has done little for the poorest fifth of Indian children, two-thirds of whom are underweight. Worldwide 870 million people were undernourished in 2012 and food prices continue to rise (Food and Agriculture Organization, 2012). Those left behind by neoliberalism and global consumerism are on occasion mobilized by national protectionism or religious populist movements with little effect on the transnational project (Kalb, 2011) while others are (at least temporarily) contained or repressed by various national and transnational state forces, from national police and armies to NATO and US- led "coalition" forces – Egypt, Syria, Thailand, and Ukraine being the more obvious examples.

Global inequality is primarily *class* inequality not simply inequality between nations. New working-class formations occur in and through transnational circuits of production-consumption, although the spread of individual consumerism, deference to the market, and the rising tide of nationalist populism (Kalb & Halmi, 2011) moderate and obscure popular recognition of the actual social conditions of production in many developed countries. Yet, one doesn't have to visit Asia or Latin America to witness the structural transformation of production: rustbelts ring formerly prosperous cities – see Gary (Indiana), Flint (Michigan), Youngstown (Ohio), Birmingham (England), and other de-industrialized corridors across the United States and United Kingdom. In fact, comparing income, life expectancy, and education across nations, the poorest Americans have a lower level of human development than the richest Bolivians or Indonesians (Grimm et al., 2010). Chinese firms and their transnational allies stride forward economically due to cheap labor as class divisions expand along with wealth. Consequently, political stability remains elusive for the TNCC as political unrest erupts across the world: the "pink" tide in Latin America; the Arab "spring" in Northern Africa and the Middle East; competing Yellow and Red shirts in Thailand; mass worker strikes in Korea and China; the list is long. The TNCC could not foresee the specifics of political fallout from its global strategy for accumulation through privatization. As the TNCC coalesced, it envisioned a new global order establishing social relations appropriate for transnational corporation (TNC) operations – consent and coercion were expected to win the day for capitalism. By the late 1970s, an uneasy consensus among members of the TNCC was reached: the TNCC determined to implement national and international structural "reforms" radically deregulating ownership, production, and trade among nations – the policies of neoliberalism.

Show Me the Money! Deregulation and Privatization

The primary strategy for accumulation of profits for the TNCC is codified simultaneously as neoliberal ideology and policy. Neoliberalism expresses the global interests of the transnational capitalist class intent on changing the architecture of global production and governance. Neoliberalism also represents an ideology the TNCC hopes will be adopted by other social classes, including nation-centered capitalists, middle classes, and the working-class majority. The popular phrases "Show me the money!" and "It costs too much" as acceptable justifications for social policy are commonsense expressions of neoliberalism. Society? "There is no such thing! There are individual men and women and their families," as

Neoliberalism

Neoliberalism is the political-ideological project of the transnational capitalist class seeking to change the balance of power in global social relations and create a new means of capital accumulation. Neoliberalism maintains that free markets best advance human happiness and good. As an economic and political policy, neoliberalism advocates the deregulation, privatization, and commercialization of everything – with the attendant promotion of consumerism. Neoliberalism as a model for transnational accumulation of wealth insists on economic restructuring in each country to increase the "free" movement of capital. Temporary employment and part-time jobs, especially in "creative" careers, appear favorably as "flexible" work hours. In country after country, transnational capitalists purchase property and rights to minerals, natural gas, petrochemicals, water and ownership of transportation, telecommunications, media, and other formerly public resources. The quality of life invariably declines for working classes.

privatization advocate and former British Prime Minister Margaret Thatcher famously said (Keay, 1987).

Neoliberalism seeks to negotiate investment and trade agreements among nations to allow transnational capital and finance to move instantaneously across borders without restriction. The market becomes an ethic in itself, capable of acting as a guide for all human action (Harvey, 2005). In practice, the size and geographical reach of a firm are seen as ever more crucial to success. Firms either expand or get swallowed up by competitors. Within nations, neoliberal policy dictates *deregulation* of production, ownership, and trade – removing public interest from economic decisions and making the "market" arbiter of all. Neoliberalism demands the *privatization* of public services and public welfare. Neoliberalism expects the "subordination and integration" of each national economy into the global economy (Robinson & Harris, 2000, p. 41). But neoliberalism expresses more than economic policy: it preaches its own ideological and cultural supremacy.

In media accounts, neoliberalism appears as a policy for free trade, efficiency, growth, prosperity, and ultimately democracy; while consumption marks the validity of neoliberalism in the diversity of choice in television and film genres, in music, sport, and everyday culture. Sklair (2001) notes that the TNCC reproduces itself through this "profit-driven culture-ideology of consumerism" (p. 6) because capitalism can only thrive by persuading humanity that the meaning of life resides in our possessions, happiness comes with consumption, and the free market is the best provider of individual goods and services.

Individualism

Neoliberalism is the global ideology of individualism with the marketplace providing all things for all people. Following privatization in India, the focus of politicians, the media, and popular culture became "what consumers want. It is no longer material if this brings about unemployment, greater economic dependency, or lack of trade union privileges" (Gupta, 2000, p. 78). For masses of middle-class consumers, this ideology has severe behavioral manifestations: individual happiness is promised in the next purchase. Bumper stickers proclaim: "I'd rather be shopping." Vacations are organized around shopping destinations. Narcissism and hyper-individualism become social norms in a global consumer culture. Neoliberal preferences in entertainment accompany the spread of transnational capitalism. The *Idol*-formatted *Super Girl* television phenomenon in China introduces individualism, self-interest, and other neoliberal ideological components into the popular cultural discourse (Keane, Fung, & Moran, 2007, p. 126).

Hyper-individualism is rampant in the United States:

> We are all inculcated into the cult of individualism – by our families, who tell us we are special; by the vision of the American Dream; by schools, who demand that we specify fields; by advertising which compels us to carve out who we are by consuming certain commodities; by capitalism which teaches us that to succeed is to win in a competition of yourself against all others; and by the ever-growing new age and pop psychology oeuvre which tells us to create our own realities … (Krasnow, 2013)

What social system best serves up this cultural existence? Transnational capitalism, the epitome of self-gratification without restriction through consumption of diverse global commodities: something for everyone awaits in the global marketplace.

The Contradictions of Accumulation by Dispossession

While neoliberalism provides a political and governmental "repertoire" for directing policies towards transnational market preferences, the privatization and commercialization strategy for capital accumulation may also "generate new contradictions, antagonisms, and dysfunctions" (Clarke, 2008, p. 144). Some can be distinguished already: the competitive heat of one billion new workers since 1989 and the two billion that may be added in the next two decades (Kalb, 2011), which will push down wages further in capitalist economies; the OECD countries edging to 100% public debt, curtailing options for alleviating social inequality and unrest; and the continuing world recession brought on by massive overproduction (Brenner, 2003) that has no realistic market outlet as workers are pummeled with national austerity programs. Basic civic functions have broken down in Detroit, Michigan – a bankrupt city devastated by transnational production realignments, like General Motors scampering to China. Non-profit foundations and volunteer groups are the last line of defense against neighborhood blight and social decay as public services have collapsed (Carey, 2013).

Above all, the TNCC needs to reproduce social relations necessary for transnational production and profit (Therborn, 2008). This takes peculiar turns. On the one hand, politicians distribute public funds for free market endeavors: in 2011, Germany provided $3.84 billion in federal tax credits for the Indian/German co-production *Don 2* (Joshi, 2010); the US Congress has an Entertainment Industries Caucus dedicated to protecting the culture industry, its jobs, and profits (Sherman, 2010). Rhetoric for competition aside, "the U.S. government has devoted massive resources to generate and sustain 'private-sector' film in the interests of ideology and money, and the industry has responded in commercial and ideological kind" (Miller et al., 2008, p. 102).

Competition and survival of the fittest become the dominant organizing principles for popular narratives and discourses (as in *Amazing Race*, *Survivor*, *Next Top Model*, and other television reality programming, as well as World Wrestling Entertainment (WWE) and Ultimate Fight Club contests, because neoliberalism and the policies it articulates are best advanced with popular consent, hence the importance of media and communication.

Combining economic control, political leadership, and cultural norms, the TNCC anticipates developing transnational state apparatuses capable of leading a new transnational world order.

Hegemony

In media and everyday political discourse, hegemony is often equated with dominance. Antonio Gramsci (1891–1937), the Italian political theorist and writer, filled hegemony with more political and cultural significance. In Gramsci's view, hegemony appears as a consensual culture and politics that meet the needs of the majority of a population while simultaneously reproducing dominant social relations and the interests of the dominant groups (Sassoon, 1987, p. 94). Rulers rule most effectively when they have the consent of the governed, when their leadership meets the needs of other social groups and classes. Given the complex cultural and social relations of contemporary society, cultural hegemony is the political preference of any leadership. In previous eras, the need for consent of the governed was not always paramount. Feudal society, for instance, was not hegemonic – dominant classes ruled largely through coercion. Landlords and nobles relied on physical force and intimidation in governing serfs and ensuring feudal relations; the plebian masses were too isolated and geographically divided to mount any consistent resistance or political organization capable of social transformation.

Hegemony in modern capitalism is predicated on the crucial structural position of a massive industrial working class. Without the continued support of working class citizens, capitalist society and social relations would collapse, and alternative social relations would be proposed, as has happened repeatedly: in France in 1968, Portugal in 1975, Nicaragua in 1979, Poland in 1980, the Soviet Union in the 1990s, and Venezuela and Bolivia in recent years, to name only a few of the more dramatic challenges to capitalist hegemony. For social stability and the reproduction of dominant social relations, any successful capitalist leadership must truly champion the *national* interest, representing the aspirations of diverse social classes and groups.

To the extent that significant non-dominant social forces conceive and assemble their own political agendas and identities (e.g., African Americans, Kurds in Iraq, indigenous nations within larger states, women), the leadership of dominant social relations will be challenged. To the extent that challenger demands can be negotiated and re-incorporated within dominant discourse and cultural and political systems, the hegemony of dominant groups may remain, albeit in a hybrid form. All states undergo this political and cultural negotiation; challengers seldom fully achieve their demands

Hegemony

Hegemony marks a society in which most citizens consent to the existing social order and its norms. Citizens support or at least tacitly accept the policies and leadership of a dominant group because the arrangement appears to provide economic, political, or cultural benefits. Consent occurs and lasts only to the extent that a leadership sufficiently meets the needs of all allied or subordinate social groups. Dominant classes that are too self-serving in their political, social, and economic leadership will create serious social contradictions, fostering resistance and challenges to the reproduction of existing social relations. As popular consent is withdrawn, hegemony shrinks and the status quo resorts to coercion. As leading groups build legitimate social and cultural support, hegemony expands.

within another's hegemony. For any social group, like the capitalist class – nationally or in transnational formation – to capture and maintain legitimacy, it must continuously organize hegemony economically, politically, and culturally.

For the emerging transnational capitalist class, hegemony must be constructed anew from existing national and international economic, political, and cultural ingredients. A new hegemony, with a new leadership drawn from multiple national hegemonic leaderships, has monumental economic, political, and cultural tasks. In each sphere, the hegemonic contenders aspire to represent broad sections of a class-divided, culturally diverse global order.

Consent through material benefit

Economically, the TNCC offers to national capitalists a production model for realizing profits. In media production, the sales of program formats have become more frequent than the sale of programming content per se. To some extent, this neoliberal model has found support among other classes, particularly the managerial and technocratic elite who benefit from the reorganization of trade, finance, production, and sales. The symbolic and ideological content of "films and global media are part of the process that associates elite status with transnational movement" and plays a role "in inciting the desire of the affluent for consumption," as Steve Derné (2008) describes in the making of the transnational middle class in India (p. 91). Some business owners, entrepreneurs, and skilled workers maintain sufficient but precarious resources and opportunities for individual success in the new competitive global environment. Gramsci amends the role of consent in hegemony by noting that material benefits need not be abundant, nor strictly economic. "Lacking options, subordinate groups may be satisfied with minimal rewards. Although consent may be reluctant, groups often consent to hegemony because the limited benefits are immediate and easily attainable. More substantial benefits may be possible, but if they can be attained only through actions that jeopardize current benefits, the risk may be too great" (Artz & Murphy, 2000, p. 25).

Consent from political benefit

No society exists solely as an economic entity. Production relations contribute to parallel social relations and require political norms for organizing and reproducing both the production and social relations of the society.

A political form must be assembled that represents the interests of the majority of essential social classes (or at least secures consent from that majority). Political consent evolves from negotiated arrangements among social forces: alliances and agreements that represent an acceptable arrangement for the civil operation of society. Conflicts over resources must be resolved according to some agreed-upon criteria, otherwise consent to the social order dissolves. Thus, political leaders often make radical adjustments when faced with organized opposition: from Britain and France, to Sweden and the United States, governments have made concessions to organized labor and civil rights protests to maintain consent. Social welfare programs, labor rights, affirmative action, environmental legislation and other "infringements" on the accumulation of profits have occurred repeatedly over the last decades whenever independently organized social groups (with enough economic and political power to disrupt the political system) mobilized their forces against the dominant hegemony. To head off challenges, dominant social forces use mass media, education, propaganda, and political agitation by their own sponsored groups in a continuous effort to maintain consent (and obstruct alternative visions) within the agenda set by the economic and political elite.

Popular support is so important that dominant social forces have institutionalized perpetual election campaigns. These elections are not about democracy, but function as rituals "that make us generally feel content with the process" while producing "both acquiescence and quiescence" (Gronbeck, 1984, p. 493). TNCC political hegemony has not yet found a suitable persuasive practice for globalization that does not appear undemocratic. Indeed, a major contradiction for the TNCC is resolving the conflict between national political rhetoric and globalization rhetoric. Making "our" country more competitive leads to protectionist policies. Allowing national corporations to freely roam the globe looking for cheap labor resonates as unpatriotic, while investments and mergers by transnational corporations appear threatening to domestic security. Political forums like the Trilateral Commission and the World Economic Forum may assemble like-minded capitalist-class members, but even with invitations to working class representatives, these transnational bodies are viewed skeptically as anti-democratic, elite formations (Graz, 2003). For now, hegemonic national capitalists and their governments have a crucial role in winning consent for transnationalizing global politics.

TNCC political leadership remains in process. Structural power is not "exempt from internal contradictions and unevenness," especially transnational class "relationships of inequality, power, and dependence" where "the politics of fear and anger incubates" (Kalb, 2011, pp. 12–13). In India, as elsewhere, affluent professionals, managers, and TNCC bureaucrats "see the opportunity for consumption as the primary benefit of globalization" (Derné , 2008, p. 99), securing hegemonic consent for transnational capitalist relations among those TNCC allies. For the majority who can afford it, consumption may become a "stronger, more affect-laden basis of shared identity than any dreary commonality of a shared position in a productive system" (Derné, 2008, p. 103).

Simultaneously, millions of workers and peasants excluded from consumption, viewing popular broadcasting of a world of plenty, may become disgruntled with the contradictions between wealth and inequity and politically oppose the new social order. Some working-class sectors may find visceral comfort in national identities fighting global forces. While instances of working class opposition to TNCC hegemony have erupted (e.g., Bolivia in 2000, France in 1995, Venezuela in 1989, and more can be expected), in other cases the more immediate challenge to global capital comes from right-wing populism and national chauvinism. Politically, the TNCC's neoliberal privatization, "gentrification and cosmopolitanism" has restructured class relations, unleashed social insecurity, and instigated global labor migration, "eroding solidarity and communal life" and fomenting right-wing racist populism across Europe and elsewhere (Kalb, 2011, p. 14). The resurgence of the right-wing in France, Golden Dawn in Greece, and anti-immigrant campaigns among the German working class demonstrate that resistance to transnational capitalism is not always progressive. Gross social inequality and insecurity unleash fractured and frightened lower middle classes prone to sudden social explosion. Neoliberal "shock therapy" may have disoriented and dislocated working classes in many regions, but the TNCC has not yet cemented its global political leadership.

Popular culture and consent

Hegemony, leadership with mass consent, is "exercised not by states but by social groups, classes or class fractions" (Robinson, 2004, p. 129). Given the complexity in reorganizing capitalist production and social relations, the construction of a transnational capitalist hegemony must rely heavily on cultural practices that interact with material conditions and promote emerging global political regimes. Culture and media entertainment are essential to establishing hegemonic social relations – culture reinforces acceptance of economic and political arrangements.

Within a stable hegemony, citizens at least tacitly consent to the existing way of life. How we live our lives and how we understand our lives roughly correspond to the political and material conditions of that hegemony, or else consent may be withdrawn and conflicts erupt. Major social groups that benefit economically from the hegemonic order support the political institutions that administer and regulate the allocation of resources. These leading social groups and classes (and their representatives and supporters) participate in the production and consumption of popular culture and the rituals and practices that legitimate the hegemonic relationship.

Television, magazines, movies, books, and electronic media tend to use understandable, popular, accepted representations drawn from the cultural values, stereotypes, and social rituals that predominate in consumer society. Because most national and transnational media are advertising-driven – selling audiences to advertisers and media products to audiences – media genres, vocabularies, languages, images, symbols, and practices mesh well with capitalist economic, political, and cultural hegemony. TNCs enhance and perfect national media practices that dominate everyday life in every nation.

Given the interactive dynamics of material, political, and cultural conditions necessary for winning consent, dominant practices and meanings appear across these lived realms. Art, law, philosophy, fashion, movies, music, religion, sports, family relations, and other cultural practices and spheres echo and contribute to the material production and political conditions of hegemony. At the same time, any of these cultural spheres of consent may become sites of contention, instigating opposition to hegemony whenever adequate material benefits or legitimate political relations falter.

The cultural basis for hegemony is perhaps the most consistently problematic for the TNCC, because hegemony depends on providing acceptable philosophical and ideological explanations defending capitalism as the best of all possible worlds. Material resources and political institutions may be difficult to manage but can nonetheless be systematically regulated. Culture and its meanings ultimately depend on self-motivated popular participation and are thus susceptible to unexpected and recurring challenges. We may laugh at jokes that release social pressures, but too incisive jokes may nurture more political consciousness.

A Transnational State

Given the class relations of transnational production, which include supra-national ownership of the means of production, cross-border production activities, and the accompanying transformation of working-class locations and social power, the transnational capitalist class needs a state capable of leading, legitimizing, defending, and reproducing social relations necessary for transnational capitalism – social relations that include massive numbers of skilled, mobile, and servile workers willing to accept minimal wages and individual responsibility for basic human services such as health, education, housing, and nutrition without health, safety, or democratic regulation; social relations that include the free flow of non-taxable profits drawn from unregulated and unsafe working conditions, including sweatshops, conscript and child labor, speed-up, piece work, extended hours, and no job security or pension. The TNCC needs a transnational state (TNS) to enforce new terms of production. No transnational state exists that can be conquered and replaced. None can be established ready-made, off the rack. We may be witnessing the birth of a transnational state formation evolving from within the existing system of nation-states and available existing international institutions that can be transformed to serve transnational political purposes.

The nation-state government maintains its apparent structural form, even as its function changes from organizing and reproducing capitalist society within national territories, to transforming economic, political, and social relations to reproduce transnational capitalism. The transnational state could not and cannot be preconceived; a TNS must coalesce from the specific social relations of transnational capitalism being inserted into existing social and political structures, including nation-states and international formations such as the United Nations, the World Trade Organization (WTO), the International Telecommunications Union, and various "treaty" regimes on trade and social policy.

The TNCC works through key transnational institutions to advance neo-liberal market globalization. The IMF, the World Bank, the WTO, the European Parliament, the International Telecommunications Union, and various trade regimes like the North Atlantic Free Trade Agreement, the European Common Market, and others legitimize market globalization and occasionally legalize deregulation and privatization through national treaties. In late 2012, 600 US corporate executives led negotiations for the Trans-Pacific Partnership (TPP), a trade agreement for New Zealand,

Australia, Peru, Chile, Malaysia, Singapore, Brunei, Vietnam, and the United States (DePillis, 2013). The TPP articulates a transnational trade regime for deregulation of FDI, financial services, and trade across the nations of the Pacific Rim. Expressing the accepted dominance of the TNCC, the Trans-Pacific Partnership (which now includes Canada and Mexico and will most likely include Japan) (Palmer, 2012) grants corporations special authority to challenge government regulations in private TPP tribunals, off-limits to citizens (Wallach & Tucker, 2012). A parallel transnational free trade agreement was negotiated among European and North American companies. The Transatlantic Trade and Investment Partnership (TTIP) provides similar protections for privatization and corporate authority with little government or public regulation.

Meanwhile, the TNCC uses its communication power expressed primarily through TNMC advertising and entertainment to promote the ideology and practices of consumerism, with "the consequence that non-business activities become more and more commercialized," as clearly demonstrated in social services, the arts, sports, science, education, and many other aspect of social and cultural life (Sklair, 2001, p. 296). TNC executives lead local, national, international, and global trade and industry associations that increasingly make global decisions in trade, production, and communication. Robinson and Harris (2000) argue that this emerging TNCC rules through its transnational corporations, financial institutions, supranational economic planning agencies, and politicians from dominant political parties, technocratic elites and transnational media conglomerates (p. 12).

Nationalizing the Global

Transnational capitalists rely heavily on governments to deregulate national markets and pursue sweeping economic restructuring and the dismantling of media and national protections and tariffs. Long considered facilitators of commercial media interests, Latin American governments since the 1990s "have promoted greater deregulation of the communications system," "allowing cross-ownership in markets" and foreign mergers and acquisitions (Mastrini & Becerra, 2011, p. 53). In 1989, the European Commission, the executive body of the European Union, convinced member states to "encourage the free flow of cable and satellite channels" and "remove the most stringent advertising rules," effectively enabling cross-border TV channels to broadcast across Europe (Chalaby, 2009, p. 58). The European Union's media policy aims to privatize media, aid in the convergence of media technologies, and promote consumerism (Rollet, 2001). In Eastern Europe, government intervention for transnational activity was even more acute in velocity and degree. Following the collapse of state-run media, citizens anticipated participatory democracy and an alternative public sphere of vibrant free speech, but governments politically controlled by former *nomenklatura* party bureaucrats rejected direct democracy and pursued "politically controlled privatization" – less concerned with "workers and citizens than with their roles as consumers and participants in popular culture" (Jakubowicz, 2007, pp. 160, 165). Eastern European governments left public media to languish. Aided by transnational state institutions like the Council of Europe's Media Division, governments immediately deregulated and entertainment content was soon dominant on every channel (Jakubowicz, 2007, p. 220). In Hungary, Poland, and the Czech Republic, 50% of the daily newspapers were soon owned by TNMCs. Leading broadcasters are all TNMCs (including Time Warner/Central European Media Enterprises, Bertlesmann's RTL, Scandinavia Broadcasting Systems (SBS), and Canal +; Bruck et al., 2004). National government "reduction of regulatory barriers is the major supporting factor" for pan-Arab and transnational media and entertainment industry growth in the Middle East (Hall & de Clerq, 2009, p. 1). Transnational marketing strategies in India, including sponsoring national cultural events and the use of national symbols, now "occur through the idiom of the nation" assisted by government policies that promote a "public culture of consumption" (Fernandes, 2000, pp. 616, 614). Korea and Taiwan governments further "liberalized" their media laws following the Asian economic crisis of 1997, opening the field to transnational co-productions by Japanese, Korean, Thai, and Chinese media firms (Iwabuchi, 2002). From Europe to Asia, "government policies were most of the time, either behind these new trends, or extended in line with economic interests towards commercialization and privatization" of media (Servaes & Wang, 1997, p. 8).

For now there is no transnational state per se, but a nascent transnational civil society exists in the formal and informal relations between the TNCC and its managers and technocrats in government and business. Global civil society is dominated by the TNCC congregated in (1) social, political, and economic clubs like the WEF; (2) economic institutions, such as the IMF, World Bank, and the TPP; and (3) policy forums, from the United Nations Development Program (UNDP), and the United Nations Conference on

The Argentina Case

In the 1990s, Argentina's "democratic" government removed restrictions on media ownership, privatized television stations Canal 13 and Canal 11, authorized press and telecom companies to own television and cable, and most importantly signed 53 treaties on foreign investments. These neoliberal policies "facilitated media centralization and concentration, on a transnational basis" (Castagno, 2012, p. 338). Spanish telecom giant Telefónica acquired Canal 11 and nine other stations, with co-productions with Dutch production studio Endemol and Argentine RGB Entertainment, the manager for Disney productions across the Southern Cone. Liberty Media bought 25% of Grupo Clarín's Cablevision network of 260 cable licenses, and Goldman Sachs purchased 18% of Grupo Clarín. Soccer is still available on public TV Pública, but the production is now owned by global media company La Corte (Castagno, 2012, p. 346). The "populist" Argentine government invites transnational capital to run the domestic media.

Trade and Development (UNCTAD) to the European Union and the Organization for Economic Cooperation and Development (OECD).

Politicians and bureaucrats shepherding transnational policy through national political terrains must continuously balance the need to win hegemony and sustain their own political legitimacy while also advancing transnational policies. For instance, Argentina's dictatorship repressed democratic social movements in the 1970s, but today Kirchner's populist policies accommodate democratic social forces while maneuvering business activity to transnational operations, similar to populist Lula de Silva's government in Brazil (Dangl, 2010). Lawmakers in the United States and elsewhere simultaneously pass protectionist legislation for some industries even as they liberalize markets for others.

Nation-state politicians are not always successful in advancing neoliberal policies, especially when crises erupt as in Greece, Spain, Italy, Mexico, and elsewhere following the 2008 recession. The inequities and contradictions of market globalization have stirred national responses from religious conservatives and national capitalists dependent on tariff protection and their internal markets. Additionally, even transnational capitalist class fragments continue to compete with other transnational capitalists over market share and access to resources, leading to recurring nation-state political responses that cannot be simply superseded by transnational actions. Nation-state resistance on behalf of French cinema and wine, Indonesian and Malaysian television, and restrictions on production and trade imposed in Zimbabwe, Singapore, and assorted dictatorial capitalist regimes in the Mideast, provide evidence that transnational capitalism may be hegemonic, but its leadership is not yet global.

The transnational capitalist class does not need individual corporations with specific brand names to cover every corner of the globe – although some do, like Coca-Cola, McDonald's, News Corp, and Time Warner. In fact, transnational capitalist strategy is to organize production *across* national borders to benefit from competitive labor and local business. Multiple regional operations linking transnationals with national firms suffice; there is no economic or political reason to bring all national productions under a single international corporate structure. Indeed, operational flexibility may be better served by regional production with corporate interlocks that maximize local political collaboration with national governments.

Even when nation-states and TNS apparatus have all the gears and cogs running smoothly, when hegemonic consent is at its peak, "class power is always backed up by coercion," because "the dominant mode of integration [is] accompanied by coercion and occasionally, actual violence backing up the imposition of capitalist discipline on an expanded scale and in novel forms" (van der Pijl, 1998, pp. 108, 117). Countries that do not follow the prescriptions of the emerging TNS institutions like the IMF or the World Bank are reprimanded with lower credit ratings, higher interest, or even investment boycotts. In Greece and Italy in November of 2011, democratically elected governments "were simply removed and replaced with technocratic administrations made up of bankers and economists" who pushed through austerity measures that fleeced the general population and protected transnational finance (Marshall, 2012). Former US Treasury Deputy Secretary Robert Altman argues that private transnational financial institutions "oust entrenched regimes where normal political processes could not do so. They force austerity, banking bail-outs and other major policy changes. Their influence dwarfs multilateral institutions such as the International Monetary Fund. Indeed, leaving aside unusable nuclear weapons, they have become the most powerful force on earth" (Altman, 2011).

Absent a TNS repressive apparatus, nation-state governments currently provide the first line of coercive defense for transnational capitalism, politically managing class polarization that inevitably arises due to job losses, wage reductions, price increases, and disappearing social safety nets. In the absence of hegemony, which disappears with suppression of wages and social welfare, "violence [is] resorted to in order to enforce a consensus of fear" and restore "class unity and discipline" (van der Pijl, 1998, pp. 128–129). Wacquant (2012) writes of two forms of coercion: "the accelerating retraction of social welfare" and "the explosive expansion of criminal justice," when transnational production and privatization began earnest downward pressure on the working class (p. 67). Extensive government surveillance (revealed in government documents released by Edward Snowden) is the most recent manifestation of preparations for mass control. Government coercion "curbs the mounting dislocations caused by the normalization of social insecurity at the bottom of the class and urban structure" and "restores the authority of the governing elite by reaffirming 'law and order' just when this authority is being undermined" (Wacquant, 2012, p. 76) by severe dislocation of previous social relations by the more mercenary social relations of transnational capitalism. For any crisis beyond the capability of national armed forces, the TNCC relies on NATO, US-led, or other "coalition" forces for military intervention. In Iraq, Yugoslavia, and Libya, for example, American forces did not win new territory or markets exclusively for the United States, but secured new conditions for transnational capitalist integration. Likewise, French intervention in Africa defends all transnational investments and operations.

National and transnational competition under the leadership of the TNCC is transforming the world, economically, politically, and culturally. In addition to a growing class polarization and ecological crises of survival proportions, we are entering an era of fundamental cultural change. Hybrid state apparatuses fabricated from transnational and national institutions protect and cultivate transnational-class relations. TNCs translate their consumerist ideology to local cultural practices primarily through entertainment media. For their part, transnational media have become adept at cross-cultural hybridization as a means for securing and then reproducing transnational capitalist hegemony at least temporarily and partially with the consent of millions of consumers and spectators.

Transnational Relations as International Leadership

While many media and communication texts neglect the historical and social context in studying micro-instances of communication, the argument here maintains that no serious investigation of media practice can be conducted outside its concrete historical context. To clarify the multiple interactions contributing to global media entertainment, social relations must be analyzed; only then will cultural symbols and media images reveal their social significance (Kalb, 2011, p. 11).

The above narrative should demonstrate the dramatic changes in national and global production, including the changes in social relations. Transnationalism is a capitalist-class project using government infrastructures alongside a complementary new transnational state apparatus-in-formation. Nation-state conflict will not disappear, but we have entered an era of global *class* battles and contradictions.

Without any doubt, "large corporations have enormous influence on how billions of people work and live" (Renner, 2000) – or don't work and don't live. And, there is no identifiable global United States, United Kingdom, or China project. There is no rising national or regional capitalist strategy. For capitalism, the local and the global are not counterposed but systematically nested in the emerging transnational system. Transnationals exploit natural resources and capture domestic markets around the world through local production. Media and cultural production and their social use are likewise not instigated by or for "Western" interests. Rather, "transnational production chains facilitate widespread cultural change and promote global capitalist culture" (Robinson, 2004, p. 32) – not Western culture, but capitalist culture. As the next chapter demonstrates, global media entertainment is a transnational class activity aimed at securing capitalist-class hegemony through consumerism and spectatorship.

This is not the only possible outcome. Transnational capitalism has no guarantees. Capitalism cannot overcome its own class contradictions, over-production, and the limits of the environment. Ongoing social movements of labor and their allies in Bolivia, Greece, Egypt, Turkey, and the "tens of thousands of Chinese workers engaging in daily struggles over hand-to-mouth issues" (Zhao & Duffy, 2008, p. 244) provide concrete evidence that working men and women around the world will remain historical agents for social change. The Venezuelan Bolivarian revolution for twenty-first century socialism sketches another trajectory for regional media integration through teleSUR (a five-nation cooperative news network) and ALBA, a regional financial and trade agreement based on equitable exchange, validating possibilities for indigenous and national independence within an international collaborative system. But for now, for much of the world's middle class, capitalism seems more reasonable, or at least more powerful, in large part due to the hegemonic cultural leadership provided by transnational media entertainment.

The next chapter addresses the extent of transnational media activity that overwhelms global culture. Then Chapter 4 explains how transnational media organize practices and produce content favorable to transnational capitalism and its social relations.

References

Altman, R. (2011, December 1). We need not fret over omnipotent markets. *Financial Times*. Retrieved from http://www.ft.com/intl/cms/s/0/890161ac-1b69-11e1-85f8-00144feabdc0.html#axzz2VqD4ba00

Armstrong, A., & McConnachie, A. (1998, July/August). The 1998 Bilderberg meeting. *Social Crediter*. Retrieved from http://www.bilderberg.org/1998.htm

Artz, L., & Murphy, B. O. (2000). *Cultural hegemony in the United States*. Thousand Oaks, CA: Sage.

Ash, T. G. (2005, February 3). Davo's man death wish. *Guardian*. Retrieved from http://www.guardian.co.uk/world/2005/feb/03/globalisation.comment

Brenner, R. (2003). *The boom and the bubble: The U.S. in the world economy*. New York: Verso.

Bruck, P. A., Dörr, D., Cole, M. D., Favre, J., Gramstad, S., Monaco, M. R., & Čulek, Z. P. (2004, November). *Transnational media concentrations in Europe*. Report by Advisory Panel on Media Diversity to the Council of Europe Steering Committee on the Mass Media. Strasbourg, France: Council of Europe.

Carey, N. (2013, July 10). Triaged giving revs up in Detroit. Street-level blight fighters. *Chicago Tribune*, p. 4B.

Castagno, P. (2012). Marxist theory in critical transitions: The democratization of the media in post-neoliberal Argentina. *Triple C: Cognition, Communication, Cooperation*, *10*(2), 334–348. Retrieved from http://www.triple-c.at/index.php/tripleC/article/view/426/391

Chalaby, J. K. (2009). *Transnational television in Europe: Reconfiguring global communications networks*. London: I.B. Tauris.

Clarke, J. (2008). Living with/in and without neo-liberalism. *Focaal*, *2008*(51), 135–147.

Crozier, M. J., Huntington, S. P., & Watanuki, J. (1975). *The crisis of democracy: Report to the Trilateral Commission*. New York: New York University Press.

Dangl, B. (2010). *Dancing with dynamite: Social movements and states in Latin America*. Oakland, CA: AK Press.

DePillis, L. (2013, December 11). Everything you need to know about the Trans Pacific Partnership. *Washington Post*. Wonk Blog. Retrieved March 15, 2014, from http://www.washingtonpost.com/blogs/wonkblog/wp/2013/12/11/everything-you-need-to-know-about-the-trans-pacific-partnership/

Derné, S. D. (2008). *Globalization on the ground: New media and the transformation of culture, class, and gender in India*. Thousand Oaks, CA: Sage.

Fernandes, L. (2000). Nationalizing 'the global': media images, cultural politics, and the middle class in India. *Media, Culture & Society, 22*(5), 611–628.

Food and Agriculture Organization. (2012, October 9). Globally almost 870 million chronically undernourished. Retrieved April 1, 2013, from www.fao.org/news/story/en/item/161819/icode/

Friedman, T. (2005). *The world is flat: A brief history of the 21st century*. New York: Farrar, Straus, & Giroux.

Gill, S. (1992). *American hegemony and the trilateral commission*. Cambridge, UK: Cambridge University Press.

Graz, J. C. (2003). How powerful are transnational elite clubs? The social myth of the World Economic Forum. *New Political Economy, 8*(3), 321–430.

Grimm, M., Harttgen, K., Klasen, S., Misselhorn, M., Munzi, T., & Smeeding, T. (2010). Inequality in human development: An empirical assessment of 32 countries. *Social Indicators Research, 97*(2), 191–211.

Gronbeck, B. E. (1984). Functional and dramaturgical theories of presidential campaigning. *Presidential Studies Quarterly, 14*, 486–499.

Gupta, D. (2000). *Mistaken modernity: India between worlds*. New Delhi: HarperCollins India.

Hall, R., & de Clerq, M. (2009). Middle East media on the move: An emerging growth industry in a pivotal region. *ATKearney: Ideas and Insights*. Retrieved July 8, 2014, from http://www.atkearney.com/documents/10192/4095877b-119c-492b-a236-219098f229df

Harvey, D. (2005). *A brief history of neoliberalism*. Oxford: Oxford University Press.

Iwabuchi, K. (2002). *Recentering globalization: Popular culture and Japanese transnationalism*. Durham, NC: Duke University Press.

Jakubowicz, K. (2007). *Rude awakening: Social and media change in Central and Eastern Europe*. Cresskill, NJ: Hampton Press.

Joshi, T. (2010, October 15). Don 2 gets bill waiver. *Mid-Day Infomedia*. Retrieved from http://www.mid-day.com/articles/don-2-gets-a-bill-waiver/98431

Kalb, D. (2011). Introduction. Headlines of nation, subtexts of class: Working-class populism and the return of the repressed in neoliberal Europe. In D. Kalb & G. Halmai (Eds.), *Headlines of nation, subtexts of class: Working-class populism and the return of the repressed in neoliberal Europe* (pp. 1–36). New York: Berghahn Books.

Kalb, D., & Halmai, G. (Eds.). (2011). *Headlines of nation, subtexts of class: Working-class populism and the return of the repressed in neoliberal Europe*. New York: Berghahn Books.

Keane, M., Fung, A. Y. H., & Moran, A. (2007). *New television, globalization, and the East Asian cultural imagination*. Hong Kong: Hong Kong University Press.

Keay, D. (1987, September 23). Interview. *Woman's Own*. Retrieved from http://www.margaretthatcher.org/document/106689

Krasnow, S. (2013, January/February). The cult of individualism. *Adbusters*, 105. Retrieved from https://www.adbusters.org/magazine/105/cult-individualism.html

Marshall, A. G. (2012). No conspiracy theory – A small group of companies have enormous power over the world. *Alternet*. Retrieved from http://www.alternet.org/world/no-conspiracy-theory-small-group-companies-have-enormous-power-over-world

Mastrini, G., & Becerra, M. (2011). Structure, concentration and changes of the media system in the southern cone of Latin America. *Comunicar*, 18, 51–59.

McGann, J. G. (2012). *Global go to think tanks report and policy advice*. Philadelphia: University of Pennsylvania, International Studies Program. Retrieved April 8, 2013, from http://gotothinktank.com/dev1/wp-content/uploads/2013/07/2012_Global_Go_To_Think_Tank_Report_-_FINAL-1.28.13.pdf

Miller, D. (2010). How neoliberalism got where it is: Elite planning, corporate lobbying and the release of the free market. In K. Birch & V. Mykhnenko (Eds.), *The rise and fall of neoliberalism: The collapse of an economic order?* (pp. 28–56). London: Zed Books.

Palmer, D. (2012, November 29). After election, pressure grows on Obama in Asia-Pacific trade talks. Reuters.com. Retrieved March 3, 2012, from http://reuters.com/assets/print?aid=USBRE8AS07M20121129

Renner, M. (2000). Corporate mergers skyrocket. *Vital Signs*. Retrieved from http://www.globalpolicy.org/component/content/article/221-transnational corporations/47142.html#

Robinson, W. I. (2004). *A theory of global capitalism: Production, class, and state in a transnational world*. Baltimore, MD: Johns Hopkins University Press.

Robinson, W. I., & Harris, J. (2000). Towards a global ruling class? Globalization and the transnational capitalist class. *Science & Society*, 64(1), 11–54.

Rollet, E. (2001). Connecting to the information age: A challenge for the European Union. *Gazette*, 63(5), 371–386.

Rupert, M. (2000). *Ideologies of globalization: Contending visions of a new world order*. New York: Routledge.

Sassoon, A. S. (1987). *Gramsci's politics*. 2nd edn. Minneapolis: University of Minnesota Press.

Servaes, J., & Wang, G. (1997). Privatization and commercialization of the Western-European and South-East Asian broadcasting media. *Asian Journal of Communication*, 7(2), 1–11.

Sherman, B. (2010, December 20). Congressman Sherman to chair entertainment industries caucus. Press release. Retrieved October 14, 2014, from http://sherman.house.gov/media-center/press-releases/congressman-sherman-to-chair-entertainment-industries-caucus

Sklair, L. (2001). *The transnational capitalist class.* New York: Wiley.

Therborn, G. (2008). *What does the ruling class do when it rules? State apparatuses and state power under feudalism, capitalism and socialism.* London: Verso.

Therborn, G. (2012). Class in the 21st century. *New Left Review, 78.* Retrieved from http://newleftreview.org/II/78?goran-therborn-class-in-the-21st-century

van der Pijl, K. (1998a). *Transnational classes and international relations.* New York: Routledge.

Wacquant, L. (2012). Three steps to a historical anthropology of actually existing neoliberalism. *Social Anthropology, 20,* 66–79.

Wallach, L., & Tucker, T. (2012, June 13). Public interest analysis of leaked Trans-Pacific Partnership (TPP) Investment text. *Public Citizen.* Retrieved from http://www.citizen.org/documents/Leaked-TPP-Investment-Analysis.pdf

Zhao, Y., & Duffy, R. (2008). Short-circuited? Communication and labor in China. In C. McKercher & V. Mosco (Eds.), *Knowledge workers in the information society* (pp. 229–248). Lanham, MD: Lexington Books.

Further Reading

Therborn, G. (2008). *What does the ruling class do when it rules? State apparatuses and state power under feudalism, capitalism and socialism.* London: Verso.

van der Pijl, K. (1998). *Transnational classes and international relations.* New York: Routledge.

3

Transnational Media

Everything is for sale. The market determines all. Meanwhile, media entertainment delights and distracts. The influence and power of media entertainment can be debated, but it cannot be denied. For many people, media is the only way of reaching beyond their own location. What we know about civil war in Syria or elections in Venezuela comes mostly from media. Likewise, how and what we learn about fashion trends, music and cultural innovation, and prevailing social norms are largely drawn from media. It is not a leap to claim that the new, emerging global order of transnational production and distribution cultivates power and mass consent (or at least acceptance) through the daily interactions of individuals and classes caught in the web of entrepreneurism and the daily struggle for survival. Simultaneously, the commodification of everything without public regulation undermines human solidarity and tends to reproduce atomized, consumerized social relations. In this unrelenting tide, the media add to the flow of tolerance and consent for capitalism, through news and information selection that validates the competitive urge and through entertainment genres that distract and gratify individuals with narratives and formats that cheer on consumerism.

Media exist within and contribute to dynamic social relations within each society and increasingly the world. Media cannot be singled out from their historical and social contexts: media practices reflect and reproduce the transnational transformation of capitalism. Media are "instruments, not instigators, of other social forces" (McQuail, 1992, p. 273). Transnational media are instruments of and for the transnational capitalist class (TNCC). Media are simultaneously technologies, forms of communication,

Global Entertainment Media: A Critical Introduction, First Edition. Lee Artz.
© 2015 John Wiley & Sons, Inc. Published 2015 by John Wiley & Sons, Inc.

programmers of content, and institutions. Media are industries and promoters of industries; media are commodities and promoters of commodities. Media have the power to create and distribute messages, images, meanings, and ideologies to millions. Media, particularly television and movies, have a crucial role in constructing and disseminating representations of what is and what is possible, thus often playing a critical role in politics through entertainment narratives. As the US occupation of Iraq and Afghanistan continued, television programming featured stories about terrorism and military actions on behalf of American security, such as *24*, *NCIS*, *Homeland*, *Sleeper Cell*, and more – all clearly advocating restrictions on civil rights (Keeton & Scheckner, 2013). Media do not begin with ideological goals; they are first and foremost capitalist institutions, for-profit enterprises contributing to and participating in the transnational capitalist transformation of social relations in every nation and territory. While economic restructuring can be conveniently defended in the United States as the need for competition in the face of global attacks on "our" way of life, elsewhere market imperatives for entertainment and ideology appear differently.

In Asia, transnational media corporations (TNMCs) try to "exploit and produce desire among the people to be members of the middle class in a modern capitalist society. Thus, Japanese capital and transnational manufacturing companies have supported Japanese media efforts with the aim of marketing consumer commodities in Asia" (Iwabuchi, 2002, p. 103). Koichi Iwabuchi (2004) notes that "transnational media flows are being reorganized in a highly dispersed and ubiquitous power structure through the intensifying collaboration of media corporations and media creators that are based in various developed nations" (p. 77). It would be inaccurate to describe transnational media development in the twenty-first century as Americanization or Westernization. It would be just as wrong to imagine that local media have secured space for their own unique cultural products.

Sony is not "Japanizing" the United States or India through its media mergers any more than Disney "Westernizes" Argentina or India with its joint ventures. Transnational capitalist investors and managers are reorganizing media production across borders and cultures to improve their net profits by lowering production costs and increasing consumer activity in new locales. Sony buys into Hollywood, Disney buys into Bollywood, Bollywood buys into China, and China's Chollywood seeks partners everywhere, all to consolidate production and distribution, to build diversified entertainment conglomerates through transnational interlocks. TNMCs party together, building networks of production and distribution. Comcast buys NBC Universal to have content to distribute. News Corp and Liberty Media/ Discovery Channel invest in DirecTV's satellite business to better distribute their content. Not all partnerships are economically or organizationally successful (as Time Warner and AOL discovered), yet the impulse and activity continues because of the capitalist drive for profits and the new transnational market reality.

Local partners are crucial for facilitating entry into new markets. If "Japanese media industries and cultural products cannot successfully become transnational players without partners" (Iwabuchi, 2002, p. 37), the "merge or die" condition is all the more pressing for other, less resourced, national and regional media firms. This is true everywhere. Australia TNMCs have turned to co-productions in other regions. In 2003, British television distributors earned $920 million from international co-productions, licensing, format, and DVD sales – three times the international income from British-produced and exported television programs (Havens, 2006, p. 33).

The transnational process entails a profound restructuring of media production and content. Transnational media efforts and successes are not separate from the universal transformation of social relations. A dialectic unfolds as capitalism reorganizes its chains of production: Entertainment media and advertising provide themes and narratives to emerging middle-class consumers that say, "This is who you are. This is what successful entrepreneurs and managers do. This is what professional lifestyles look like." In other words, TNMCs and their advertisers only enter nations where privatization and the accumulation of wealth through increased wage labor production has become accepted. Increased productivity of labor provides capitalist wealth as well as income for middle classes who then become dedicated consumers. Conversely, during the prolonged economic recession in Asia, unemployment ramped up, consumer spending collapsed, advertising revenues declined, and regional TNMCs retreated from lower-profit nations (Iwabuchi, 2002, p. 107). Transnational media influence is not independent of social relations, material conditions, or, for that matter, creative expertise in delivering popular messages. Transnational media do not fly solo; they ride in tandem with capitalist development.

Global expansion has become a matter of survival and consequently media have developed in line with the transnationalization of all capitalist production. Having flooded their own markets, national media must inevitably consolidate and expand to other countries to maximize revenues and profits. Mergers and acquisitions of all or part of another nation's media provide one form of expansion, but national regulations restricted foreign ownership until recently. Satellite technology opened the possibility for unregulated cross-border broadcasting, often making national regulations unenforceable. Meanwhile, the influence and leadership of segments of the TNCC in each country secured policy changes and dramatic media deregulation in all but the most authoritarian countries (e.g., Zimbabwe, Burma), permitting increased foreign direct investment (FDI), transnational mergers, and joint ventures. Driven by TNCC thirst for consumer audiences, most nations soon privatize media, while TNMCs gobble up the best outlets – startling citizens concerned with pluralism and media democracy (Bruck et al., 2004). TNMCs expand program diversity in many places, but curtail public media and media democracy in all places.

Direct foreign investment, strategic partnerships, and mergers and acquisitions create a geographically dispersed and culturally diverse media enterprises that quickly outpace media that rely on selling globally standardized products abroad (Flew & Gilmour, 2003, p. 12). The rapid growth of News Corp, Rupert Murdoch's media empire, testifies to the efficacy of transnational strategies. Standardized production practices, consumer market segmentation, and customized localized media supplement the more traditional single global media product. Licensing formats in television programming assure not only transfer of cultural content, but perhaps just as importantly for long-term effects, formats also bring professional media management protocols, expertise in production, distribution and marketing, training and supervision in corporate media entertainment norms, and transnationalized "commonsense" notions about branding, audience creation, competition, business ethics, shared industry values, and how to deal with local government protocols.

In Europe, the Council of Europe and the European Union led the way with the "Television Without Frontiers" directive that enforced unrestricted television broadcasting across borders (Aubry, 2000). In other regions, IMF structural adjustment programs and WTO guidelines on media overrule national regulations. Deregulation in every case contributed to a recognizable loss of political diversity and democratic access to the media (Boas, 2013; Bruck et al., 2004; Jakubowicz, 2007; Hallin & Papathanassopoulos, 2002; Hong, 1998; Zhao, 2008). "The incapability of national authorities to deal efficiently with cross-national developments [in media] is increasingly evident" as the Council of Europe "obliges Member states to remove obstacles to the operation of the internal [media] market" (Bruck et al., 2004, pp. 15, 17). Changes and contradictions in transnational production have had repercussions on political, ideological, and cultural formations; media production has been no exception.

Media and culture are also prime commodity-producing, profit-making industries. The global entertainment and media market is estimated to reach $2 trillion in 2015 (Li, 2008; Bond, 2013). A few examples should verify the economic possibilities for telecommunication, entertainment media, and culture industries. In the twenty-first century, media can make some people very rich.

Media for Profit

Carlos Slim, *Forbes* magazine's richest man in the world ($65 billion), became a billionaire following a sweetheart deal takeover of Mexico's public telephone company TELMEX and his subsequent acquisition of América Movile, the Western Hemisphere's fourth largest telecommunications company. Slim owns stakes in Independent News & Media (a large newspaper chain with outlets in Australia, Ireland, New Zealand, Northern Ireland, and South Africa) and the New York Times Company. Incidentally, as part of the TNCC, Slim also sits on the board of the RAND Corporation, a TNCC global policy research center serving government and corporations (Menotti, 2011).

Billionaire Vladimir Potanin, owner of Interros, an industrial and financial consortium, owns Profmedia, Russia's largest media group, with magazines, radio stations, movie theaters, and Russia's dominant television network (Menotti, 2011). Profmedia broadcasts Russian versions of transnational programming, such as MTV, relaunched as Pyatnitsa with $100 million investment in 2012 (Profmedia, 2013). Profmedia "works with the premium target audience" through a number of famous Russian brands, including TV3 and 2×2 in television, Avtoradio, Energy, Radio Romantika, and Humour FM in radio, Central Partnership in film production and distribution, Cinema Park in cinemas, Afisha in print media, and rambler.ru, lenta.ru, afisha.ru, 101. ru, and other major Internet brands in RuNet (Profmedia.ru, 2013). Profmedia joined George Soros in Syaszinvest, a leading Russian telecom firm. In 2013, Profmedia joined with Dutch-based TNMC Sanoma Independent Media to publish 20 new magazines (Russian joint, 2013), which has Russian partnerships with Hearst, Wall St. Journal, and Financial Times (Sanoma, 2013).

Alisher Usmanov, primary shareholder of Metalloinvest, Russia's primary iron ore producer and the fifth richest man in Russia ($17.7 billion), owns *Kommersant*, Russia's leading business-oriented newspaper, owns 59% of Telecominvest, and is the head of MegaFon, Russia's third largest mobile phone company. Usmanov's Digital Sky Technologies has investments in Facebook, Zynga, and Groupon. He also has shares in South Africa-based TNMC Naspers and is co-owner of a TV media holding company that includes a sports channel, a music channel, and 33 regional TV broadcasting stations. Usmanov owns the Sekret Firmy Publishing House, as well as the Internet website Livejournal.com, the Internet newspaper Gazeta.ru, and several popular web portals, including Mail.ru, Odnoklassniki.ru, and Vkontakte.ru. (Menotti, 2011).

More than 100 other Russian billionaires made fortunes in their gallop from state bureaucracy to private enterprise. To consolidate political power, many branched out into media, as lucrative venues for accumulating more wealth, while ensuring direct media access to 150 million people across nine time zones, promoting consumerism and the market ideology essential to winning popular Russian support for transnational capitalist practices.

Rupert Murdoch's News Corp brings in on average $34 billion in revenues annually and $700 million in profits, demonstrating the enormous wealth that can be generated from media commodities and selling audiences to advertisers, but smaller transnational corporations (TNCs) have snatched some profits from telecommunications and media entertainment on the global periphery. In India, the Ruia brothers, Sashi and Ravi, control the Essar Group – a highly diversified TNC with global interests in shipping, steel, energy, and telecom. Essar clinched a $350 million deal with Dhabi Group's Warid Telecom to acquire a majority stake in firms in Uganda and the Democratic Republic of the Congo (Menotti, 2011). Essar owns several global ICT companies and a UK joint venture in Paprika Media magazine. Essar underscores that transnational media are capitalist enterprises: telecommunication, media entertainment, and information and communication technologies (ICT) contribute to the Ruias' wealth as clearly as profits generated by selling steel or transporting commodities.

As these and other examples testify, media and culture are not peripheral to transnational capitalist economic formation (e.g., see ketupa.net; mediedatenbank.com). Media "contribute to the commodification of all productive forces and become a commodity in their own right" (Mosco, 2012, p. 571). In general, media gain capitalist profits by selling media products for more than producers and creators are paid for their labor

Berlusconi/Mediaset

Mediaset earns $4 billion in annual revenue. Much less global than other TNMCs, Mediaset is Silvio Berlusconi's political and economic power base in Italy. Mediaset comprises three national television channels that collectively cover half of the national television audience and 58% of advertising revenue (Mediedatenbank, 2013). Berlusconi owns Publitalia, the leading Italian advertising and publicity agency, reaping profits from advertising sales and production on both ends of the audience commodity exchange. Berlusconi owns Arnoldo Mondadori Editore, Italy's largest publisher, including *Panorama*, a popular news magazine. Berlusconi is major shareholder of Fininvest, a multimedia company, which is among the 10 largest private companies in Italy. Berlusconi has interests in cinema and video distribution (Medusa Film and Penta Film) and owns AC Milan, one of Italy's most popular football teams. Mediaset has US, Canadian, and British shareholders with additional French, German, and Dutch investors. Mediaset has joint ventures with Comcast's CNBC and Time Warner, is majority holder in the largest television network in Spain and has shares in Telecinco TV, Digital Plus, and Prisa TV in Spain, as well as a 25% partnership with Nessma TV, an Arabic station in Tunisia. Mediaset owns 35% of Pegaso (which has 83% of the Caribevision network broadcasting in New York, Miami, and Puerto Rico) and has a 49% partnership with the China Media Group, which broadcasts the China Sport Network (Mediaset, 2013). Mediaset illustrates the hegemonic appeal that the transnational agenda pledges for all TNMCs: adopting a cross-border production and distribution regimen brings economic rewards; failure to adapt means death by national and domestic attrition as audiences migrate to larger, more appealing TNMC programs.

and creativity. Transnational media are important contributors to TNCC wealth and the transnational capitalist transformation as media firms join other TNCs in border crossings to build alliances for producing and distributing multicultural, multinational entertainment and its consuming audiences.

Media Entertainment and Transnational Capitalism

Those who own and control media production and distribution have more ability to determine media content and practice. Yet, the structure of media is not the complete picture. Beyond concerns about owner abuse of power, the shifting relations of transnational media raise questions about how production practices and commercial strategies influence cultural production, including the standardization of entertainment formats and the consequent reduction in political diversity and citizen access to the media.

Political economy provides a lens for understanding the relations between ownership and content, because it encompasses the full complement of social relations, particularly power relations that mutually constitute the production, distribution, and consumption of resources; political economy addresses the totality of social relations that constitute the economic, political, social, and cultural fields (Mosco, 2009; Boyd-Barrett, n. d.). Political economy approaches consider ownership with production norms; production practices with programming choices; programming choices with commercial goals (or public service aims); advertising revenues with audience programming; audience effects with cultural norms; material commodities with symbolic meanings; economic relations with ideology; and more. In other words, the production, distribution, and consumption of media are not simply economic or structural conditions – in each process a panoply of social relations is forged and implemented.

Media structures frame production practices and programming content. Programming forms and themes that dominate transnational media set political agendas, contribute knowledge, and influence attitudes and behaviors – depending on the social and cultural background, skill, consciousness, and interest of the audience. Media institutions, professional practices, and the social consequences of media are stirred by existing social class relations, their antagonism and contradictions. This does not suggest structures are insurmountable or predeterminant; rather, it recognizes the concrete conditions under which reproduction or change is possible.

Michael Keane (2006) imagines "Asianess is colonizing international communication" (p. 839). Jan Nedverteen Pieterse (2006) claims global culture is being "Easternized" (p. 122) and Dayan Thussu (2007) argues that new networks from the global South are circulating "subaltern flows" (subordinate groups expressing alternative worldviews) which construct new identities for international viewers (pp. 23, 25). What is sorely lacking is recognition of the structure of capitalist social relations. Keane, Thussu, and Hafez (2007) and disparate others are astute enough to see the changing global media environment, but as they don't admit that social classes exist their conclusions are handicapped.

Insights from international media studies need the backbone of international political economy to explain the changing relations of production globally, and in each country: increased labor productivity from technology and industrial rationalization creates such wealth that fewer humans are needed to produce the necessities of life; capitalism has flooded national markets with the overproduction of goods and has been forced to increase pressure on the working class and also to look globally to accumulate more profit; cross-border production and distribution depend on the deregulation of public interest. Neoliberalism forcefully requires international integration of production and trade; and finally, as former state-controlled nations collapse and authoritarian regimes lose power, structural adjustment programs and rapid privatization create new capitalists in nations previously off the market economy grid. In other words, a political economy lens makes sense of what all can see, but is not yet fully explained, including making sense of global entertainment media as an expression of global class relations.

Transforming the Political Economy of Global Media

The production and distribution of global media entertainment conforms to transnational capitalist social relations of production. Capitalism has grown and re-formed as transnational. There is a dominant, irrefutable influence on global cultural production, but it is not from Western culture per se. Rather, a transnational capitalism regime demands low-cost labor to produce mass entertainment, world citizens to be consumers, all cultures to be commodified, and the entire world to become a source of accumulation of wealth for a voracious transnational capitalist class. Media are at the center of this economic, social, and cultural process.

Significantly, media around the world have signed up with the transnational media corporations. Local media are not "striking back" against transnational media (Rantanen, 2002) because TNMCs appear as paternal guides to riches. Local commercial media seek their own advertising revenues and audience share, bringing side dishes to the transnational buffet of consumerism, as they line up for admission to transnational markets in response to the invitation by TNMCs to make more local productions. Meanwhile, TNMCs "thrive on respect for and exploitation of local cultural values" (Mooij, 1998, p. 299).

Shifting alliances and antagonisms among transnational media play out like a world domination board game – with human costs. Leaving old partners for new often means abandoning workers in one locale for a cheaper labor force in another. National interests do not explain Lenovo's purchase of US-based Motorola, or its investment in Germany and Brazil. The same American and Asian workers will produce and distribute IBM ThinkPads and Motorola Razr phones across borders, while shareholders of diverse nationalities will reap profits across borders. The more complete picture shows that US capitalists, Chinese capitalists, Indian capitalists, and Finnish capitalists are each poised to prosper from Indian and Chinese labor productivity and consumer sales without any regard for labor in their

Nokia: Transnational Competition and Consolidation

In 2010, Finnish-based Nokia had $57 billion in revenue from information technology (ICT) produced in seven countries. Nokia also has joint ventures with Microsoft, Sanyo, Siemens, and dozens of other firms in China, India, Kenya, Switzerland, United States, and the United Kingdom. Yet as Nokia discovered, transnational joint ventures do not preclude transnational competition – capitalist investors expect a continuous return of profit. Exploiting lower labor costs and a more efficient software platform, Huawei and ZTE are gobbling up Nokia's market. Microsoft's "Windows" rescue of Nokia may not even save the once former leader in cellular phones (Gasseé, 2012). Vodafone, Telefónica, Deutsche Telekom, Ericsson, Sony, Motorola (now owned by Lenovo), China's Huawei (the world's largest telecom equipment maker, which works with all of the world's top telecoms), and other telecom and ICT manufacturers are also transnational in structure, production, and distribution (UNCTAD, 2011). In 2013, Japan's Sofbank investment firm paid $21.6 billion for a 78% stake in Sprint-Nextel, instantly making it one of the world's largest transnational mobile operators (Gabriel, 2012). All of them are circling the wounded Nokia and attacking its lingering market share, even as they each look for new transnational partnerships.

own nations. Smaller TNMCs are involved in the transformation of global telecommunications as well: Qatar Telecom has a joint venture with Korea Telecom, IndoSat (Indonesia), and ATT; Nippon TT owns shares in Singapore's StarHub Cablevision; Telecom Italia owns 30% of Globo.com; and Microsoft is a major investor in Globo Cabo, Brazil's largest cable provider.

The impact of global class realignments cannot be ignored, with the TNCC implementing cross-border, cross-media production relations among social classes, eroding democracy and destroying the environment in the process. We have entered the transnational era. Transnational capitalism's cultural aspirations are not US dominance, but profits for the few and consumerism for all (Sklair, 2001, p. 289).

Media in all nations reflect existing social relations. Today media relations are transnational capitalist relations. This is not a denial of agency; but absent conscious, organized alternative social movements, the TNCC will continue in myriad ways to influence nations and peoples on behalf of market values. We can identify the owners of entertainment media, ascertain their financial interests and goals, discover the norms of their content production, list the participants and agents in their production and distribution chains, and ascertain the social, cultural, and ideological character of their programming. Transnational media have transnational owners, managers, and co-producers attempting to create programs that will attract audiences that can be sold to advertisers. Those advertisers want audiences "ready to buy" consumer goods, so programming has structures, themes, narratives, and ideologies conducive to individual consumption. Global, national, regional, local, and cultural signs and symbols appear according to the intents, skills, expectations, resources, and commonsense practices of the creators of programs – all in line with transnational accumulation goals.

Accordingly, the maturing political economy of transnational entertainment media predicts that programming genre diversity will flourish, but democratic access will recede. More diversity, less democracy. In Latin America, for instance, "a competitive radio market essentially means multiple music options rather than different news perspectives" (Boas, 2013, p. 5). In the Middle East, where there is "a high number of channels available, there is a wide variety of genres and content on offer for the pan-Arab audience" (Dubai Press Club, 2010), but there is scant democratic participation in media or society.

Transnational media have morphed beyond the previously known and recognized species of Western, national, or international media to become new agents of cross-border entertainment feeding on local, regional, national, and linguistic ingredients. Although TNMCs broadcast programs across borders to countries not hosting TNMC production (Bruck et al., 2004, p. 6), it is a "misconception that global and local are mutually exclusive and contradictory processes" (Sklair, 2001, p. 256); both are part of the transnational production and distribution system. Media partnerships may not exist beyond an individual project, but local producers welcome TNMC collaboration "because it leads to increased production funding and increased revenues, which can be used to cross-subsidize local producers' other projects" (Havens, 2006, p. 51). Additionally, TNMCs recruit and hire a multitude of local firms for technical, logistical, and creative assistance for almost every aspect of production, from building sets to providing lighting, from script editing and translation to wardrobe and makeup, to post-production editing and distribution via multiple media platforms – all flowing within the current of TNMC production practices for local and cross-border distribution.

Diversity in Transnational Media Operation

Multi-territory channels broadcast locally with independent programs for local audience interests. Over 100 pan-European networks specialize in niche genres broadcasting over country-specific or region-specific channels. Time Warner's Cartoon Network, Fox Kids, MTV, and Discovery are typical examples: they each attempt to localize their broadcasts by dubbing or subtitling language and split the satellite or cable feed to allow local programming windows under the international brand. Pan-European broadcasters that have combined local adaptability with country-specific channels have been more successful. These channels share a brand style as well as network resources. Networks benefit from creative contributions of local co-producers that can be shared across channels. Viacom/Paramount has been particularly active with a headquarters in Rome, co-productions with Spanish cable giant Sogecable, and other ventures with British, French, German, and Belgian companies (Havens, 2006, p. 51). Firms based in Europe have struggled to combine their support of economic neoliberalism with national film subsidies for co-production of pan-European-based regional and "world" projects (Miller et al., 2008, pp. 175, 178–182). Chalaby (2005) concludes that transnational networks transcend national cultures by respecting and incorporating cultural difference in their programming.

Pan-European channels have not displaced smaller multi-territory transnationals, but find common ground in co-productions and other joint ventures in a shared drive for audience share. David Fernández-Quijada (2013) relates how TNMCs like Endemol, Sony, Fremantle, Banijay,and Zodiak contract co-productions or merge with domestic "independent" media like Shed, Tinopolis, and Boomerang to create TNMC webs of production and distribution in Britain and Spain. Across Europe, TNMCs of all types recruit local media producers to maximize profits. There are no global/local barriers that cannot be reduced to parameters for making media and profits.

Media are crucial to the transnational production circuit (distributing information and advertising for other products) and to the potential success of TNCC hegemony (producing and legitimizing consumerist and market ideologies). Summarizing years of research, Chalaby (2009) observes that "transnational television does not merely participate in the globalizing process, it also reflects our globalized world" (p. 227). As part of transnational capitalism, media production shares many of the same structural and procedural characteristics of other transnational corporations – including the inexhaustible drive for profits as national markets become saturated or concentrated. Media are an industrial segment of transnational capitalist production, making commodities for profit in the global market. Transnational media extract content and revenue from around the world. *Hard Rain* (1993), the Paramount action adventure movie, was co-financed by UGC (France's largest theater chain), the BBC, Telemuchen, and the Danish Nordisk Studio, as well as Marubeni and Toho-Towa, Japanese film distributors.

In general, transnational media production chains in multiple nations gather local directors, television and film studios, local technicians from videographers to editors and manufacturing workers, advertising, public relations, and marketing staff, actors, writers, copyeditors, lighting crews, and all the other necessary and ancillary workers. The location of these workers and their work is secondary. Thailand has become "the top production destination and post-production site for many international projects for low-cost labour, scenery, facilities, and logistics," while other Euro-Asian productions set up shop in Europe, India, and Australia to tap talent, resources, and markets elsewhere (Davis & Yeh, 2008, pp. 97, 99–105). Media corporations have trajectories similar to other TNCs. Whether appliances, automobiles, or movies, transnational capitalism has rearranged production and distribution of commodities across borders.

Media Apparatus

Media's unique characteristics make them instrumental for transforming the global social order. Yet, the complexities of their characteristics, forms, and functions often complicate discussions. Media can be understood as:

1. Technology: AM/FM/Short wave radio, television, print, cellular, digital, with attendant material processes: sound, print, electronics, ether broadcast, coaxial cable, and more.
2. Form: poster, book, magazine, newspaper, radio, television, video, film, Internet, mobile.
3. Content: news, information, entertainment, education, advertising, propaganda. Media content may also be understood stylistically as genre: news, news magazine, drama, melodrama, situation comedy, sports, game show, documentary, factual entertainment, and more.
4. Institution: public, private, government, community.
5. Social function: information, socialization, identification, persuasion, and so on.

Of course, media have additional distinctions or categories and can be further sub-divided. Often disagreements or confusions about media arise because individuals are talking about different media dimensions using different vocabularies and assumptions.

Media Content as Social Lubricant

Media entertainment content is crucial for assembling consent for TNCC policies and practices, providing messages and symbols promoting, representing, and legitimating transnational production social relations with "global 'semiotic constructions,' through images of the world, nations, institutions, people and activities, that media create and distribute, or not" (Boyd-Barrett, 2006, p. 28). Media, particularly entertainment media, supply the consensual lubricant for cultural hegemony among diverse cultures, nations, and classes.

> The goal of dominant political groups and classes [is to] disseminate their own ideas throughout a society such that these ideas become dominant, cohering a social formation in a process of cultural and political leadership and absorbing

or articulating in this way the discourses of other groups and classes in order to nullify their potential antagonism. (Castagno, 2012, p. 334)

MediaAsia, one of the most active pan-Asian TNMCs, courts upscale youth across Asia with movie characters fluent in a variety of cultures, proficient in languages, fashion, food, and stylish travel as well as the latest technology in a "pointedly twenty-first century amalgamation of commodity and entertainment values" (Davis & Yeh, 2008, p. 107). The movie and media industries replicate the structure and practice of other transnational industries, while TNMC commodities carry symbolic content that further advocates cultural behaviors appropriate for a transnational capitalist system. Media are influential as a primary means of communicating values in every society. Thus, the Chinese bureaucracy has begun substituting state propaganda with consumerist media entertainment as an improved means of social control (Hong, 1998; Zhao, 2008, p. 123).

Media: Industries for Profit

Media are capitalist industries. Capitalist entertainment media have become transnationalized in production and distribution for private profit, generating billions in revenues from sales of media products, including newspapers, magazines, DVDs, CDs, and audiences for cinema, radio, television, and digital media. Whatever the medium, TNMCs profit from commodities produced by the wage labor of creative workers, either as salaried or hourly wageworkers, or as private contractors hired for their labor power, their creative ability to produce content which is essential for print, broadcast, music, and film. Media profit from the wage labor of production workers, who create value through their production of magazines, newspapers, CDs, DVDs, and other material goods. Media profits are extracted by paying workers less than the value of the products they produce.

Estimates put global media revenue at $2.2 trillion in 2012. Media produce and sell products. Each medium has a specific commodity form as determined by its capitalist producers and their target consumer market. In their various divisions, media produce and distribute: (1) programs and other content; (2) advertising; (3) audiences; and (4) ideologies (expressed in the values and beliefs manifest in the messages and narratives of news and entertainment programming). Media products have a more profound social consequence than most other commodities because they exude meaning as their essential appeal and effect. Media explicitly transmit and elicit symbolic meanings, values, norms, and beliefs. Indeed, meaning as a primary ingredient in media provides a major motivation for consumer behavior. Thus, ideology (including consumerism) is produced and distributed through all media goods and services.

Revenue streams for the media industry depend on the sale of commodities, including:

1. Media technology (phones, computers, televisions, radios, and other devices)
2. Media access (cable and satellite connections, premium channels, pay-per-view, downloads, movie admissions, concerts, and other user access fees)
3. Media content as commodity (DVDs, books, magazines, comics, and other media commodities that can be retailed)
4. Media program formats may be sold, especially internationally, and producers can add training, supervision, promotion, and other add-ons
5. Media programming sold through syndication to distribution networks, when programs are sold per episode or season to a broadcaster
6. Non-media commodity spin-offs (toys, games, video games, clothing, and other goods featuring media content, characters, or icons)
7. Media audiences attracted to programming are sold to advertisers directly or through product placement in programs and movies.

Not all TNMCs produce and distribute every media commodity or for every media use, but all global entertainment media either contribute to or profit from each of these commodity forms in one way or another.

Profits can be generated in several ways. Most media now profit from multiple delivery systems. Film is produced for a "per viewing" consumption. Movie-goers pay for each single viewing. Film producers also copy their movies into discrete consumer products in the form of DVDs. Broadcasters purchase films for distribution on television, including through pay-per-view and traditional "free" TV. Record companies likewise mass produce copies of music as CDs or other digital formats. Books and other printed material are produced for individual sale, as well. Newspapers and magazines are material goods sold to individual consumers. With the Internet, publishers now also garner revenue through on-line reader subscriptions.

Phones for Fun and Profit

The demand for mobile phones is not a "mechanical outcome of technical progress, but the product of the balance of forces that shape society. [For individuals] it is an attempt to wrest a measure of personal control in a social world out of control" (Schiller, 1999, p. 8). For corporations, cell phones are lucrative consumer products and a means for further software sales and advertising. Rather than becoming a means to improve human communication, mobile phones have been configured as consumable media commodities and a means to access other media commodities. The transnationalized telecommunication industry has developed multiple revenue components: the phone itself is technology sold as individual commodity; the monthly or per use purchase of phone connectivity is another major source of revenue; finally, consumers may purchase special applications and services for their phones as a one-time buy, per use, or through monthly service fees. Multiple revenue streams explain why transnational telecommunication equipment makers and service providers are among the richest TNCs (ATT, Vodafone, Telefónica, NTT, Huawei, Nokia, Deutsche Telekom). Digital technology for cell phones, cable, and Internet broadband opens the transmission of media content by telecommunications firms, which are challenging traditional broadcasters and publishers for audiences (Bain & Company, 2012; Mastrini & Becerra, 2011, p. 54).

Cable, satellite, and pay-per-view systems collect subscription and user fees directly from audiences. China Telecom, Jiangsu, Comcast, DirecTV, BSkyB, T-Sky India, and other Sky systems, Dish Network, Time-Warner, TelMex, Nippon, Naspers, and another 100 regional TNMCs have millions of subscribers and collectively turn revenues in the hundreds of billions annually (Zhao, 2013).

Some content creators like Disney make programming decisions anticipating the potential market for toys, games, music, clothes, and other spin-off consumer goods based on characters in their films. Larger firms contain costs and increase income through vertical and horizontal integration. Vertical integration refers to a company's control over resources for all the steps in the production process: a newspaper might own a paper

Super Girl, Super Profit

Social media have added to the revenue stream of integrated TNMCs. Text message voting generates millions for networks and telecommunication firms. TV voters for their favorite contestant on *Super Girl* – the Chinese version of the *Idol* format broadcast on Hunan Satellite TV – were charged 13 cents per vote. At the end of the 2004 first season, revenues from text messaging gave Hunan Satellite $11 million, Shanghai Tianyu, the local producer, $4 million, Internet providers $3.5 million, the merchandizing firm $12 million, and the telecom provider $1.5 million. The show's sponsor, Mongolian Cow Yoghurt, which paid millions for access to the television audiences, raised $89 million in revenues from products advertised on *Super Girl*. (Keane, Fung, & Moran, 2007, p. 133). The model quickly caught on with other TNMCS. By 2005, 55 million text message and phone call "votes" to *Indian Idol* were generating almost $2.5 million in telecom revenue (Pudnathambekar, 2010, p. 247).

mill, or even timber, as the *New York Times* does, printing presses, and delivery trucks. Horizontal integration means a company has expanded its holdings of other companies in the same medium: Clear Channel purchases multiple radio stations in single markets to increase its leverage with advertisers and encompass more radio audiences with diverse genres. Multi-platform media (vertically and horizontally integrated) promote synergy among their offerings and holdings: a movie provides music CDs, a cartoon provides characters for a video game, a movie becomes a stage performance, a television program markets a theme park, and similar cross-promotion activity (Gershon, 2005, p. 23). Although cross-promotion revenues do not accrue directly from cross-promotion, the ability to advertise its own products is value-added to any media company.

While all media commodities must elicit some desire in the consumer, self-acting, power-broking audiences aren't the source of demand for any particular product; calculations of distribution, sales, and profits based on whether media content elements can be marketed and promoted more often determine what will be produced (Miller et al., 2008, pp. 260–266). Concentration among TNMCs tends to standardize formats, increase entertainment diversity, and decrease political diversity because commercial interests are paramount and consolidation improves a TNMC's ability to influence markets, labor costs, and national and international media programming. Increased profits may result from the successful negotiation of these economic and political variables.

Audience as Commodity

The kernel of capitalism is the market imperative for all production-for-profit: commodities are produced for sale. There are no profits until the products are sold. In this process, modern-day capitalism relies on advertising to promote and speed up the circulation/sale of commodities. Production for consumption is what drives, organizes, and over-determines all production, including the content of media programming.

Television networks produce programs, but programs are not their primary product. Viewers don't buy network television shows. Advertisers don't buy television shows. Advertisers don't buy "time," either. Advertisers pay big bucks to networks for viewers: advertisers buy audiences. Advertisers need viewers who are potential consumers essential to the sale of products.

Media profit from the "sale" of audiences to advertisers – about $350 billion annually for television, some $65 billion for Internet advertising. Advertisers "buy" readers, viewers, and listeners as discrete demographic units, so the production of audiences requires an appropriate programming form and content. In the 1960s, Dallas Smythe (1994) first explained this process: advertisers "buy the services of audiences" who will pay attention to their messages (p. 270).

Television networks have little interest in audiences per se; their primary concern is to attract audiences that have commercial value to advertisers. Networks do not care about audiences any more than automobile manufacturers care about cars or fast-food restaurants want hamburgers. Audiences, autos, hamburgers are products, a means to an end. Each product must appeal to its buyer. Audiences are not the end-goal of the networks, any more than automobiles are the end-goal of auto manufacturers. Cars are sold; audiences are sold.

Programs are thus produced and broadcast for different audiences, largely according to social class, but also delineated by gender, ethnicity, and culture (Garnham, 1990, p. 29). Audiences have more or less worth depending on the value of their demographic to product producers: denture manufacturers value over-50 viewers, candy manufacturers prefer younger viewers, beer producers target males 21–34, and so on. An award-winning television series will be canceled in an instant, if advertisers don't want that particular viewing audience.

Transnational broadcasting in Europe depends on the class character of viewing and consuming audiences, explaining programming and even station choices of TNMCs. Fashion TV, Travel Channel, Eurosport, and documentary channels have a "more upmarket audience than that of terrestrial stations" (Chalaby, 2009, p. 91). The audience profile of news and business channels, like CNN and Bloomberg, translates into maximum advertising exposure to the desired elite audiences and "minimum audience wastage" for luxury goods, technology firms, and elite service providers because these stations "offer an advertising environment that is adapted to an affluent business audience" (Chalaby, 2009, pp. 91–92).

Wherever other niche audiences are desirable due to their available disposable income (women or youth in Europe and North America, for example) programmers provide low-cost shows expected to have significant appeal to that demographic. "Small town audiences with their cut-price tickets and queues of eager young fans don't matter as much as they used to" since more profits can be made from multiplexes catering to affluent, upper-middle-class youth in India (Mishra, 2006, p. 175). For years, STAR TV, Zee TV, and Sony provided no local language programming in Northeast India "simply because the region did not represent a commercially viable market" – advertisers had little interest in the economically distressed states. Thus, Zee TV, Eenadu, and Sun TV broadcast in Hindi, Tamil, and Telugu to audiences in the more prosperous southern regions (Punathambekar, 2010, pp. 245–246).

Reality shows, relatively cheap to produce, are now the leading drama format on television. Although some active-audience advocates celebrate reality television as the "feminization" of the public sphere, the emergence of the format can best be understood as a cost-cutting measure and an instance of niche marketing (Miller et al., 2008, p. 95).

Mass-produced, advertiser-supported transnational media depend on the audience commodity to realize profits at the end of the production-distribution-consumption chain. Understanding the audience as commodity admits that audiences are assembled as marketable units that have exchange value for programmers and advertisers. Audiences are sold to advertisers for their exchange value – they are useful to advertisers who need viewers and readers who will attend to their persuasive messages. The larger the audience and the more the audience has demographics matching the buying characteristics of potential consumers, the more value that particular audience has to an advertiser.

The real significance of transnational media content is this: "in economic terms the main function of the mass media in this system is to produce audiences prepared to be dutiful consumers ... The real end-product is the commodity to be sold, and the audience produced by the mass media is but part of the means to that end" (Smythe, 1994, p. 251). The primary task facing transnational media content producers is how to attract, capture, and deliver those local audiences (and their attention) as consumers to transnational advertisers. Content producers create programming not for global audiences per se, but for specific localized audiences which have exchange value – that is, audiences which are desirable and can be sold in discrete time blocs to advertisers. Audiences that will be consumers.

For transnational media that means the standardization of localization – creating hybrid media with local translations of global consumerist themes. Programming content or form must facilitate the intended purpose for broadcast: priming audiences to buy.

Pay Per View

Pay television – direct consumer purchase of content – has earned billions for TNMC cable and satellite systems, such as Comcast, Liberty Global, and News Corp's Sky TV. Programs produced for premium cable stations are bought by content aggregators and media distributors, as well as consumers. In most cases, viewers buy programming without advertising: media profits are skimmed off the difference between program costs and monthly subscription fees or per-view purchases. This system of financing runs in tandem with advertising-funded media. Movies or programs on one system often appear later on the other. Still, even with pay-per-view television and DVR recording devices that allow viewers to "skip" commercial advertisements, television and film producers can market audiences to advertisers. Products appear directly in programs, either as logos, incidental spots, or background shots of the product, or when the characters use the product. Just about every product seen in a film or TV program is the result of a product deal.

Audiences must be attracted and stimulated, but not reflective or thoughtful. Programming must include appropriate cultural norms and ideological preferences that prepare audiences for consuming the products advertised and consumerism in general (Garnham, 1990, pp. 24–29). Audiences must be nurtured and raised so they may be harvested by networks and delivered to advertisers as retail consumers.

A crucial part of audience cultivation is ideological. Media entertainment must share the virtues of consumerism. Entertainment programming must flow with commercial spots to socialize viewers to self-interest, celebrity worship, and instant gratification – ingredients valuable to advertisers and marketers. Messages important for transnational capitalism.

From this more critical political economy position, we can better understand television programming decisions as actions based on market projections and share dividends, not on public preferences. Within these parameters, hegemonic programming must have compelling cultural ingredients, sensibilities, and themes to carry the larger purpose of bringing local audiences to the market Jesus.

As all TNMCs share the same economic imperatives, it is not surprising that few stray from standard formats, themes, and genres best suited for advertising and consumerism.

The costs of producing a marketable audience are high, requiring scriptwriters; directors, producers, and editors; animators, amateurs, or actors and their attendants; set designers, lighting staff, camera crews, technicians, and diverse skilled assistants; audience researchers, promoters, and more. Networks continually search for low-cost, low-risk advertising-audience friendly programs such as reality television, game shows, and animation.

Advertisers have little interest in content, because they are concerned with one criterion: will the desired audience be available for my commercial? Thus, in general, advertisers have little motivation for the censorship of ideas. Indeed, a little controversy or titillation might even improve audience size and enhance attention. Viacom's Comedy Central network routinely airs programs that challenge decency standards that many citizens would find offensive, but because advertisers are purchasing 18–34 year old (mostly white male) audiences, they "are not particularly concerned with offending other viewers" (Crouteau & Hoynes, 2001, p. 124). Advertisers only balk at content that might "damage" the desired audience product or disrupt the smooth delivery of that audience to the advertising spot. Status quo local cultural values rule – with a dash of trendy edginess or cosmopolitan seasoning for some targeted audiences.

Images and representations, as part of the creative process of communication, arise with the material production of audience-as-commodity in mind. The battle for legitimate news, creative culture, or educational programming is meaningless disconnected from the fight to wrench media production out of the hands of transnational commercial networks and their transnational capitalist allies and advertising clients. Capitalist entertainment media content and advertising have no existence separate from one another. Media content and advertising are symbiotically connected with separate agents and sites of production; recognizing audience-as-product is central to any understanding of transnational media practice. Media are industrial institutions with similar strategies and goals as all TNCs, but media function more complexly with additional communication features that are deployed by the TNCC for its global political strategy.

Transnational Media Production

Evidence of transnational ownership of corporations through mergers, joint ventures, and FDI verifies the incomplete but continuing development of transnational production. "Joint production arrangements are now well established between U.S. enterprises and French, British, Swedish, Australian, and Italian companies, with connections to television, theme parks, cable, satellite, video, and the Internet" (Miller et al., 2008, p. 124). Multiple capitalist-class institutions and formations indicate an emerging transnational capitalist class that owns and controls cross-border production and plans and leads transnational planning and policy groups.

Satellite broadcast, mobile devices, and digital technology have spurred transnational media expansion, as TNMCs, advertisers, and consumer product manufacturers seek to tap into the disposable income of middle class audiences across the world. Media technology should not be construed as a cause of globalization, but seen for what it is: a tool of transnational capital and TNMCs that are driven to secure more profit. Technology appears as both a media product for sale and an efficient means to increase profits using the speed and ease of technology for transnational transactions. Although consumers treasure their mobile devices, Paul du Gay (1997) argues that mobile, privatized, personal devices atomize citizens and comprise a technological sabotage of collective identities and socially responsive human relations – recognizable side effects of transnationalism.

Undeterred by human costs, transnational co-productions provide the means for media expansion, audience attraction, and profits across borders. TNMC networks transcend national boundaries even as channels share a common broadcasting philosophy, produce well-defined, branded television content, and attract and sell a clearly defined audience. TNMCs benefit from local adaptations within their networks. Centralized resources like Turner Classic Movies (TCM), for instance, appear across the network but are never shown at the same time. TNMCs can acquire material for a specific market: Time Warner's Boomerang buys and airs *Babar* cartoons in France and *Pink Panther* in Britain. Local content is produced both at national and regional levels. MTV's partners produce local music shows. Disney and Time Warner co-produce and commission original content for specific European channels (Chalaby, 2009, pp. 212–213). All TBS entertainment properties are fully localized, including TCM, Boomerang, and the Cartoon Network.

Consolidation of media across nations and territories is a necessary process for capitalist media profit. Diversification and vertical integration mitigate financial risk. Transnational media do not promote a particular national ethos (Iwabuchi, 2002, p. 28), although a few established brands appear distinctly American – McDonald's, Coca-Cola, Disney, to name the obvious. An astute transnational leadership hammers out strategies for expansion and control, including the promotion of its free market policies and its ideology of neoliberalism, which insists on national deregulation of ownership and production, privatization of all human activity, and the commercialization for profit in the production of goods and services. As the TNCC through its national and transnational institutions and legions of managers rearranges the legal, political, commercial, and technological environments within nation-states, TNMCs thrive.

To summarize: transnational media are multi-faceted producers, profiting from global sales of many media products, including audiences. TNMCs communicate on behalf of the TNCC, providing the technological means for global advertising and communication for global transnational production and finance.

Finding the Choke Point for Profit: TNMC Planning and Policy Groups

In the last several decades, corporate media, their managers, and transnational agencies have been advancing cross-border capitalist practices and free market perspectives. The World Economic Forum (WEF), for example, organizes "select Member companies" from transnational media firms in "Industry Partnership Meetings on Media, Entertainment & Information" and "Global Agenda Councils" (World Economic Forum, 2013). The WEF also hosts international conferences on media strategy and public affairs and sponsors media industry workshops in East Asia, Rio, and New York to advise transnationals in content production, aggregation, and distribution.

In 2011, the WEF challenged transnational media to grab "the 'choke point' of the new [digital] value chain" by "making a concerted effort across industry sectors (content, platforms and devices) … to transform this potential business opportunity into real profit" (World Economic Forum, 2011). The report includes fact sheets on media infrastructures and strategies from around the world that demonstrate successful transnational strategies, like the media city twofour54 in Abu Dhabi that has attracted Fox, CNN, BBC, Sky, Viacom, and others to the "only content creation community in the Arab world" (Orsten, 2011).

Media for profit, not for humanity. Democracy appears only as consumer-responses to media content production or as social media providing "user generated content" to "drive a number of business goals" for TNMCs (Bain & Company, 2012).

Consumer choice is cultivated as the essence of freedom. Diversity is to be filtered by media firms that must "reinforce their competitive position across the video ecosystem" (Bain & Company, 2012). Diversity to shut down democracy. TNMC content produced to "choke" information flow.

Other international media conferences like the UN's World Television Forum also serve transnational media, linking investors and content producers from Europe and the United States with media from Africa, Asia, and Latin America. Television worldwide is now governed by the General Agreement on Trade in Services (GATS) as part of the World Trade Organization's protocol on culture as commodity. WTO talks "entrench privatization and deregulation," voiding most domestic democratic controls over media corporations (Gould, 2001). The pending Transatlantic Trade and Investment Partnership and the Trans-Pacific Partnership are set to ensure more corporate control without any democratic oversight (Monbiot, 2013).

The World Bank Institute has its own media programs for building a TNMC development model (World Bank Institute, 2012). The International Telecommunications Union (ITU), the United Nations' agency for communication, once was a collaboration among nations working on international media policies. Under pressure from the transnational capitalist class, the ITU opened its membership to private business in the late 1980s (Thussu, 2000). The 193 member nations have since added over 700 private-sector entities and academic institutions. The ITU now functions essentially as a pseudo-transnational state agency enforcing commercialized media policy (ITU, 2013).

TNMCs also convene their own industry-led conferences to network on concepts and strategies, including: the MIPTV (Marché International des Programmes de Télévision), an international entertainment conference and trade show, arranging financing and joint ventures, selling programs, and networking on media business models and trends (MIPTV, 2013); the Telenovelas and Fiction Industry annual conference which shares formats and discusses "new ways to profitability" (Telenovelas, 2009); the Global Business Dialogue on Electronic Commerce, which gathers governments with hundreds of top media executives, so "basically global business leaders [tell] governments what to do in the governance of CyberSpace" (Hamelink, 2001, p. 15).

These international policy-making organizations (and other regional groups) contribute to transnational entertainment production and distribution norms under the leadership of global entertainment media. Joint ventures, investments, and collaborations are cooperatively organized by media firms and facilitated by governments favoring transnational capitalist relations. Parallel to media industry practices based on market projections, audiences are treated to appealing entertainment that promotes similar social practices of consumerism and other audience market impulses. Media profit economically, while they politically and culturally represent and promote transnational capitalism. Some of the leading TNMCs and their collaborations on behalf of transnational capitalism are presented in the next chapter.

References

Aubry, P. (2000). The "television without frontiers" directive, cornerstone of the European broadcasting policy. *European Audiovisual Observatory*. Retrieved from http://global.asc.upenn.edu/fileLibrary/PDFs/18_valcke_reading1.pdf

Bain & Company (2012). Forces transforming the content landscape. Report prepared for World Economic Forum Annual Meeting 2012. Retrieved April 12, 2014, from http://www.bain.com/Images/WEF%20report%202012.pdf

Boas, T. C. (2013). Mass media and politics in Latin America. In J. I. Domínguez & M. Shifter (Eds.), *Constructing democratic governance in Latin America*. 4th edn (pp. 48–77). Baltimore, MD: Johns Hopkins University Press. Retrieved from people.bu.edu/tboas/media_LA.pdf

Bond, P. (2013, June 4). Study: Global media industry poised to top $2 trillion in 2016. *Hollywood Reporter*. Retrieved from http://www.hollywoodreporter.com/print/562694

Boyd-Barrett, O. (2006). Cyberspace, globalization and empire. *Global Media and Communication, 21*(1), 21–41.

Boyd-Barrett, O. (n. d.). *The political economy approach*. Retrieved from http://users.ipfw.edu/tankel/Syllabi/Spring%202010/COM%20330/BBarrett Politicaleconomy.pdf

Bruck, P. A., Dörr, D., Cole, M. D., Favre, J., Gramstad, S., Monaco, M. R., & Čulek, Z. P. (2004, November). *Transnational media concentrations in Europe*. Report by Advisory Panel on Media Diversity to the Council of Europe Steering Committee on the Mass Media. Strasbourg, France: Council of Europe.

Castagno, P. (2012). Marxist theory in critical transitions: The democratization of the media in post-neoliberal Argentina. *Triple C: Cognition, Communication, Cooperation, 10*(2), 334–348. Retrieved from http://www.triple-c.at/index.php/tripleC/article/view/426/391

Chalaby, J. K. (Ed.). (2005). *Transnational television worldwide: Towards a new media order*. London: I.B. Tauris.

Chalaby, J. K. (2009). *Transnational television in Europe: Reconfiguring global communications networks*. London: I.B. Tauris.

Crouteau, D., & Hoynes, W. (2001). *The business of media: Corporate media and the public interest*. Thousand Oaks, CA: Pine Forge Press.

Davis, D. W., & Yeh, E. Y. (2008). *East Asian screen industries*. London: British Film Institute.

du Gay, P., Hall, S., Janes, L., Mackay, H., & Negus, K. (Eds.). (1997). *Doing cultural studies: The story of Sony Walkman*. London: Sage.

Dubai Press Club. (2010). *Arab media outlook: Inspiring local content*. Dubai, UAE: Dubai Press Club.

Fernández-Quijada, D. (2013). Transnationalism and media groups in independent television production in the UK and Spain. *Global Media and Communication, 9*(2), 101–118.

Flew, T., & Gilmour, C. J. (2003, July). A tale of two synergies: An institutional analysis of the expansionary strategies of News Corporation and AOL-Time Warner. Paper presented at Australia and New Zealand Communication Association Conference. Brisbane, Australia. Retrieved from http://eprints.qut.edu.au/195/1/Flew_Tale.PDF

Gabriel, C. (2012, October 15). Sofbank confirms $20.1 bn deal for Sprint. *Rethink Wireless*. Retrieved October 14, 2014, from http://www.rethink-wireless. com/2012/10/15/sofbank-confirms-201bn-deal-sprint.htm

Garnham, N. (1990). *Capitalism and communication: Global culture and the economics of information*. Thousand Oaks, CA: Sage.

Gasseé, J.-L. (2012, April 23). Nokia: Three big problems for deposed king of mobile phones. *Guardian*. Retrieved from http://www.theguardian.com/ technology/2012/apr/23/monday-note-nokia

Gershon, R.A. (2005). The transnationals: Media corporations, international trade and entertainment flows. In A. Cooper-Chen (Ed.), *Global entertainment media*. (pp. 17–35). Mahwah, NJ: Lawrence Erlbaum & Associates.

Gould, E. (2001). The 2001 GATS negotiations: The political challenge ahead. Retrieved July 1, 2013, from http://www.thealliancefordemocracy.org/html/ eng/1332-AA.shtml

Hafez, K. (2007). *The myth of media globalization*. Malden, MA: Polity Press.

Hallin, D. C., & Papathanassopoulos, S. (2002). Political clientelism and the media: southern Europe and Latin America in comparative perspective. *Media, Culture & Society*, *24*, 175–195.

Hamelink, C. (2001). Remembering Herbert Schiller: Our common efforts. *Television & New Media*, *2*(1), 11–16.

Havens, T. (2006). *Global television marketplace*. London: Palgrave Macmillan.

Hong, J. (1998). *The internationalization of television in China: The evolution of ideology, society, and media since the reform*. Westport, CN: Praeger.

ITU. (2013). International Telecommunications Union. Retrieved from http:// www.itu.int/en/about/Pages/default.aspx

Iwabuchi, K. (2002). *Recentering globalization: Popular culture and Japanese transnationalism*. Durham, NC: Duke University Press.

Iwabuchi, K. (2004). How Japanese is Pokémon? In J. Tobin (Ed.), *Pikachu's global adventure: The rise and fall of Pokémon* (pp. 53–79). Durham, NC: Duke University Press.

Jakubowicz, K. (2007a). *Rude awakening: Social and media change in Central and Eastern Europe*. Cresskill, NJ: Hampton Press.

Keane, M. (2006). Once were peripheral: Creating media capacity in East Asia. *Media, Culture & Society*, *28*(6), 835–855.

Keane, M., Fung, A. Y. H., & Moran, A. (2007). *New television, globalization, and the East Asian cultural imagination*. Hong Kong: Hong Kong University Press.

Keeton, P., & Scheckner, P. (2013). *American war cinema and media since Vietnam*. New York: Palgrave Macmillan

Li, P. (2008). International cooperation and globalization of the magazine industry in China. *Public Relations Quarterly*, *24*, 59–63.

Mastrini, G., & Becerra, M. (2011). Structure, concentration and changes of the media system in the southern cone of Latin America. *Comunicar*, *18*, 51–59.

McQuail, D. (1992). *Media performance, mass communication and the public interest.* Thousand Oaks, CA: Sage.

Mediedatenbank. (2013). Media database. Institut für Medien- und Kommunikationspolitik. Retrieved from http://www.mediadb.eu/en/database/international-media-corporations/

Mediaset. (2013). Corporate website. Retrieved from http://www.mediaset.it/corporate/chisiamo/azionariato_en.shtml

Menotti, V. (2011, December). Individuals of undue influence. In *Outing the Oligarchy: Billionaires Who Benefit from Today's Climate Crisis* (pp. 1–57). Special Report by the International Forum on Globalization. Retrieved May 17, 2013, from http://ifg.org/v2/wp-content/uploads/2014/04/IFG_OTO_report.pdf

Miller, T., Govil, N., McMurria, J., Wang, T., & Maxwell, R. (2008). *Global Hollywood 2.* 2nd edn. London: British Film Institute.

MIPTV: The world's tv market and creative forum. (2013). MIPTV. Retrieved June 22, 2013, from http://www.miptv.com/en/the-event/overview/

Mishra, P. (2006). *Temptations of the West.* London: Picador.

Monbiot, G. (2013, November 4). This transatlantic trade deal is a full-frontal assault on democracy. *Guardian.* Retrieved from http://www.theguardian.com/commentisfree/2013/nov/04/us-trade-deal-full-frontal-assault-on-democracy

Mooij, M. (1998). *Global marketing and advertising: Understanding cultural paradoxes.* London: Sage.

Mosco, V. (2009). *The political economy of communication.* 2nd edn. Los Angeles, CA: Sage.

Mosco, V. (2012). Marx is back, but which one? On knowledge labour and media practice. *Triple C: Cognition, Communication & Cooperation, 10*(2), 570–576. Retrieved from http://www.triple-c.at/index.php/tripleC/article/view/377/379

Orsten, T. (2011). Content creation in the Arab world. In *World Economic Forum, The Future of Content* (pp. 29–32). Retrieved February 9, 2014, from http://reports.weforum.org/future-of-content-2011/#chapter-content-creation-in-the-arab-region

Pieterse, J. N. (2006). Globalization goes in circles: Hybridities East-West. *Social Theory.* Retrieved June 18, 2014 from http://www.social-theory.eu/texts/pieterse_globalization_goes_in_circles.pdf

Profmedia to spend $100 million to replace MTV with new channel. (2013, May 17). *Moscow Times.* Retrieved from http://www.themoscowtimes.com/business/article/profmedia-to-spend-100m-to-replace-mtv-with-new-channel/480075.html

Profmedia.ru. (2013) Retrieved from http://www.profmedia.ru/eng/about/

Punathambekar, A. (2010). Reality TV and participatory culture in India. *Popular Communication, 8*(4), 241–255.

Rantanen, T. (2005). *The media and globalization.* Thousand Oaks, CA: Sage.

Russian joint venture promises to produce 20 titles. (2013). FIPP website. Retrieved May 17, 2013, from http://fipp.com/news/russian-joint-venture-promises-to-produce-20-title

Sanoma Independent Media. (2013). Retrieved from http://english.imedia.ru/about/

Schiller, D. (1999). *Digital capitalism: Networking the global market system.* Cambridge, MA: MIT Press.

Sklair, L. (2001). *The transnational capitalist class.* New York: Wiley.

Smythe, D. (1994). *Counterclockwise: Perspectives on communication.* Boulder, CO: Westview.

Telenovelas, series, and fiction formats. (2009). VII World Summit of Telenovelas and Fiction Industry. Retrieved June 9, 2013, from http://www.tvmasnovela.tv/cumbre09/newsite/indexen.html

Thussu, D. K. (2000). *International communication: Continuity and change.* London: Arnold.

Thussu, D. K. (2007). Mapping global media flow and contra flow. In D. K. Thussu (Ed.), *Media on the move: Global flow and contra flow* (pp. 11–32). New York: Routledge.

UNCTAD. (2011). The world's top 100 non-financial TNCs, ranked by foreign assets, 2010. Retrieved from http://unctad.org/Sections/dite_dir/docs/WIR11_web%20tab%2029.pdf

World Bank Institute. (2012). IMAGE: WBI's media program. Retrieved March 4, 2013, from http://wbi/worldbank.org/content/wbis-media-program-image

World Economic Forum. (2011). *World Economic Forum on East Asia. Industry partnership meeting for media, entertainment, & information.* Retrieved February 8, 2013, from http://reports.weforum.org/wp-content/uploads/future-of-content/east-asia/WEF-Firing-Up-Asias-Creative-Engine-Summary.pdf

World Economic Forum. (2013). *Industry agenda. Industry partnership for media, entertainment, & information 2013.* Retrieved February 8, 2013, from http://www3.weforum.org/docs/WEF_MEI_IndustryPartnershipOverview_2013.pdf

Zhao, Y. (2008). *Communication in China: Political economy, power, and conflict.* Lanham, MD: Rowman & Littlefield.

Zhao, W. (2013, May 13). Global top pay TV operators and broadband providers. *SNL Kagan Global Multichannel.* Retrieved from http://www.snl.com/InteractiveX/Article.aspx?cdid=A-17689563-10537

Further Reading

Chalaby, J. K. (2002). Transnational television in Europe: The role of pan-European channels. *European Journal of Communication,* 17(2), 183–203.

Derné, S. D. (2008). *Globalization on the ground: New media and the transformation of culture, class, and gender in India*. Thousand Oaks, CA: Sage.

Jakubowicz, K. (2007). *Rude awakening: Social and media change in Central and Eastern Europe*. Cresskill, NJ: Hampton Press.

Zhao, Y. (2008). *Communication in China: Political economy, power, and conflict*. Lanham, MD: Rowman & Littlefield.

4

From Regional to Global
Transnational Media Leaders

Transnational Media Integration

Media are transnational. They organize production and distribution chains across borders with multiple owners and shareholders. Like other transnational corporations (TNCs), transnational media corporations (TNMCs) have established networks and institutions to advance their transnational practices. And, just like other TNCs, media collaborate with and rely on national governments as well. Increasingly, nationally concentrated firms have solicited foreign investment in their domestic operations while seeking acquisitions and joint ventures abroad.

The condition of transnational media cannot be fully assessed because the relations among and between media corporations remain in such flux that descriptions of holdings and interests are outdated almost before the reports are in. Nonetheless, a compilation of diverse transnational media in 2014 serves as a snapshot of interlocking interests and primary global trends. To present transnational media in some geographic order, such as Europe, Middle East, Africa, Asia, Latin America, and North America, would seem logical. However, the transnational character of media production does not conform to neat national markers. With the exception of a handful of established TNMCs headquartered in the United States, Germany, and Japan, media production can no longer be so easily unpacked geographically. Transnationalism is a class relation more than a geographic phenomemon. Thus, to emphasize the spatial and organizational

Global Entertainment Media: A Critical Introduction, First Edition. Lee Artz.
© 2015 John Wiley & Sons, Inc. Published 2015 by John Wiley & Sons, Inc.

complexities, several TNMCs are presented randomly as representative of the changing global media relations.

Reliance Entertainment

Although most accounts of global media begin with US-based firms, the largest English-speaking population in the world is India, the third largest television market in the world. India illustrates the stage and the direction of transnationalism in media, driven by the capitalist need for continual growth. Over 1 billion people live in India and 70% are under 34 – the prime advertising demographic. Indians own 865 million cell phones and 134 million homes have televisions (Stilson, 2007). India's television industry is valued at over $11 billion with a projected 15% growth per year (Machado, 2010).

Such a lucrative television and mobile phone market attracts transnational interest. In 2010, CBS partnered with Reliance Broadcast, part of Reliance Entertainment, one of the largest entertainment companies in India, with holdings in film, radio, and digital production. Reliance is a newcomer to Indian television, launching 20 channels in 2008 using part of a $100 million investment by financier George Soros (Lakshman, 2008). The joint venture arms Reliance with an experienced, content-rich international television content producer, while CBS can greatly expand its local operations with an Indian partner.

Big CBS Networks, as the merger is called, offers three channels in English, with Big CBS Spark aimed at youth, Big CBS Love aimed at women, and Big CBS Prime a general entertainment channel (Machado, 2010). Reliance takes CBS show formats and localizes their content for Indian audiences in Hindi, Punjabi, and other regional language channels.

In 2013, Reliance attracted Bertelsmann's European broadcast giant, RTL, into a joint venture television station, Big RTL Thrill, broadcasting Endemol, FremantleMedia, and A + E content in Hindi. Reliance-RTL plans regional multi-lingual broadcasts to Nepal, Sri Lanka, Bhutan, Pakistan, Bangladesh, and Afghanistan (Webdale, 2013). Bloomberg gave Reliance 66% in a 2011 TV joint venture for television in India.

Reliance Entertainment is also a significant player in Bollywood (India's Mumbai-based movie industry), producing films in Hindi, Tamil, Bengali, Mayalam, and Kannada for multi-linguistic Indian audiences. Reliance has joint ventures with LionsGate, Paramount, and 20th Century Fox, perfecting an action-adventure format in *Don* (2006) and *Don 2* (2011) among other movies. Filmed in Berlin with $3 million in German support, *Don 2* was released internationally to the United States, Britain, Australia, Pakistan, Germany, and the Middle East. A Hindi-language film, *Don 2* grossed $38 million, earning more from marketing tie-ins with McDonald's, Google, YouTube, Facebook, and Microsoft.

By 2012, Reliance investments in DreamWorks surpassed $500 million, establishing 50% control of the studio, which has additional joint ventures such as *Help* (with Abu Dhabi's Imagenation) and Oscar-nominated *Lincoln* (with 20th Century Fox). In 2012, DreamWorks Animation/ Reliance announced Oriental DreamWorks, a joint venture with China Media Capital, Shanghai Media Group, and Shanghai Alliance Investments to produce animated and live action Chinese movies (DreamWorks, 2012). DreamWorks theme parks are planned for New Jersey (2014) and Shanghai (2016). Last year, Reliance launched a US theater chain for Bollywood cinema, as part of its transnational BIG Cinema chain, with theaters in the United States, Malaysia, Nepal, and the Netherlands (with Pathé Theaters).

Together with China-based partner Galloping Horse, Reliance purchased Digital Domain, a visual effects firm with studios in London, Los Angeles, Vancouver, and Mumbai. Reliance plans further transnational ventures with its recently completed 7 acre, eight-stage studio in Mumbai, built to attract international partners. The studio recently acquired Classic Media (He-Man, Gumby, Felix the Cat, and Casper the Ghost) (Sun, 2013) and has invested in HBO's Electric City and Image Entertainment, Ron Howard's movie studio (Masters, 2012). Meanwhile, Reliance continues to purchase US firms and studios, including the digital film restoration company Lowry Digital.

Reliance also has a vibrant mobile video game division, Zapak, which distributes to 40 countries. Reliance owns 50% of the UK-based Codemasters that makes software for Sony's Playstation, has another partnership with Sony to make mobile games, and an agreement with BhartiAirtel, India's largest cell phone provider, for data connections across the Asia Pacific region. Across West India, Reliance Entertainment comprises BIG Movies, BIG Music, and digital ventures BIG Animation, Zapak (online gaming), Jump Games (mobile gaming), BIG Flix, Willow.tv (online streaming, offline video rental), and BIG Adda (social networking).

Reliance Entertainment and Reliance Media Works do not appear on any top media lists, due in part to a less than transparent corporate accounting structure. However, the Reliance Group, parent of Reliance Entertainment, is the third largest company in India, with more than $33 billion in assets and $15 billion in revenue, acquired through its increasing transnational activity in media, as well as transportation, telecommunications, financial services, health care, mutual funds, coal and hydroelectric power, and insurance. Media transnational activity by Reliance Entertainment is but one highly visible manifestation of the transnational capitalist class (TNCC) in India.

Liberty Media

Another less widely recognized TNMC operation is Liberty Global/ Discovery Communications. Organized as separate companies, these two TNMCs have interlocking directors and overlapping ownership. With assets in cable, entertainment, book publishing, satellite radio, and telecommunications Liberty Global, Liberty Media, and Liberty Interactive draw in $14 billion annually. John Malone, major shareholder in Liberty and Discovery, maneuvered his control of cable networks to secure interest in Turner Broadcasting Systems and Rupert Murdoch's News Corp (18%). Most of Liberty Media's revenue comes from QVC, the home shopping network, received by over 160 million households worldwide, and pay-TV networks Starz and Encore. Liberty has major shares in Vivendi, owns 11% of Hallmark Entertainment; 20% of Live Nation, the concert promoter; 67% of public television news programmer MacNeil/Lehrer Productions; 4% of Time Warner; 49% of Sirius XM Radio; 17% of Barnes & Noble, the world's largest bookseller; and owns the Atlanta Braves. Liberty Global owns 58% of Telenet, Belgium's largest cable service, and has merged with European UnitedGlobalCommunication, one of the largest broadband providers outside the United States. Chorus Communications in Ireland is a 50/50 partnership. Liberty also has joint ventures with CBS, A + E, and ZON Multimedia, the largest cable and cellular provider in Portugal and owner of Lusomundo, film studio and video distributor for Disney, DreamWorks, and Warner Bros.

Through its European division, Chellomedia, Liberty produces content for some 125 countries, broadcasting to 382 million homes. Chellomedia joint ventures with Scripps; HiT Entertainment (Mattel), the British producer of *Bob the Builder*, *Thomas the Tank Engine*, and other children's shows; MeteoConsult, a European weather channel; and Outdoor Channel. In all, Chellomedia has 66 active joint ventures in dozens of countries from Europe to Latin America.

Following media deregulation in Argentina in the 1990s, Liberty acquired 25% of Grupo Clarin's Cablevision system. In 2007, Liberty paid $484 million to purchase Fun Technologies, the Canadian on-line game company with 35 million subscribers. In 2010, Liberty acquired UnityMedia, a broadband provider in Germany. Additionally, Liberty has merged with a diverse group of Internet, cellular, cable, and satellite businesses, from Swiss Cablecom and Romanian Astral Telecom, to firms in Slovenia and across Europe. In 2013, Liberty acquired Virgin Media, the second largest pay-TV network in Britain with a 30% share of the cable TV market. With Virgin Media, Liberty provides television, Internet, phone, and cellular services, and partners with News Corp's BSkyB TV in the UK.

Liberty Media's board of directors includes directors from Sony, ABC-Disney, Expedia, Oracle, Citigroup, Bank of New York, and more – all companies in various stages of transnationalizing their operations. The directors oversee the strategic direction of Liberty Media, but local and domestic co-owners and producers like Grupo Clarin and Lusomundo run the daily operations of Chellomedia and other Liberty divisions to ensure favorable national licensing, cultural translation, and local connection.

Small compared to Comcast or Time Warner, Liberty Global represents the unrelenting sweep of transnationalism, as "market share leads companies to the crossroads of either growing through the takeover of smaller companies, or being bought out by international groups … the traditional company structure has become a group structure" of transnational co-production (Mastrini & Becerra, 2011, p. 53).

Discovery

Discovery Communications has followed a similar transnational trajectory. Discovery Channel split off from Liberty in 2005, with Liberty's Malone retaining 29% ownership. Newhouse Publications owns 31%, the balance held by a variety of investors and funds. Discovery's board of directors includes interlocks with Comcast, Sprint, Bank of New York, Newhouse/Advance Publications, and Landmark Communications. Discovery has major joint ventures with Sony and Harpo Productions, Oprah Winfrey's television and film studio.

A series on continental drift, icebergs in the North Atlantic, or the secret life of urban deer? Not the most likely content for marketing audiences to advertisers, but the beauty of nature documentaries is their universal, cross-border, apolitical appeal to audiences and advertisers alike. Natural science and cultural narratives find space on cable systems looking for inexpensive programming. Discovery offers Animal Planet, Travel Channel, Learning Channel, Discovery Kids, and more. With a successful formula marketing non-fiction entertainment, Discovery expanded internationally, from 156,000 US viewers in 1985 to 187 million viewers in 146 countries by 2000 (Mediedatenbank, 2013). The global reach of Discovery spreads through multiple joint ventures with content providers, including BBC, Liberty Media, Newhouse's Cox Communications, and Advance Publications. In 2002, Discovery partnered with Sony Entertainment Television to form The One Alliance – a leading network in India (Mjos, 2009, p. 31).

> Each Discovery feed in Europe is localized in a variety of ways ... language, schedule and on-air promotional elements, some shows are reversioned for each territory. They can be introduced by a different host, be rescripted or have segments taken in or out so local experts can be brought in. (Chalaby, 2009, p. 211)

Discovery's only local programming teams are in Germany and the United Kingdom, but the TNMC has alliances with Spiegel (Germany), Voyage (France), BBC (UK), O Globo (Brazil), Venevisión (Venezuela), Televisa (Mexico), Sony (India), Shanghai Media Group (China), and companies elsewhere. Discovery's globalization of local production has delivered local audiences to advertisers through factual entertainment in culturally and linguistically acceptable presentations.

Co-productions are not only more likely to meet audience cultural preferences, they also grant Discovery domestic status to meet local regulations. With production centers in London, Singapore, Miami, and Mumbai, Discovery creates formats that can be locally produced and "customized for a specific territory" (Mjos, 2009, p. 82). Discovery broadcasts of animals and nature are "repurposed" in 170 countries in 38 languages by outsourcing translation and editing to local producers. The "hybridization" of Discovery content reflects the preoccupation that programmers and advertisers have with demographics of local audiences – the primary commodity produced by Discovery – underscoring that localization is "purely driven by commercial needs" (Mjos, 2009, pp. 37, 108).

Localization is standard practice for Discovery and other TNMCs, just as hybrid feed supplements are part of cattle growers' regimen: in both cases, the goal is to nurture a desirable commodity that can be delivered to market. Inserting local or national inflections into global formats with shows like

Big Brother (Endemol), *Millionaire* (Celador), *Survivor* (CBS), *Idol* (ITV/ Fox), *Weakest Link* (ECM), *Dancing* (BBC), *Ugly Betty* (RCN), or *Funny Home Videos* (TBS Japan/ABC), TNMCs better appeal to national or local markets, garnering more profits for TNC shareholders.

Discovery may not challenge TNMC giants, but it has found sustainable local habitats in the entertainment environment of the transnational world. Discovery accumulates wealth for members of the same TNCC that run other, more diverse media firms. Moreover, Discovery faithfully contributes to a global culture of consumerism, providing viewers with a universal culture of spectatorship of the spectacular, another complementary entertainment form suited for political passivity and individual gratification.

Central European Media Enterprises (CME)

Transnationals migrate to the most profitable markets and resource-rich regions. Media are no different. TNMCs tend to consolidate in regions with large, high-consuming populations, from Western Europe and the United States, to East Asia and Latin America. Africa and the Middle East offer smaller markets due to lagging consumer demand – a condition reflecting the historical legacy of colonialism, underdevelopment, and gross economic inequality, not population size per se. Nigeria, for instance, is the fifth most populous country in the world, but has a comparatively small consumer market. Nonetheless, in each region TNMCs have emerged relative to the size of the consumer audience and incursions of global advertising and consumer product sales. Transnational media develop in tandem with rising wage labor employment, middle classes with disposable income, and the willingness of advertisers to pay for audiences.

The transition to transnational production and distribution received a world-historic assist with the collapse of the Soviet Union and Eastern European regimes – state-regulated command economies imploded, opening each nation to snatch-and-grab privatization and deregulation. Neoliberal advisors assisted foreign investors and former bureaucrats who rushed in to scoop up previously public enterprises, from industrial production of steel, oil, gas, and other primary manufacturing to public services like telecommunications, public utilities, and media. Karol Jakubowicz (2007) places the development of media enterprises in post-communist Eastern Europe within the context of "systematic social transformation" – media are both an indicator and consequence of political developments, economic privatization, and globalization trends in media production (pp. 1, 9–10).

Each country in Eastern and Central Europe took its own path to privatization, but none successfully built vibrant civic societies with adequate democratic opportunities for full citizen participation. In post-Soviet countries, laws are not designed for democratic media: "legal regulation is at best incomplete, and at worst expressly designed to subjugate" media to government and investors (Jakubowicz, 2007, p. 346). The TNCC, through the IMF, World Bank, European Union, and other institutions, *required* deregulation and market-oriented media policies, effectively preventing public service broadcasting and democratic community-based media. Democratization appeared in the rhetoric of reform, but was shunted aside for commercial interests that are "enemies of popular expression and popular democracy" (Sparks, 2000, p. 40). Across Eastern and Central Europe, TNMCs have purchased, merged, or partnered with major media outlets, particularly in broadcasting.

Investors followed the waves and floods of privatization across Central Europe. SBS (Scandinavia Broadcasting Systems) and the German ProSieben (both of which are now run by private equity firms, Permira and KKR) invested quickly and widely, buying radio and television stations in Hungary, Romania, and Serbia.

A more startling example is Central European Media Enterprises (CME), founded in 1994 by Robert Lauder, of the Estée Lauder cosmetic empire. CME has become the market leader in every Central European country where it operates. CME claims 50 million viewers from Bulgaria, Croatia, Czech Republic, Romania, Slovakia, and Slovenia. In 2009, CME acquired Media Pro Entertainment, which owns the largest TV production facility in Central Europe. In 2011, CME added the leading content distributors from Slovakia and the Czech Republic. Once CME found a lucrative revenue stream, Time Warner invested heavily. As of 2012, Time Warner owns 49.9% of CME (Jannarone, 2012).

CME's operations are managed by local directors (like Constantine Mocanu, Romanian VP of Voyo and Anca Budinchsi at ProTV) and financed with locally based advertising. CME targets the advertising-desired high-end demographic (Investor, 2012, pp. 3–4, 14). A mid-size European media transnational, CME blends investment and production expertise from Time Warner with cross-border production and distribution by locally run firms in each of the six countries of its operation.

Naspers

The largest media company in Africa is Naspers, grabbing almost $6 billion in revenue in 2012 (Mediendatenbank, 2013). Beginning as a newspaper group in Cape Town in 1915, Naspers grew out of its pay-TV network, M-Net, in the 1980s. Following the deregulation of media in some 48 sub-Saharan nations, Naspers rapidly grew to a diversified TNMC. Naspers broadcasts from sub-Sahara to the Maghreb, making it the dominant media distributor on the continent.

There are more than 1,000 indigenous languages on the continent, but transnational capitalism has "moved the tide substantially in favor of English, especially among the urban privileged of Africa" (Adeosun, 2012, p. 7). In commerce and politics, French remains dominant in Mali, Niger, Guinea, Senegal, Ivory Coast, Togo, Chad, and a few other former French colonies, while Portuguese maintains a toehold in Angola, Guinea-Bissau, and Mozambique. The class divide in media reception is largely expressed linguistically: in 2002, 22 satellites were transmitting some 250 stations in English, French, Arabic, and Portuguese – only three in African languages, and two of those were in Afrikaans, the language of white South Africa (Teer-Tomaselli, Wasserman, & de Beer, 2007).

Nasper's M-Net television network, with 6 million subscribers in 40 African countries, is responding to the language and cultural gap by "focusing on rolling out digital terrestrial TV services in a number of markets across Africa" (Hedley, 2012). Naspers has new film channels in Yoruba and Huasa, featuring African cinema, especially Nigeria's "Nollywood" locally produced videos that might attract sizable audiences and profits. Of course, filtered by M-Net and Naspers, the more commercial, more universally familiar, Hollywood-like videos are given wider distribution.

Naspers' growth strategy plunges into transnationalism, undertaking partnerships with "local entrepreneurs or state broadcasters, in which each party has a partial shareholding and a joint management strategy" (Teer-Tomaselli, Wasserman, & de Beer, 2007, p. 157). Africa and the Middle East combined account for less than 2% of worldwide TV revenue (TV, 2009), so Naspers has been keen to go beyond Africa and its limited middle class consumer market, investing in TV stations in Greece, Cyprus, Thailand, Poland, Ukraine, India, Turkey, China, Romania, and the United States. Naspers has a satellite joint venture with Canal + in Nethold, which has a bouquet of channels in Belgium, Luxembourg, Holland, the Nordic countries, Central Europe, Italy, and Greece (Chalaby, 2009, p. 156). Naspers also markets its television content directly to Kenya, Zambia, Tanzania, Uganda, Nigeria, Ghana, and other countries.

Naspers is increasing its television content production to improve vertical integration of its media: from content creation and ownership to content branding and delivery through television, pay-TV, Internet, and mobile phones (www.naspers.com). Naspers owns 30% of Editor Abril, the largest magazine publisher in Latin America and Media24 (Nasper's publishing arm) is Africa's largest publisher, but the Internet has been the major driver of Nasper's transnational growth (Hedley, 2012). Naspers has expanded web operations to the Czech Republic, Poland, Hungary, Slovakia, and Slovenia, as well as holding 46.5% of social media site Tencent (China), and joint ventures with Dubai-based Souq.com and Russian on-line retailer Mail.ru. With Mail.ru, Naspers holds a 28.7% stake in Digital Sky Technologies.

Naspers purchased 49% of ComperanTime/Movile, a major cell provider in Brazil, Mexico, and other countries. Naspers has alliances in social networking services in Spain, Portugal, Mexico, and other Latin American countries and e-commerce joint ventures in Turkey and Central Europe.

Naspers may only be ranked 31 on the list of the world's largest media corporations (Mediendatenbank, 2013), but like its larger cousins, Naspers has become thoroughly transnational in structure, operation, and political and cultural effect. In addition to its programming content, Naspers' transnational media in Africa and Latin America complement the global masters of transnationalism by modeling production practices, promoting business values and norms, and distributing other TNMC content. Naspers' TNCC leadership echoes the transnational hegemonic ideology through its media content: individualized entertainment and consumerism.

Disney

Perhaps no global media has been better at weaving entertainment with consumerism than the quintessential American entertainer, the Walt Disney Company. Disney exemplifies the drive for transnational production and distribution that spurs the global transformation of capitalism. As part of the transnational economic system and a stable source of capitalist profit, the Disney Company has major non-media shareholders, including the Bass Brothers, Berkshire Hathaway, Capital Group, the Norwegian Norges Bank Investment Fund, Goldman Sachs, and others.

The world's second largest media entertainment company with revenues of $40 billion, Disney is known for children's animation, theme parks, movie divisions (Touchstone, Buena Vista) and television production (ABC, ESPN, Jetix, and cartoon channels) (Mediendatenbank, 2013). Disney TV channels reach 560 million viewers worldwide, not counting subsidiaries or other local Disney channels.

With multiple interlocks in myriad joint ventures – A+E, History Channel, Lifetime, ESPN, and others – Disney continually expands through selective mergers and acquisitions, purchasing Lucasfilms and Marvel Comics (2012) and distributing films by Reliance/DreamWorks and Studio Ghibli, a Japanese TNMC. Wherever regulations allow, Disney directly owns subsidiaries, in Qatar, Egypt, and other Mideast countries, in much of Europe, Latin America, and Asia. Meanwhile, Disney has quietly but dramatically partnered with television and media producers around the globe in some incredibly successful ventures.

Disney has 13 joint ventures in Western Europe, including partnerships with Bertlesmann's RTL, Box TV in Britain, Bauer in Germany, and NetTV in Spain. In 2006, Disney moved into Central Europe, with localized productions in Poland reaching 1.3 million. Disney's Buena Vista division partners with HBO Central Europe and TNMCs Time Warner and Sony, broadcasting movies, concerts, special events, and local content productions from Hungary, Czech Republic, and Poland (Chalaby, 2009, p. 144). Disney XD, formerly Jetix, buys half its programming locally – establishing local production chains and distribution relations transnationally. In each country, firms have economic and political interest in Disney. Disney brands and partners in Europe (ESPN, A+E [Hearst], Toon Disney, Cinemagic) have similar transnational–local relations. The advantage of transnational production is that "networks can acquire material that is specific to a market" while "local content is produced at both national and regional levels" (Chalaby, 2009, p. 212).

Disney has a major presence in India, jointly producing Hungama TV in three languages. Disney's Indian television subsidiary, UTV, has partnerships with Zee TV, Star India, and Sun TV. UTV also co-owns Smriti Irani Television, UMP television in Mauritius, and co-produces video games with Sony and Nintendo. Disney Channel Asia distributes local productions such as the Malaysian animated series *Upin and Ipin*, *Waktu Rehat* (based on an Italian children's cartoon), and co-produced *Bo Boi Boy*, with Animosta Studios, a leading Malaysian animator.

Disney has perfected a transnational formula for local audience creation, global product branding, and advertising profit from domestic and transnational advertisers:

> UTV's Motion Pictures business spans the integrated model of creative development, production, marketing, distribution, merchandising and syndication worldwide. UTV's portfolio includes Hindi Movies, Regional Movies, Animation Films, international productions and co-productions …
> [UTV believes that] well segmented channels targeting likeminded people will score over others by creating an engaged consumer; thus offering us as well as advertisers myriad possibilities to deliver content to a defined audience. (UTV, 2013)

Disney's rhetoric and success trumpet the value of transnational production for capitalism.

Disney brands appear in synergistic tie-ins (television spin-offs, video games, theme park rides, clothing, games, and consumer home products), generating additional profits. Even unsuccessful films merchandize products manufactured by cheap subcontractors employing low-wage workers from Asia to Latin America and the Caribbean. In the 1990s, garment workers in Haiti made 28 cents an hour sewing Disney t-shirts, workers in other nations about the same (IPS, 1996). (Following public outcry, Disney and others relocated garment production to Burma, where wages average 45 cents an hour.)

Using its massive global profits from animated features like *Lion King*, *Mulan*, *Winnie-the-Pooh*, and Pixar's *Monsters, Inc.* and *Cars*, Disney has aggressively pursued transnational expansion. Disney's Miravista has produced more than 25 films in Latin America in the last 10 years and co-produced several with domestic studios in Brazil and Mexico. Disney acquired 30% of Patagonik Film Group in Argentina (entering its productions in foreign film competitions in the United States and Europe). Disney co-produces movies with Elinas Salinas Group in Santo Domingo, Venezuelan film studios, and Village Roadshow in Australia. UTV has become one of the largest film studios in India, turning out typical blockbuster Bollywood extravaganzas as well as art cinema for niche audiences in several Indian languages. Disney has partnered with Yash Raj Films, a major Indian studio to co-produce films in Hindi. Disney's Buena Vista International has production and distribution agreements with firms in Singapore, Malaysia, and Thailand.

Disney has other transnational ventures through local subsidiaries that are not readily transparent. Of course, its theme parks outside of the *United States* are only possible with transnational investment and management: Disney Hong Kong (53% non-US), Euro Disney Paris (50% non-US, including 24% Saudi Prince Al-Waleed), Disney Shanghai (57% non-US), and Disney Tokyo which has major Japanese sponsorship.

Thorn EMI

Not all media partnerships or productions are successful. Figuring out the optimum corporate structure, co-production decision-making, and advertising strategy, while also building audience share in diverse, competitive markets is fraught with obstacles and pitfalls. As an early entrant in Central and Eastern Europe, CME had corporate experience, resources, and size advantages in a relatively underdeveloped media environment. TNMCs stepping into Western Europe or Latin America face fiercer competition, oftentimes with inadequate TNCC commitment or expertise. Music Box/ Super Channel/Children's Channel (1984–2000) in Europe illustrates extreme TNCC hubris that led to corporate failure.

Thorn (a British telecom/computer hardware company) merged with EMI (a film and record company) in the late 1970s. Thorn EMI launched Music Box in 1984 in a joint venture with Virgin Records and Yorkshire TV – envisioning a European equivalent to MTV. Music Box attracted 3 million satellite viewers, but never turned a profit. Music Box aired British and American videos, with limited contributions from other nations or languages – curbing its pan-European appeal from the start. In 1987, a consortium of ITV stations, the largest commercial network in Britain, bought Music Box and relaunched it as Super Channel. Super Channel created the Children's Channel with Thorn EMI, Central Television, British Telecom, and DC Thomson – but Thorn EMI and British Telecom were adrift in the industry and soon withdrew. Cable companies in the Netherlands, Ireland, and Sweden joined in distribution, but the channel lacked funding for programming. In 1990, Flextech, a British oil-industry-turned-media-cable-company, bought 25% of the Children's Channel. In 1994, John Malone's TCI cable company (precursor to Liberty Media) was looking for a quick and easy expansion to the European mass media market and acquired 60% of Flextech in exchange for 100% Bravo Europe, 25% of the Children's Channel, and two UK lifestyle cable channels. Flextech/TCI was still unable to attract enough viewers and advertisers to profit and the

Children's Channel ended in 2000. Flextech held on to its lifestyle stations and merged into Virgin Media only to be taken over by News Corp's BSkyB. In the end, each of the British, Dutch, Scandinavian, and US partners fared poorly in their attempt to form and build a TNMC in Europe. Ultimately, Music Box/Super Channel/Children's Channel could not compete against larger, better-organized firms with more capital and, above all, better local networks.

MTV/Viacom

Viacom's MTV did what Music Box could not: build a music-based TNMC in Europe. By 1997, MTV abandoned its simplistic pan-European approach and was co-producing over 2,500 hours, with 70% locally produced content (Gershon, 2005, p. 29). With MTV Nordic, MTV Italy, MTV North, MTV Central, and MTV UK, Viacom sidestepped charges of cultural imposition and the "Americanization" of national media. In 2000, MTV added Polish, Spanish, French, and Dutch editions. Viacom built an independent management structure with local production studios. Local partners also produced their own marketing and promotional material (Chalaby, 2002, pp. 195–197). Although part of a European 128 million household network, MTV's 40 regional and 40+ localized channels look and sound quite different. MTV underwent a similar localization process with partners in Asia (Sowards, 2003). MTV now has 141 channels broadcasting to 507 million households across 160 territories (Chalaby, 2009, p. 164).

MTV illustrates one variation of transnational media: a global network of local channels "centralized around a core broadcasting philosophy and structure" (Chalaby, 2009, p. 207). MTV content is organized transnationally, across hundreds of national borders, with thousands of firms and thousands of creative, technical, and production workers socially and economically connected in a vast capitalist enterprise to accumulate profits for Viacom's shareholders and audiences for MTV's advertisers. MTV not only organizes its own production, it stimulates sales for the production of hundreds of other TNCs, promoting an ideology of individual consumerism. Celebrity-focused news, game shows, reality TV, and infotainment nurture a culture of immediate gratification driven by the latest music, fashion, or cultural trend promoted by MTV, its artists, and its advertisers. Local production, local management, and local creative workers accepting low wages assure the accumulation of wealth for a small coterie of transnational capitalists: Sumner Redstone and investors in National Amusements (including Gabelli Assets Management, JP Morgan Chase, Goldman Sachs), and dozens of nationally dispersed smaller businesses and investors who receive a minor share of the $28 billion Viacom pulls in annually.

Even this brief of Music Box and MTV demonstrates how the conditions of transnational capitalism are asserted. TNCC survivors learned the lessons of grow or die. Iconoclast Richard Branson from Virgin Records admitted the downside of independent smallness, merging with Liberty Media and thereby maintaining his position as a TNMC player. Liberty Media's size assured survival, and Malone's subsequent TNMC success resulted from running many operations through local joint ventures. News Corp's BSkyB bested all competing joint ventures for satellite and cable audiences due to its overwhelming economic dominance, picking up the remains of failed companies. Transnational capitalism privileges collaborative TNCC activity; it also raises the mercenary stakes and capital rewards as some TNCs consolidate while others become fodder or fade away.

Rotana/LBC

Joint local production has become the strategy of choice by transnationals everywhere, including the Middle East. The Rotana network, majority owned by Saudi Prince Al-Waleed bin Talal (with 9% News Corp), has multiple channels dedicated to diverse entertainment and music genres, from Egyptian classical and Lebanese pop music to more traditional Gulf folkloric songs and Rotana cinema (Kraidy & Khalil, 2007). With satellite networks and six free-to-air television stations, Rotana is the leading broadcaster in more than 20 Mideast and North African countries. Rotana is a vertically and horizontally integrated transnational, producing and distributing music and film by Arab artists under exclusive contract. Rotana owns more than 85% of Lebanese Broadcasting Corporation (LBC), a satellite broadcasting operation of Christian militia forces in Lebanon.

Rotana/LBC distributes international programs (e.g., Star Academy, Fear Factor) in local formats across the region. Al-Waleed also owns 5% stake in News Corp, minority shares in AOL-Time Warner, 35% of the largest media marketing group in the Mideast, 3% of Twitter, 25% of Euro Disney, and is the largest shareholder in Citigroup. Al-Waleed also has joint ventures in African tourism and telecommunications (Jalloh, 2013). With Rotana/LBC, Al-Waleed, the 26th richest man in the world according to *Forbes* magazine, is part of the new TNCC, meeting with the world's top CEOs at summits in the United States and Middle East (Alwaleed, 2013), and partic-ipating in joint media ventures on three continents.

A reduction in regulatory barriers has allowed a rapid growth of transna-tional media and entertainment in the Middle East, a small but attractive market estimated at more than $10 billion a year. With a younger, wealthier, middle class population expected over the coming years, Arab countries have drawn the attention of many transnationals from BBC, CNN, Showtime, and Dubai's Middle East Broadcasting Center, a multimedia news, entertainment, and music business, owned 55% by Visi Media Asia, an Indonesian transnational media firm (Buchta, Fabel, De Clerq, & Hall, 2009, p. 4).

As these examples have illustrated, the "optimum model for creating high-value cultural exports is the transnational media corporation" (Keane, Fung, & Moran, 2007, p. 51). The horizontal and vertical integration of the structure of TNMCs, along with their interlocking boards and production hierarchies, allow them to translate globally standardized formats into locally appealing media content, especially where partners share regional connections. Co-productions and joint ventures increase financial and creative resources while limiting potential risk. Cross-promotional marketing and merchandizing contribute even more revenue. TNMCs also benefit from their dispersed production systems that press down wages and taxes under the new international division of cultural labor (discussed in Chapter 5). Meanwhile, firms that do not join the legions of TNMC partners and contractors struggle to attract audiences and advertisers and are severely restricted in their abilities to distribute their media without a TNMC alliance.

Transnational Media in East Asia

Global media have become less about export flows and more about production strategies and cross-border operations. East Asia, for example, has multiple transnational arrangements for sharing concepts, models, and networks of production and broadcasting, making it very difficult to isolate the original impetus or identify the nationality of the participants. Despite language and culture barriers, Asian content travels across national boundaries because the transformation of national to transnational media has followed a much different path in East Asia than elsewhere. The political economy of media in Asia arises from the legacy of colonialism, both

European and regional, including Japanese and Chinese, four decades of Mao-style communism in China, and protectionist policies encouraged by authoritarian regimes.

Despite geographic and linguistic borders, capitalism's harsh entry into the region over the last two centuries has nonetheless made the "conception of rigidly demarcated national and cultural boundaries implausible and tenuous" (Iwabuchi, 2002, p.15). Meanwhile, "traditional values are fading as Chinese society [and other Asian nations] undergoes restructuring and competition under the market economy" (Kim, 2007, p. 143) and the crush of consumerism. National media in Asia, as elsewhere, exist as manifestations and challenges from the economic and political inequalities of inherited social relations. Japanese media and cultural exports totaled over $1.5 trillion from 1992 to 2002, while media exports from South Korea barely reached $100 million in 2005 (Siriyuvasak, 2010). Such differences in regional media production reflect the diverse power relations in each country and their past and present links with transnational capital.

Sony

As the most developed nation in East Asia, Japan nurtured a muscular private media system, adhering to the same interlocking corporate structure of other Japanese industries, reflecting and contributing to the development of an active consumer culture. For decades, Japanese media reaped sufficient profits within the nation to focus production and distribution internally. It was a non-media company that first ventured abroad for media mergers. The company is now one of best-known global media brands: Sony.

Sony was a leading manufacturer of consumer technology long before it stepped into the media entertainment world. Sony Walkman, CD players, and Blu-Ray DVD players improved the delivery of media content, and Sony soon recognized its interest in providing content as a means for increasing technology sales. At first Sony sponsored karaoke contests as a lever to drive sales of its technology (Iwabuchi, 2002, p. 102). In the late 1980s, Sony became one of the first Japanese companies to enter the US media market, quickly becoming a global media player with the purchase of CBS Records (1988) and Columbia Pictures (1989). Sony successfully handled the economic and corporate transition from media distribution to media production, becoming the seventh largest media company in the world, with over $21.5 billion in revenue in 2012 (Mediendatenbank, 2013).

Columbia/Tristar and Sony Pictures are present in more than 67 countries. Sony TV studios produce some 60 formats from *Jeopardy* and *Wheel of Fortune* (from Germany) to *Young and the Restless* and other soaps and game shows, broadcasting over six East Asian channels, including AXN, the leading international channel in Asia. AXN has a joint venture with CU Media in Korea to produce local Korean content and a partnership with CJ Hellovision and On Media in a Hong Kong cable channel (AXN, 2011). In partnership with Discovery and India's SAB Television, Sony formed One Alliance, leveraging the three firms' content and distribution resources. As of 2012, the firms combined to distribute 22 of the top 100 shows in India, and Sony's SET is one of the leading channels across the subcontinent (Star plus, 2013). Produced jointly by Optimystix Entertainment and Miditech, Sony's *Indian Idol* regularly attracts 40 million viewers and 55 million SMSs (Punathambekar, 2010, p. 247).

Sony owns or co-owns dozens of stations across Europe, Latin America, and West Asia, with investments in television channels in Brazil, Russian, India, and China (Stilson, 2007). Sony has partnerships with Comcast (broadcasting), 3D Impact Media in Switzerland (technology), and Rotana in the Middle East (music videos and technology). Sony Music Entertainment (which includes its deal with Bertelsmann in Sony BMG) is the second largest music label in the world, and Sony's Playstation system profits from Sony's license for each game sold (Mediendatenbank, 2013).

Sony is a preeminent transnational with direct corporate interlocks with Bertelsmann, News Corp, Hulu (the distribution joint venture of News Corp's Fox and ABC/Disney), and Comcast/NBC's Telemundo, as well as non-media firms, Toyota, Mitsubishi, Ericcson, British Telecom, and Fuji Xerox. Morgan Stanley, Goldman Sachs, Deutsche Bank, and Credit Suisse are major shareholders.

With the exception of Sony, Nintendo, and Sega, which dominate video gaming hardware and software, transnationalizing media from Asia have sprung more from an uneven regional intermingling than from bursting the limits of their national markets in search of foreign audiences. Until recently, the legacy of Japanese imperialism, fear of US cultural invasion, and the protectionist media policies in almost all Asian nations restricted the export of media across borders. With the triumph of transnational trade regimes, especially the World Trade Organization, reforms permitting media import, investment, and co-production were adopted. However, the increase in TNMC operations across East Asia has not led to "foreign" power cultural invasion; rather, media entertainment and consumer culture are the primary markers of transnational capitalism. "Japanese" culture in particular is "odorless," almost invisible. The universal appeal of "Japanese" TNMC products has erupted without the appearance of any culturally explicit "Japaneseness" (Iwabuchi, 2002). It seems that *mukokuseki* (the erasure of physical signs of origin) cloaks transnational hegemony in East Asia, providing counsel for successful transnational production and distribution internationally.

Capitalist dominance is not an externally based Western cultural dominance. The arrival and seduction of advertising-driven entertainment has been sufficient to nurture individual consumerism as a complement to the illusion that private industry, consumer technology, and market-based politics offer social progress. "Competition has turned to co-operation and regional consolidation" that extends the size, reach, and resources of pan-Asian TNMCs (Davis & Yeh, 2008, p. 87). Already churning out 21% of world television revenue (IDATE, 2010), Asia constitutes an attractive market for transnational media with 17% growth projected in media entertainment in China alone (Child, 2012).

China: TNMC joint ventures and co-productions

China is the market everyone wants. China: the land of 4,500 TV channels, 400 million television sets, and 1 billion mobile phones. More than 550 million use Baidu.com, China's leading website (Stilson, 2007), which churned out $3.5 billion in revenues in 2012. China is the second-largest FDI destination, with $106 billion invested in 2012 (Li & Sligo, 2012). Since *Crouching Tiger, Hidden Dragon* (2000) (Huayi Brothers, Taiye Film, United China Vision UK, and Sony Tristar), TNMCs are yearning for the next big co-production with Chinese studios. Sony, Comcast Universal, Warner Bros., and Bertelsmann's Fremantle all have established joint projects in China, (Wang, 2005; Bertelsmann, 2012). The big question for media entertainment producers and advertisers is, "How many China's are you going to address?" Given that there are 40 regions with different languages and cultures (Stilson, 2007), transnational media hope that as more private stations go on the air a growing demand for programming will translate into a need for more TNMC content. In 2006, Gruner + Jahr reported that Chinese publishers were "desperately looking for international partners, because they [were] having problems generating content" and they were already buying "ready-made media products" (Rohn, 2011, pp. 204, 207).

Even as TNMCs seek local producers, talent, and distribution outlets, Chinese companies are reaching out aggressively for collaborators for transnational markets. By 1998, China had become the third largest exporter of media and culture (UNESCO, in Miller et al., 2008, p. 59) despite a shortage of entertainment content for Chinese broadcasters.

Chinese companies are investing heavily in diversified industrial production and natural resource extraction in Latin America, Africa, and Asia (China global, 2012). Chinese transnationals have also turned to American companies: Lenovo now owns Motorola's mobile phone division and has shares in IBM; auto firms are partnered with GM; and Chinese investors hold substantial shares in Morgan Stanley, Visa, and Shell, among others. In 2013, Shuanghui International bought Smithfield, the world's largest pork producer. Perhaps less widely known is Chinese-based transnational media ventures in the United States. In 2012, the Dalan Wanda media group purchased AMC Entertainment, the second largest US theater chain – as part of a planned $10 million investment project. Galloping Horse Films partnered 70–30 with Reliance Entertainment to purchase the Hollywood-based visual effects firm, Digital Domain, in 2012. In 2013, Chinese LCD-television manufacturer TCL invested in Disney's *Iron Man 3* with a product placement agreement (Tsui, 2013). The Chinese government has launched multi-language satellite TV, sponsors over 200 Confucius Institutes around the world, and expanded the global reach of Central China Television (CCTV) (Xiaoling, 2010).

Chinese rules on FDI and joint ventures have been loosened, bringing global television producers into the Chinese film and broadcasting market. As China opens broadcasting to privatization and advertising, News Corp, Time Warner, and Viacom provide stations for Chinese TV. Hollywood filmmaker Legendary Entertainment partnered with Huayi Brothers Media Group and a Hong Kong construction company in 2011 to create a $220 million movie venture, bypassing restrictions on foreign movie imports. Disney has partnered with Huayi on several co-productions, including a remake of *High School Musical*. DMG Entertainment financed Tristar's *Looper* (2012) and co-produced *Iron Man 3* (2013) with Disney's Marvel Comics. Relativity Media joined Huaxi Films in producing movies in China; Sony remade *Karate Kid* with the state-owned China Film Group, while News Corp's Fox Searchlight has a deal with IDG China Media to co-produce several films (Rushe, 2011).

In 2012, China increased the number of imported films allowed each year from 20 to 34. Harvest Seven Stars, a private production firm, is building "Chinawood," a 8.6 million square foot production site for international filmmakers, which will recruit further joint ventures exempt from Chinese import quotas. Harvest's CEO, Bruno Wu, expects the East Asian film market to be worth $10 billion by 2015 and wants TNMC joint ventures to capture half of that market (Coonan, 2012). In anticipation, China, already the second largest cinema market in the world, expects to have 25,000 more movie screens by 2016 (Child, 2012).

East Asian waves

Given small national markets in Korea, Taiwan, Hong Kong, Singapore, and other East Asian countries, national media have been keen to partner in content and broadcasting. In 1997, Sumitomo Trading Co. launched JET pay-TV with Japan's leading commercial station, TBS, broadcasting to Taiwan, Hong Kong, Thailand, Singapore, Malaysia, Indonesia, and the Philippines. Sumitomo also invited Universal Studios to build a theme park in Osaka, partnering with 40 other shareholders, while Universal struck deals with 23 separate Asian marketing partners for the project (Miller et al., 2008, p. 277). Korea sponsors regional conferences on co-financing and marketing of regional transnational productions. Hong Kong offers the Asia Film Financing Forum as a co-production market for Japan, Singapore, Korea, Thailand, China, and Iran (Davis & Yeh, 2008, pp. 85–86).

Alliances are many and varied, from Euro-Asian (e.g., Fortissimo, Sud Fond) and pan-Asian co-productions (e.g., Huayi Brothers, Shanghai Film Group, Sidus, CJ Entertainment) to Hollywood–Asian ventures (Warner, Colombia Pictures) (Davis & Yeh, 2008, p. 90). The "national" response to Hollywood transnationals has been to vigorously become transnational, starting with East Asia as a market, "not out of any cultural idealism, but from sheer necessity," as filmmaker Peter Chan explained to the Asian Cultural Cooperation Forum (cited in Davis & Yeh, 2008, p. 91). Pony Canyon, a subsidiary of Fuji Entertainment Japan, has branches in Hong Kong, Taipei, Singapore, and Kuala Lumpur, searching for local amateur talent.

The pan-East Asian market is potentially 250 million consumers, rivaling that of the United States – not including 1.4 billion Chinese. To reach the largest commercial market, TNMCs, including pan-Asian firms, seek to maximize audience size by hybridizing the local/national into synthesized "pan-Asian" commodities. At the same time, transnational firms from Asia, Europe, and the United States are wooing state and private firms in China, seeking access to billions of eager media consumers, threatening prospects for nationally based media content even as localization of production grows. Asian cinema spreads internationally, with Pokémon, anime, and manga, kung-fu movies, and K-pop entertaining new generations around the world, while TNMCs increasingly trade internationally in Asian genres and sources.

Following regional media deregulation in the 1990s, TNMCs have had a 30% return on Asian media investments. *Tokyo Eyes* (1998) was a successful French–Japanese co-production. Sony and Columbia Asia partnered on *Double Vision* (2002) and *20:30:40* (2004), both produced by Taiwanese filmmakers. Fortissimo, a Dutch/Hong Kong international film distributor co-produces Chinese, Thai, Japanese, and Singaporean films (as well as films in Europe). Blind Spot Pictures, a small transnational Finnish filmmaker, which has co-produced with firms from Denmark, Estonia, the Netherlands, United Kingdom, Italy, Sweden, Russia, and Germany, collaborated on the production of the Chinese kung-fu movie *Jade Warrior* (2006) and other Chinese joint ventures over the last few years.

Media Asia (Hong Kong) partnered with Warner Bros. and Singapore's Media Corporation on *Departed* (2006), a remake of *Infernal Affairs* (2002), which was a success in China and Hong Kong. In 2004, Warner established a production partnership, Warner China Film HG Group, with additional operations in Spain and Italy. With *World Without Thieves* (2004), Media Asia secured a Chinese joint venture with state-run China Film Corporation and Huayi Brothers, a Hong Kong advertising firm, which sold product placement to Nokia, BMW, and China Mobile.

The leap in cultural production and subsequent transnationalization in the 1990s across East Asia can be attributed to several conjunctural factors: insistence by global financial institutions on deregulating media; the normalization of relations between Japan and Korea, China, Hong Kong, and Taiwan; digital technology development; the increase in regional industrial production; and the accompanying concerted push towards consumerism. In this mix, transnational capital combines with local and national capital to produce media in partnership with economic and political elites. Samsung and Daewoo invest in film production. Disney distributes Japanese anime. News Corp promotes Taiwanese musicians. The Australian production studio Beckers Group co-produces and distributes international remakes of Japanese melodramas.

Media co-productions and cross-border exchanges are frequently not recognized because television programs and music are difficult to culturally identify. Japanese exports in particular, from technologies to cartoons and comics, mix elements of diverse cultures to scrub away any ethnic or cultural identifiers. Japanese transnationals act as "transformer sub-stations" to refashion Western commodities (and Japanese commodities) to suit the tastes and material conditions of consumers across Asia. Media TNMCs with Japanese TNCC input increase their capital and market share by distributing apparently non-Western, non-Japanese media content and commodities.

Korean waves and transnational tides

Importantly, the rise of Asian TNMCs confirms the "shifting nature of cultural power in a context in which intensified global cultural flows have decentered the power structure and vitalized local practices of appropria-tion and consumption of foreign cultural products and meanings" (Iwabuchi, 2002, p. 35). Korean cultural exports hit $4.2 billion in 2011 (Beattie, 2012); Japanese creative industry exports now exceed $10 billion a year (Otmazgin, 2008). Transnational media production practices are encouraged by the TNCC and its politically organized transnational planning groups, national governments accepting neoliberalism, an aggres-sive international financial apparatus, and TNMCs that organize production in similar ways. "The conjunction between a new [transnationally organized] external environment, which was receptive to Korean cultural products, and the transformation of some segment of the cultural industries in the 1980s paved the way for the actual spurt of trans-Asian flow" (Siriyuvasak, 2010).

Transnational production disrupts the national identity and symbolic meaning of formerly culturally encrusted communication. "Geo-linguistic regional markets spread over many countries have become increasingly important components in the business strategies of [transnational] Asian media producers" (Chadha & Koovri, 2000, p. 425). Consequently, TNMCs adopt and adapt whatever local ritual or artifact can be commodified, or whatever cultural icon or meaning will attract an audience that can be sold to an advertiser. "Chinese or Japanese or Korean, nobody cares," says Hong Kong director Fruit Chan. "Young people just want to watch good movies," so film ventures in the region are cross-cultural from the start (quoted in Beals & Platt, 2001, p. 52). Here decentering only refers to the national origin of entertainment media, not to the removal of central power – the new TNCC firmly holds power through national firms partnered with TNMCs or pulled along in their market-driven wake. Transnational capitalism integrates markets and capital, employs new communication technologies, attracts affluent middle classes in every nation and region, and reorganizes transnational cultural production and distribution.

Hybrid media content reflects the appropriation, production, and transmission of cultural forms selected by TNMCs and their national, regional, and local partners for purposes of advertising and corporate profit. Media globalization is not simply (or even primarily) a Western media strategy; rather, transnational capitalism and transnational media increase "integration, networking, and cooperation among worldwide" capitalists (Iwabuchi, 2002, p. 36), undermining cultural specificity, obstructing citizen reflection and action, and simultaneously dressing up consumerism as democracy and progress.

ABC's *America's Funny Home Videos* is actually Japanese, first broadcast from 1986 to 1992 as part of a TBS variety show. ABC bought the rights to the program in 1989 and has since exported the format to more than 80 countries. *Funny Home Videos* in every land demonstrates transnational media's contribution to democracy: viewers get to vote for their favorite videos. Not surprisingly, neither the technology nor the participatory model are available for actual democratic debate and vote on social or political issues. Can you imagine: a weekly presentation of short arguments on climate change, education, or health care by citizens, ending in a vote by viewers for their preferred policy?

In larger operations, transnationals structurally reinforce their entire market lines. Sony (and Panasonic, Sumitomo, and Itochu) partnered with US firms (Columbia, Universal, TCI, and Time Warner) not for cultural influence, but to profit by merging production and distribution. Japanese television networks buy global television formats such as *Who Wants to Be a Millionaire?* (Celador, UK), *Weakest Link* (BBC, UK), and *Survivor* (Planet 24, Sweden/UK), while Japanese networks TBS and NTV sell formats to Western broadcasters. TBS has sold formats, including the original *Funniest Home Videos*, to more than 40 countries. Fuji TV developed the competitive cooking show, *Iron Chef*, purchased by Paramount in 2001. Japanese manga comics, anime television, music idols, and soaps are exported widely across East Asia, usually with "joint production ventures spanning several different markets" (Iwabuchi, 2007, p. 74), including Hong Kong, Taiwan, Korea, Thailand, and China. Although Japanese media and culture industries cannot become global players without partners, these media mergers cannot be unpacked by reference to national interest: transnational media contribute to transnational capitalism and strengthen the hegemony of

Pikachu's Global Adventure

Transnational media aim to offer a total cultural package. The multimedia strategy of Nintendo's international phenomenon Pokémon is a case in point. Comics, animation, playing cards, toys, and video games intertextually complement each product line. Introduced as kids' card game in 1996, Pokémon has since sold over 200 million video games. The international success required a transnational strategy: "Pikachu's [a Pokémon hero] global adventure carried him not from Japan to the world, but from Japan to the United States, where he was given a makeover before sending him on to the rest of the world" (Tobin, 2004, p. 267). Nintendo, Shogkukan, TV Tokyo, Creatures, Inc., and other Japanese firms that first developed the game and characters recruited others with expertise and resources to jointly share in the creation, distribution, and profit. Nintendo America, Hasbro, 4Kids Entertainment, and Warner Bros. earned a large share of the profit, because they partnered in the production of global versions of Pokémon. Clever names were devised for Pokémon's French, Italian, and German versions, but for smaller market countries and languages translations were not as thoroughly localized (Tobin, 2004, p. 266). Still, the cartoon was shown in more than 70 countries in 30 languages (Iwabuchi, 2007, p. 69).

consumer entertainment media. Manga Entertainment (75% owned by Starz/Liberty Media) produces and distributes Japanese animation in North America and Europe. Disney distributes Miyazaki Hayo's Studio Ghibli animation around the world. Warner Bros. partners with Nintendo to broadcast Pokémon in the United States and distribute an American version internationally. In each case, "apparently opposing forces are working simultaneously and interactively" (Iwabuchi, 2007, p. 68): nationality is secondary, while TNCC profits, formations, and interests are paramount.

There is ample evidence of the decentering of US-dominated media and cultural flows; evidence that doesn't require theoretical hallucinations of contraflow (which imagines significant media export from smaller nations to major capitalist countries) but reflects the expansion of a shared transnational capitalist power based on wage labor making profits for globally connected corporations, including TNMCs. As Iwabuchi (2007) observes,

"Asian markets have become even more synchronized, joint East Asian projects in film and music have become more common, and singers and actors from around the region are engaged in activities that transcend national borders" (p. 74).

Complementary Media Flow as Transnational Consent

Perhaps instead of reference to contraflow, which sees media from developing nations challenging Western media dominance, a more accurate description of global media processes might be "comple-flow." Transnational media in East Asia supplement, parallel, and *complement* the cross-border flow of commodities, advertising, and cultural practices by more global TNMCs, which are also present in the region. Comple-flow indicates local differentiation among transnational media according to their reach, interlocks, and hegemonic influence. "Imitation, localization, co-productions, and niche programming are a strategic means for new or under-capitalised production companies to compete against high-budget international programs" (Keane et al., 2007, p. 5), but global competition is not a consideration for most national or local firms. Rather, survival and financial return drive media that cannot actually compete against the transnationals.

Smaller transnational media cannot challenge Sony, News Corp, or Reliance Entertainment, but do offer complementary assistance through joint ventures, provide sustenance through mergers, or simply confer hegemonic legitimacy on the transnational operation by complementing through myriad smaller transnational productions that include local and regional producers, directors, celebrities, and technicians. Korean-based Seoul Broadcasting Service (SBS), for instance, has invested in Japan's Nippon Television Network, Beijing TV, Shanghai Media and Entertainment Group, Hong Kong's TVB, Taiwan's Gala Television, Hanoi TV, and ABS-CBN and GMA in the Philippines (Thailand Ministry of Commerce, in Siriyuvasak, 2010) – making SBS a key transnational player in the region, but essentially unknown worldwide. SBS does not contribute media flow against dominant TNMC producers; it *complements* the flow of TNMC media with localized production and hybridized content. Hong Kong-based TVB (a superstation airing soaps and game shows) has partnered with Taiwan's Era International to launch 15 satellite channels broadcasting to Hong Kong, China, Taiwan, Singapore, Japan, Australia, Malaysia, Macau, and North America (TVBI, 2010) – exceeding STAR TV's audience reach in the region, but TVB programming content complements the more global content on offer by dominant TNMCs.

Domestic transnational applicants fill important gaps in the global media environment. Co-productions by regional transnationals target multiple markets and facilitate the mutual promotion of transnational media culture, which is being "recentered through the alliance of major media corporations" entering the East Asian market (Iwabuchi, 2007, p. 78). Transnational media do not standardize media culture in Asia (or worldwide), but join and profit in the dissemination of hybrid difference and cultural diversity, albeit "governed by the logic of capital and organized within the context of globalization" and transnational capitalism (Iwabuchi, 2007, p. 78).

East Asian integration illustrates that it "is no longer tenable for any country [or media corporation] to contain its cultural orientation and agendas within clearly demarcated national boundaries" (Iwabuchi, 2007, p. 79). National governments reorganize their economic and cultural policies to attract TNMC investment to national co-productions. The Korean government deregulated ownership guidelines in the 1990s, which brought investment, mergers, and co-productions, directly contributing to the "Korean Wave" of media "exports" throughout the region. Increased FDI underwrote regional expansion by Korea's two national private television networks: MBC television signed with 17 transnational partners; Korea's SBS found 21 transnational partners. Complementary entertainment media flow from everywhere.

Market "liberalization" was not simply pushed on India by the World Bank and other international lenders during the 1990s, because the Indian government lifted restrictions and passed reforms designed to "solicit" non-Indian FDI investment and "recruit" foreign media investors (Govil, 2007, pp. 87–88). By 1999, the government allowed 100% foreign equity in film, giving preference to Hollywood distributors of Indian producers. As media transnationalize, cultural and territorial borders become more porous and transnational capitalist wealth and power expand. As Korean media exports increased, so did sales of Korean consumer goods, including televisions, phones, cars, clothing, and cosmetics due to the strategic placement of advertising in media entertainment across the region (Kim, 2007). Korea's transnational culture industry was developed economically and politically by the government in service to the Korean TNCC segment, commodifying and marketing the entire country as an export brand.

Capitalist Interlocks

Global cultural power may be dispersed in location and diversified in form as experienced in East Asia, Europe, and the Americas, but this does not mean that power has disappeared or been muted. Rather, capitalism is evolving into a new transnational formation. In service to global capital, transnational media (despite their consumer popularity) exclude "a tremendous number of people and their unprofitable cultural expressions and concerns ... underpinning the logic of transnational capitalism ... benefitting a few, while acting freely beyond the confines of national interest in accord with the fundamental tenets of consumerism" (Iwabuchi, 2007, p. 81). TNMCs and their local partners perform within the parameters of transnational capitalism, promoting and profiting from the production and consumption by a multitude.

The following paragraphs include a partial list of the eight largest TNMCs, their subsidiaries, joint ventures, and director interlocks primarily related to broadcasting and film. In addition to transnational joint ventures with local names, many of these TNMCs brand their co-productions as their own. So Bertelsmann, the largest transnational operator in Europe, has its RTL TV brand in 10 European countries, Viacom has local productions in dozens of countries under its MTV and Nickelodeon brands, while Disney, Time Warner, and the others have done likewise with well-known brands such as CNN, ESPN, and the Cartoon Network.

The list of major TNMCs has remained fairly stable over the decades, although their families of partners have grown. Comcast entered the echelons of TNMCs with its purchase of NBC Universal from GE. Others like Liberty Global, Reliance, and Naspers have consolidated and expanded their transnational operations. Many national media have disappeared in mergers, entered partnerships with larger TNMCs, or else struggle to survive – especially if they operate in small markets. TNMCs of all sizes and locations engage in joint ventures, co-productions, and organizational interlocks. The most successful TNMCs achieve what all transnational capitalists aspire to: they "control all points in the promotion, production, and distribution process ... Merchandising, product licensing, and international revenue [are] all part of the return on the investment" (Pecora, 2004, pp. 35, 37).

The relationships presented below are incomplete in terms of print, Internet, or radio broadcasting. The lists are also tentative, as every TNMC has additional joint ventures and unpublicized mergers and acquisitions around the globe. Not included in these lists are connections each TNMC has with other transnational corporations (McDonald's, Caterpillar, Novartis, Fuji, GM, Ford, AIG, Procter & Gamble, Coca-Cola, Nike, and more) or financial institutions (like Citigroup, JP Morgan, Goldman Sachs, Banco Santander, Deutsche Bank, and private equity funds). Nonetheless, the breadth of inter-corporate connections across national boundaries is astounding. Many of the TNMCs listed may have origins in the West, but they are now transnational in production and programming.

Bertelsmann/RTL

RTL Television (Europe), RTL Radio (Europe), VOX TV, Fremantle Media, Grundy Media, Sportfive (Europe), UFA Film, Gruner + Jahr, Bookspan, BMG Music, Bertrand (Portugal), Bertelsmann (China), BOL China, BOL Britain, Arvato Media Services, Prinovis, Random House, Doubleday, Bantam Books, Ballantine, Anchor Books, Knopf, Virgin Books (UK), Discovery, Disney, RCA/Sony Music, Playboy, IBM, Hewlett Packard, AOL, Univisión, New York Times, Freedom Communications, Activision/ Blizzard, Newspaper Association of America, Freedom Communications (US), RCA Records, News Corp, Comcast, Talpa Media (Netherlands), Russian satellite and cable, MaXposure publishing (India), India NetworkPlay, Vodafone, Pearson.

Comcast

NBC, CNBC, HBO, MSNBC, SciFi, E!, Style, G4, Oxygen, Sundance, Bravo, A + E, History Channel, Universal Studios, Aegis-Dentsû, Time Warner, Hearst, ATT, DeLoitte, WNYC, CBS, DirecTV, Cox Communications, Hallmark, GemSTAR TV Guide, PBS, HIT Entertainment/Mattel (UK), National Geographic Channel, Hulu, BSkyB, News Corp, Disney, Vivendi, Sumitomo, Hitachi, Calle 13 (Spain), Steel (Hungary), Telemundo, USA network, Bravo, Universal theme parks, Televisa (Mexico), RTI (Italy), Caracol (Colombia), Microsoft, ATT, WNYC, Discovery, CBS, TV 18 (India).

Disney

ABC, ESPN, Lifetime, Jetix, Disney Channel, Soap, A + E, History Channel, Touchstone, Buena Vista, Axel Springer, Bertelsmann, Patagonik Films (Argentina), Cisco, Jetix, Univisión, ImpreMedia, La Opinion, Google, Facebook, UTV (India), Hugama (India), Nintendo, Microsoft, Sony, Fox, Comcast, Hearst, Smriti Irani Television, UMP and UTV (Mauritius), Doordashan, Bauer (Germany), Box TV (UK), Yash Raj (India), Zee TV, Sun TV (India), Doordarshan (India), Tata T-Sky (India), National Geographic, Hearst, Net TV (Spain), RTL (Germany), BVS, Saban Group, Lucasfilms, Miravista, Reliance/DreamWorks, Village Roadshow (Australia), Tele-München (Germany), SBS (Sweden), Tesauro (Spain), Hammster Media, Sport France, BSkyB (Europe), RCN (Colombia).

News Corp

Fox Television, TV Guide, Speed, National Geographic, STAR TV (Asia), Wall St. Journal, BSkyB (Europe), Harper Collins, 20th Century Fox, Wall St. Journal, New York Post, London Times, Sky Global, Sky Brazil, Los Angeles Dodgers, National Rugby League (Australia), Phoenix TV (Asia), New York Times, O Globo, Sky Mexico, Televisa, Liberty Media, MGM, Rotana (Middle East), Gateway, Disney, Bertelsmann, Comcast, Time Warner, Sony, Hulu, Facebook, Gateway, DirecTV, Haim Saban, ESPN, History Channel, National Geographic, Marvel Comics, Dell, Turner, Zee TV (India), Anand Bazaar Patrika (India), DEN (Digital Entertainment Network, India), Vijay TV (Asia), Balkan News Corp., J Sky Sports (Japan), SKY PerfecTV (Japan), Taiwan Cable Systems, UTV Software (Asia), Yesky. com (Asia), NDS (Europe), Hathway (India), DTH Tata-Sky (India), Star Ananda (Tamil-India).

Sony

MGM, Animax, AXN (Asia), AXN (Europe), Sony Pictures, Playstation, Blu-Ray, Colombia-Tristar, Sony BMG Music, Columbia, Epic, Arista, Bertelsmann, News Corp, Viacom/CBS, Time Warner, Disney, Hulu, Blu-ray, Telemundo, Fuji Xerox, Berlitz, McKinsey & Co., Comcast, CBS, Discovery, Rotana (Middle East), Star India, Weather Channel, 3D Impact (Swiss).

Time Warner

CNN, TBS, TNT, CW, Turner Classic Movies, HBO, Cartoon Network, Boomerang, Time, Fortune, Sports Illustrated, Warner Bros., DC Comics, Little Brown & Co., Atlanta Hawks, Atlanta Braves, Warner Music, Atlantic Records, Rhino Records, Legendary Entertainment, Comcast, Bertelsmann, ATT, Netscape, Verizon, Disney, Axel Springer, Omnicom, CME (Eastern Europe), Disney, News Corp, Viacom, AOL, AOLTV, Time Warner (Europe), Boing (Italy), Dogan Media (Turkey), Fanda (Czech), Axel Springer (Germany), New Line Cinema, Google, Trion World Network, Hewlett Packard, VIVA (Europe with EMI, Sony), Warner China Film HG (China), Shanghai Media Group, Electronic Arts, Dell, Pokémon, Nickelodeon, China Film Group (China), Hengdian Group (China), 21Communications (China), STAR, Zee TV (India), DEN (Digital Entertainment Network, India), CNN-IBN (India), TV 18 (India).

Viacom/CBS

MTV, VH1, BET, Nickelodeon, TV Land, Spike, Comedy Central, CMT, CBS, Showtime, CW, Movie Channel, Flix, Paramount Movies, VIVA, Infinity Radio, AOL, Teenage Mutant Ninja Turtles, Simon & Schuster, Scribner's, Comcast, United International, Melange Pictures, Reliance Entertainment (India), Time Warner, Tyco, Sony, Verizon, GAMCO, Oracle, Akamai Tech, Scholastic, Liberty Meida, Chellozone (Europe), TV 18 (India), SBS (Korea), Winx/Rainbow (Italy), Tanglong Culture Company (China), Abril Music (Brazil), Bonnier (Sweden), Sogecable (Spain), Ufa (Germany), Nelvana (Canada).

Vivendi

Canal+, TV Cyfra (Poland), Canal Overseas (Africa, Vietnam), Bolloré's Direct 8 and Digital Star Television, StudioCanal (Europe), Universal Studios, EMI Records, Universal Music Group, Vevo, Havas, TPS Pay TV (France), Comcast, NBC Universal (20%), BMG Music, Houghton Mifflin, Activision, SFR mobile phones, GVT telecom (Brazil), Dish TV (Brazil), Vodafone, BSkyB, Yahoo!, Sony, Carolco, Lagardère, Random House, Warner Music, GVT (Brazil), Houghton Mifflin, Bertelsmann Digital, Marco Telecom (Mauritius, Gabon, Mali), Abril (Brazil).

Table 4.1 Top transnational entertainment media, 2014 (by revenue)

	Revenues $ billions
1. Comcast	64.5
2. Google	52
3. Time Warner/TW Cable	52
4. Disney	46
5. 21st Century Fox/News Corp	40.8
6. DirecTV	32
7. Vivendi	31.6
8. Viacom/CBS	29
9. Liberty Global/Liberty	18.5
10. Cox Enterprises	15
11. Dish Network	13.9
12. Thomson Reuters	12.7
13. Rogers Communications	12.3
14. British Sky Broadcasting	11.7
15. Lagardère	9.5
16. Reed Elsevier	9.4
17. Nippon Hoso Kyokai	8.4
18. ARD	8.2
19. Bloomberg	8
20. Charter Communications	8
21. Sony Entertainment	8
22. Bertelsmann	7.8
23. BBC	7.7
24. Cablevision	7
25. Fuji Media	7
26. Advance Publications	7
27. Pearson	7
28. Virgin Media	6.7
29. Globo	6.6
30. Clear Channel	6.3
31. Naspers	6.1
32. Grupo Televisa	5.8
33. MediaSet	5.5
34. Discovery	5.5
35. Gannett	5.2
36. Shaw Comm	5.1

(Continued)

Table 4.1   (*Continued*)

	Revenues $ billions
37. Yahoo!	4.7
38. Wolters Kluwer	4.7
39. McGraw-Hill	4.5
40. Bonnier	4.4
41. Axel Springer	4.4
42. Tokyo Broadcasting	4.2
43. Washington Post	4.1
44. Quebecor	4
45. France Télévision	4
46. ITV	3.7
47. Hearst	3.7
48. Netflix	3.7
49. ProSiebenSat.1	3.5

Sources: Mediadatenbank (2013); CNN Money Global 500 (2014)

Transnationalism for All: Diversity without Democracy

Transnational media corporations have reorganized the global media environment through mergers, acquisitions, joint ventures, and local co-production chains. In some regions, transnational media have earned respect and followings. "Al Jazeera is now an integral part of the Arab identity and satellite channels are perceived to be at the heart of media and cultural changes in South East Asia ... [In Europe] international TV brands and channels have outperformed national television in recent times" (Chalaby, 2009, p. 115). National commercial media that remain fight for survival, as audiences and advertising shift to the more integrated, resourced, and talent-laden production systems of TNMCs. Despite the remarkable increase in television stations and genres, the Council of Europe's Media Advisory Panel concluded in 2004 that as a result of media transnationalism "fewer media companies exist, market access is hindered for new entrants and editorial freedoms are interfered with, thus limiting the number of independent voices which can make themselves heard and diminishing the diversity of cultural and social life" (Bruck et al., 2004, p. 4).

The move towards media transnationalism continues and deepens, confirming the concerns of the Council of Europe's Media Advisory Panel. Smaller media firms must either merge, form alliances with TNMCs, or face extinction. Transnational operations cannot "be conducted effectively without partners" locally and transnationally (Iwabuchi, 2002, p. 119). "What matters spatially is not the company's headquarters, or the location of its major shareholders, but the site of its actual product development and management" (Miller et al., 2008, p. 92), which remains under the control of TNMCs. Consequently, there is a diminishing access to production as national, regional, and local producers link with transnational production chains. A diversity of genres appears through subcontracting, re-purposing existing transnational productions, adapting transnational media models, and creating local productions that conform to the advertising needs of the transnational programmers. Primarily seeking affluent audiences, TNMCs begin with programming entertainment for the cosmopolitan elite, inevitably expanding their media offerings targeting larger mass audiences for personal consumption, but always offering little for the millions of world citizens who have limited disposable income.

As an outcome of the privatization process, transnational media concentrations have devastated the public sphere by dismantling public media and curbing media production by alternative voices and social groups, access that is crucial to the functioning of democracy. Diversity in genre and programming has increased, as advertisers and producers narrowcast to target markets, but political and cultural democratic media access has been overwhelmed by the globalization of commercial standardization. Karol Jakubowicz's (2007) summary of media reform in Eastern Europe speaks to TNMC expansion in general: "Very little has been done to achieve true democratization of the media system or media organizations" (p. 314). As becomes apparent in media entertainment content, all TNMCs tend towards entertainment, distraction, and diversion. Reflection, thoughtfulness, and critique are not traits that nurture individual consumers concerned with personal gratification necessary for increasing consumer product sales and avoiding citizen involvement or action.

The next chapter delves into the process and impact of transnational media production and distribution of entertainment that attracts and delivers viewers to TNMCs, advertisers, and transnational capitalist norms. The following chapters also note the collapse of active citizenship in a consumer society.

Table 4.2 Media companies in the Forbes Global 2000 in 2014 (ranked by revenues, profits, assets, market value)

Media rank	Forbes rank	Company	Country
1	57	Comcast	United States
2	100	Walt Disney	United States
3	152	21st Century Fox	United States
4	156	Time Warner	United States
5	252	Time Warner Cable	United States
6	300	DirecTV	United States
7	368	CBS	United States
8	380	Viacom	United States
9	479	Rogers Communications	Canada
10	520	Dish Network	United States
11	548	Vivendi	France
12	621	Liberty Global	United States
13	635	British Sky Broadcasting	United Kingdom
14	671	Virgin Media	United Kingdom
15	747	Thomson Reuters	Canada
16	793	Discovery Communications	United States
17	805	RTL Group	Luxembourg
18	837	Pearson	United Kingdom
19	851	Naspers	South Africa
20	865	Reed Elsevier	United Kingdom
21	877	Grupo Televisa	Mexico
22	922	News Corp	United States

23	1038	Lagardère	France
24	1040	McGraw-Hill Cos	United States
25	1072	Shaw Communications	Canada
26	1074	SES	Luxembourg
27	1160	Dai Nippon Printing	Japan
28	1268	Liberty Media	United States
29	1308	Charter Communications	United States
30	1378	Toppan Printing	Japan
31	1447	ITV	United Kingdom
32	1455	ProSiebenSat1	Germany
33	1499	Scripps Networks	United States
34	1507	Wolters Kluwer	Netherlands
35	1565	RR Donnelley	United States
36	1754	Gannett	United States
37	1808	Cablevision	United States
38	1851	Eutelsat Communications	France
39	1874	CC Media Holdings	United States
40	1999	Mediaset	Italy

Sources: FactSet; Bloomberg; Forbes: http://www.forbes.com/global2000/list/

References

Adeosun, O. (2012, Winter). Tongue tied. *World Policy Institute.* Retrieved from http://www.worldpolicy.org/journal/winter2012/tongue-tied

Alwaleed, Bill Gates discuss joint projects at The Savoy. (2013, February 3). *Arab News.* Retrieved June 9, 2013, from http://www.arabnews.com/alwaleed-bill-gates-discuss-joint-projects-savoy

AXN. (2011, January 3). AXN partners CU MEDIA to expand reach in Korea. Retrieved from http://www.indiantelevision.com/content/axn-partners-cu-media-to-expand-reach-in-korea

Beals, G., & Platt, K. (2001, May 21). The birth of Asiawood. *Newsweek (Pacific Edition), 137*(21), 52–56.

Beattie, A. C. (2012, June 11). Marketing's next wave: The Korean pop star. *Advertising Age, 83,* 6.

Bertelsmann forges ahead with growth in China. (2012, October 26). Bertelsmann. Retrieved July 9, 2013, from http://www.bertelsmann.com/Press.html

Bruck, P. A., Dörr, D., Cole, M. D., Favre, J., Gramstad, S., Monaco, M. R., & Čulek, Z. P. (2004, November). *Transnational media concentrations in Europe.* Report by Advisory Panel on Media Diversity to the Council of Europe Steering Committee on the Mass Media. Strasbourg, France: Council of Europe.

Buchta, D., Fabel, M., De Clerq, M., & Hall, R. (2009). *Middle East media on the move.* Chicago: AT Kearney, Inc. Retrieved from http://www.atkearney.com/documents/10192/4095877b-119c-492b-a236-219098f229df

Chadha, K., & Kavoori, A. (2000). Media imperialism revisited: some findings, from the Asian case. *Media, Culture & Society, 22*(4), 415–432.

Chalaby, J. K. (2002). Transnational television in Europe: The role of pan-European channels. *European Journal of Communication, 17*(2), 183–203.

Chalaby, J. K. (2009). *Transnational television in Europe: Reconfiguring global communications networks.* London: I.B. Tauris.

Child, B. (2012, November 29). China will be the world's biggest film market by 2020. *Guardian.* Retrieved March 14, 2013, from http://www.guardian.co.uk/film/2012/nov/29/china-biggest-film-market-2020

China global investment tracker interactive map. (2012). Heritage Foundation. Retrieved June 9, 2013, from http://www.heritage.org/research/projects/china-global-investment-tracker-interactive-map

Coonan, C. (2012, April 30.) China plans $1.27 billion production hub. *Variety.* RetrievedMarch14,2013,fromhttp://variety.com/2012/film/news/china-plans-1-27-billion-production-hub-1118053284/

Davis, D. W., & Yeh, E. Y. (2008). *East Asian screen industries.* London: British Film Institute.

DreamWorks Animation in joint venture in China. (2012, February 17). *Seattle Times*. Retrieved February 14, 2013, from http://seattletimes.com/html/entertainment/2017532169_apusdreamworksanimationchina.html

Gershon, R. A. (2005). The transnationals: Media corporations, international trade and entertainment flows. In A. Cooper-Chen (Ed.), *Global entertainment media* (pp. 17–35). Mahwah, NJ: Lawrence Erlbaum Associates.

Govil, N. (2007). Bollywood and the frictions of global mobility. In D. K. Thussu (Ed.), *Media on the move: Global flow and contra flow* (pp. 84–99). New York: Routledge.

Hedley, N. (2013, January 3). Naspers 'head and shoulders above its rivals'. BIZCOMMUNITY.com. Retrieved January 22, 2013 from, http://www.bizcommunity.com/Article/196/15/87463.html

IDATE. (2010). *TV 2010: Markets & trends, facts & figures*. IDATE: Montpellier, France. Retrieved from http://www.international-television.org/tv_market_data/world-tv-market-2010.html

Investor Fact Sheet. (2012, November). Central European Media Enterprises website. Retrieved May 17, 2013, from http://www.cetv-net.com/file/u/presentations/Q312_IP_November.pdf?20130107

IPS Correspondents. (1996, September 9). U.S.-Haiti: Groups target Disney's link to Haitian firms. Inter Press Service News Agency. Retrieved July 9, 2013, from http://www.ipsnews.net/1996/09/us-haiti-groups-target-disneys-link-to-haitian-firms/

Iwabuchi, K. (2002). *Recentering globalization: Popular culture and Japanese trans-nationalism*. Durham, NC: Duke University Press.

Iwabuchi, K. (2007). Contra-flows or the cultural logic of uneven globalization? Japanese media in the global agora. In D. K. Thussu (Ed.), *Media on the move: Global flow and contra flow* (pp. 67–83). New York: Routledge.

Jakubowicz, K. (2007). *Rude awakening: Social and media change in Central and Eastern Europe*. Cresskill, NJ: Hampton Press.

Jalloh, A. (2012, June 6). Saudi Arabia's billionaire prince honors President Koroma's invitation. *Sierra Express Media*. Retrieved from http://www.sierraexpressmedia.com/?p=57565

Jannarone, J. (2012, July 3). Time Warner increases stake in Central European Media. *Wall Street Journal*. Retrieved from http://online.wsj.com/article/SB10001424052702304708604577505372445636642.html

Keane, M., Fung, A. Y. H., & Moran, A. (2007). *New television, globalization, and the East Asian cultural imagination*. Hong Kong: Hong Kong University Press.

Kim, Y. (2007). The rising East Asian 'wave': Korean media go global. In D. K. Thussu (Ed.), *Media on the move: Global flow and contra flow* (pp. 135–152). New York: Routledge.

Kraidy, M. M., & Khalil, J. F. (2007). The Middle East: Transnational Arab television, in L. Artz and Y. Kamalipour (Eds.), *The media globe: Trends in international mass media* (pp. 79–98). Lanham, MD: Rowman & Littlefield.

Lakshman, N. (2008, April 15). Why Reliance is buying U.S. cinemas. *Bloomberg Business Week.* Retrieved October 3, 2014, from http://www.businessweek.com/stories/2008-04-15/why-reliance-is-buying-u-dot-s-dot-cinemasbusinessweek-business-news-stock-market-and-financial-advice

Li, M., & Sligo, F. (2012). Chinese media going global: Issues of perception and credibility. *China Media Research, 8*(3), 116–127.

Machado, K. (2010, August 18). Reliance Broadcast, CBS in India pact. *Wall Street Journal.* Retrieved from http://online.wsj.com/article/SB10001424052748703649004575436930748453518.html

Masters, K. (2012, February 24). Reliance rethinks its big Hollywood experiment amid an uncertain future. *Hollywood Reporter.* Retrieved March 5, 2012, from http://www.hollywoodreporter.com/news/reliance-dreamworks-caa-indian-conglom-hollywood-292383

Mastrini, G., & Becerra, M. (2011). Structure, concentration and changes of the media system in the southern cone of Latin America. *Comunicar, 36*(18), 51–59.

Mediedatenbank. (2013). Media database. Institut für Medien- und Kommunikationspolitik. Retrievedfromhttp://www.mediadb.eu/en/data-base/international-media-corporations/

Miller, T., Govil, N., McMurria, J., Wang, T., & Maxwell, R. (2008). *Global Hollywood 2.* 2nd edn. London: British Film Institute.

Mjos, O. J. (2009). *Media globalization and the Discovery Channel networks.* New York: Taylor & Francis.

Otmazgin, N. K. (2008). Contesting soft power: Japanese popular culture in East and Southeast Asia. *International Relations of the Asia-Pacific, 8*(1), 73–101.

Pecora, N. (2004). Nickelodeon grows up: The economic evolution of a network. In H. Hendershot (Ed.), *Nickelodeon nation: The history, politics, and economics of America's only TV channel for kids* (pp. 15–44). New York: New York University Press.

Punathambekar, A. (2010). Reality TV and participatory culture in India. *Popular Communication, 8*(4), 241–255.

Rohn, U. (2011). Emerging, attracting and challenging: How some of the world's largest media companies perceive their challenges and opportunities in China. *Chinese Journal of Communication, 4*(2), 198–217.

Rushe, D. (2011, August 22). Hollywood targets Chollywood as LA studio enters $220 m joint venture. *Guardian.* Retrieved from http://www.guardian.co.uk/business/2011/aug/22/film-china-legendary-entertainment-joint

Siriyuvasak, U. (2010). Cultural industry and Asianization: The new "imagined" inter-Asia economy. Retrieved from http://bookrepublic.org/wp-content/uploads/2012/10/UBONRAT-Asianization-Jan-2010-FINAL1.pdf

Sowards, S. (2003). MTV Asia: Localizing the global media. In L. Artz and Y. Kamalipour (Eds.), *The globalization of corporate media hegemony* (pp. 229–244). Albany, NY: State University of New York Press.

Sparks, C. (2000). Media theory after the fall of European communism. Why the old models from East and West won't do any more. In J. Curran & M. J. Part (Eds.), *De-westernizing media studies* (pp. 35–49). London: Routledge.

Star plus and Sab gain in TAM week 22. (2013, June 6). IndianTelevision.com. Retrieved October 10, 2014, from http://www.indiantelevision.com/mam/marketing/mam/star-plus-and-sab-gain-in-tam-week-22

Stilson, J. (2007, November 5). Golden BRIC road: Brazil, Russia, India and China. *Mediaweek, 17*(40), 12–16.

Sun, L. (2013, February 7). Is stability a pipe dream for DreamWorks Animation? The Motley Fool Blog. Retrieved July 1, 2013, from http://beta.fool.com/leokornsun/2013/02/07dreamworks-pipe-dream-or-sweet-dream/23814/

Teer-Tomaselli, R., Wasserman, H. J., & De Beer, A. S. (2007). South Africa as a regional media power. In D. K. Thussu (Ed.), *Media on the move: Global flow and contraflow* (pp.153–164). New York: Routledge.

Tobin, J. (2004). Conclusion: The rise and fall of the Pokémon empire. In J. Tobin (Ed.), *Pikachu's global adventure: The rise and fall of Pokémon* (pp. 257–292). Durham, NC: Duke University Press.

Tsui, C. (2013, January 25). Will China buy a Hollywood studio? (Analysis). *Hollywood Reporter*. Retrieved from http://www.hollywoodreporter.com/news/will-china-buy-a-hollywood-414056

TV 2010: Market and trends, facts and figures. (2009). IDATE. Retrieved from www.idate.org/2009/pages/download.php?

TVBI. (2010, April 10). International business – Taiwan TVBS. Retrieved from http://b.tvb.com/tvbi/category/international-business/taiwan-tvbs/

UTV. (2013). UTV website. Retrieved from http://www.utvgroup.com/

Wang, T. (2005). PRC. In T. Miller, N. Govil, J. MacMurria, R. Maxwell, & T. Wang (Eds.), *Global Hollywood 2* (pp. 149–151). London: British Film Institute.

Webdale, J. (2012, October 29). Reliance, RTL ready for big thrill. *C21Media*. Retrieved from http://www.c21media.net/archives/91044

Xiaoling, Z. (2010). Chinese state media going global. *East Asian Policy, 2*(1), 42–50.

Further Reading

Chalaby, J. K. (Ed.). (2005). *Transnational television worldwide: Towards a new media order.* London: I.B. Tauris.

Havens, T. (2006). *Global television marketplace.* London: Palgrave Macmillan.

Iwabuchi, K. (2002). *Recentering globalization: Popular culture and Japanese transnationalism.* Durham, NC: Duke University Press.

5

Cultural Hegemony
Leadership with Consent

Legitimizing Transnational Relations

Transnational media corporation (TNMC) structures and practices conform to, express, and reproduce social relations of production that establish
hierarchies of decision-making. A new transnational division of labor alters
the global access to the means of production, changes the relations of
production, and determines what will be produced. Social relations are
not analytical abstractions. Social relations in media production include:
(1) the labor process necessary for production; (2) the social hierarchy in
decision-making and implementation of production; (3) the means by
which labor is recruited to participate in the production process; (4) the
contribution of creative workers to media production; (5) the organization
of consent by labor for an unequal social system; (6) the complementary
process of involving labor in the production process as consumers and
audience commodities; and (7) the symbolic production of meaning through
media content. Several of these components will be at least minimally
addressed in this chapter, especially the role of consent in reproducing
transnational capitalism.

The structure of media production under capitalism frames the possible
range and social terms of media consumption, so media production must
be investigated for its ideological and cultural contribution to the functioning of the broader society. Media content programming – its images,
narratives, and representations – roughly conforms to the structure and
material relations of production: commercial media broadcast entertainment

Global Entertainment Media: A Critical Introduction, First Edition. Lee Artz.
© 2015 John Wiley & Sons, Inc. Published 2015 by John Wiley & Sons, Inc.

to attract audiences; religious media broadcast entertainment for uplifting souls; public media broadcast entertainment for edification and education. Transnational media build consent for transnational capitalist relations.

Structures of ownership, financing, and regulation organize production norms and practices that create content that social groups interpret and use to reinforce or challenge the existing social relations of production. In shorthand: ownership → programming content → social use.

Ownership does not simply dictate norms, but social relations among groups inform and organize practices. Capitalist owners, corporate managers, production supervisors, writers and creative workers, technical professionals, and more all have differential effects on the production process relative to their social position and the relations of power that have been lost or won in previous negotiations for control (Therborn, 2008).

Content parallels media ownership structures and production practices. Content underwrites TNMC marketing goals, anticipates profits from media products and audiences sold as commodities, and provides a fertile culture for advertising other consumer goods. In the process, media content popularizes and legitimizes explanations for dominant social relations and cultural norms. Television and movie genres are not selected for their cultural creativity, but for their expected capacity for attracting audiences and advertisers relative to their production costs, restrictions that express and parallel their ideological function of promoting consumerism and spectatorship.

The industrial organization of media directly impacts the dominant style of performance and artistic creation. The concentrated capitalist relations of production reserve power for executives who create performers from scratch, coordinate all artistic production by all employees, plan long-term marketing, and control all media content (Marx, 2012, p. 36). Likewise, media buyers exhibit a shared occupational screen, an insular business culture, and a bias in favor of established transnational media producers (Havens, 2006, p. 160). Richard Butsch's 50 year study of working class images on US television finds that network structures, economic imperatives, and the closed culture of network media creators produce negative images of male working class characters couched in an affluent consumerist ideology.

The political economy of transnational capitalism depends on the cooperation of working classes around the world. Capital is nothing without labor. The transnational capitalist class (TNCC) in all of its national and local manifestations must have at least tacit consent from the workforce to produce and distribute goods. Mass consumer participation is also required to realize corporate profit. The social contradictions of capitalist inequality and overproduction cannot be avoided, but they may be mitigated or dispersed if TNCC leadership has mass popular consent for the social order and if the working class majority sees no alternative possibilities. These social and political conditions describe cultural hegemony – mass consent for a leadership that reproduces social relations for its own dominance and at least minimal benefits for others.

Capitalist cultural hegemony occurs to the extent that social groups consent to the political and cultural leadership of the transnational capitalist class and its representatives. Media entertainment and the commercial culture it nurtures contribute to mass consent for the larger social order led by transnational capitalism, while social structures and social relations that organize daily life at work and home provide ample experiences echoed in media depictions.

Cultural Hegemony and Mass Consent

Cultural hegemony embraces a political economy paradigm that stresses not just structures of production, but social relations that organize human actions and socialize participants to norms and practices necessary for the smooth functioning of transnational capitalism. Social structures of production and politics organize society; culture includes all those practices and meanings that help us make sense of our lives. Culture, understood as "a whole way of life," includes language, signs and symbols, rituals, norms, beliefs, and everyday practices that help us understand the world and express our understanding of our way of life. Yet, the construction of cultural meaning is arguably a matter of political and economic power (Vujnovic, 2008, p. 435).

Capitalism depends on contributions of distinct social classes that have unequal access to the means of production and unequal benefits from the wealth created by labor's use of technology and machinery. Because we are socialized from birth to accept the norms of inherited hierarchy, individual responsibility, and economic requirements for life, we internalize these norms as natural, internalizing explanations, beliefs, and ideologies that support the free market, corporate power, and social hierarchy as we experience them. Hegemony describes a social order that has broad consent for its way of life. Hegemony, as reconsidered by Antonio Gramsci (2000), explains that social contradictions between classes, including disparities in

Cultural Hegemony

Cultural hegemony understood as the social process of "moral, philosophical, and political leadership that a social group attains only with the active consent of other important social groups" (Artz & Murphy, 2000, p. 1) expresses the current status of transnational capitalism and the social relations that sustain it. Cultural hegemony posits that "commonsense" beliefs about the world arise from daily activities organized according to existing social relations, including wage labor and corporate profit. The hegemonic leadership of the capitalist class depends on widespread consent for social relations by other social classes and groups. Consent depends on how a leadership provides material, political, and cultural benefits to allies, supporters, and subordinate classes and social groups.

wealth and lifestyle, can be muted and accepted as the unfortunate weakness of an otherwise acceptable social order. Hegemony, as a political relationship, can only exist with the widespread consent of allies and subordinate classes willing to follow the political and cultural leadership of the hegemonic group (Artz & Murphy, 2000; Sassoon, 1987). Without consent, hegemony dissipates, challenges by new leaders emerge, and attempts to renegotiate consent may be supplemented with coercion to defend the dominant group.

In the twenty-first century, building hegemonic relations requires concerted, focused strategies for winning consent across classes, nations, and cultures. The political economy of transnational capitalism encompasses all of humanity engaged in accumulating wealth for corporate shareholders and owners – the notorious 1% and their upper class subordinates. Transnational capitalism has been able to temporarily forge widespread tolerance for its competitive, neoliberal order organized through its global chains of production and distribution. The cultural success of transnational capitalism depends on cross-class alliances with a global perspective that is attuned to the needs and demands of all social forces (Gramsci, 2000; Therborn, 2008, p. 158). Ironically, wageworkers unknowingly deliver surplus value to their capitalist employers, who thus acquire resources to maintain and continue exploitation (Therborn, 2008, p. 164) and sporadically win support for the social order.

The political economy of transnational capitalism includes all the structures, practices, and norms of commodity production from design and mass manufacturing through sweatshops, casual labor, and new media and the so-called new economy. The transnational capitalist political economy includes multiple levels of participation that build consent from different classes of people that sufficiently benefit economically, politically, and culturally (Artz & Murphy, 2000, pp. 24–29). *Economically*, working men and women benefit from employment and adequate wages which can be used to obtain food, housing, and leisure activities. Other social classes are involved in material production in diverse ways – from ownership, to management, to design, and quality control. *Politically*, labor has accepted modest political reforms and competitive electoral systems as evidence of representation, which has partially brought them into the political process. Other social classes are involved in political organization in diverse ways – from policy planning, to administration, enforcement, political party campaigning, and publicity. *Culturally*, TNMC media obscure the existence of social class, providing diverse and entertaining positive images of most social groups and providing a pleasing and confirming outlet for challenges and criticisms (Alper & Lestyna, 2005; Butsch, 2003; Dines & Humez, 2010). Ready access to affordable consumer goods reinforces self-interest and individual choice for all, while middle class professionals create and promote culture in diverse ways – from creation of content, to promotion, participation, and reporting on culture. All social classes contribute to the reproduction of capitalism materially and symbolically in contradictory and complex ways (Bourdieu, 1987; Garnham, 1990; Therborn, 1983). In all, for now, capitalist cultural hegemony has broad (albeit partial) consent across social classes, genders, and ethnic and religious groups in most nations – punctuated by some dramatic class conflicts rejecting capitalist assumptions, as seen recently in Greece, Bolivia, and Venezuela.

Local labor, creative workers, and subcontractors build sets, write dialogue, and translate consumer values to local cultures. They not only contribute to the hegemony of transnational capital, they contribute to their own consent by directly participating in the capitalist production process, receiving economic and political benefits while they confirm capitalist cultural hegemony in their own cultural work. The transnational capitalist class does not personally run this social system. It relies on the commitment and expertise of experts to manage social relations that ensure TNCC profits. Supplementing political practices, advertisers, publicists, and media programmers are charged with building consent for the social order. In return, these "intellectuals for transnational consumerism" (Gramsci, 2011, Vol. 2, p. 242) are well-compensated and thereby exemplify living proof of the validity of assumptions about market economics.

Deregulation and privatization open access to personal consumption for the elite, while films, television serials, and advertising glamorize global standards of consumption (Derné, 2008, p. 99). Consequently, the capitalist bureaucracy, from technocrats and managers to government politicians, willingly consent to free market rules and values as expressed in the transnational order. "Thus both direct economic pressures and the cultural investment required for successful competition for cultural dominance ensure a tendency for the class structure of the dominant class to reproduce itself and its control over symbolic production" (Garnham, 1990, p. 85) with the increased likelihood of popular consent for its cultural hegemony.

By far the largest class in the world consists of millions of workers who actually produce the wealth of the world through their creative labor power. Their sheer immense majority would suggest that democratic decisions would quickly rearrange the socio-economic order, but for now this working class majority is not sufficiently organized politically to challenge capitalist social relations. Part of the responsibility of the managerial social class is to keep labor oriented away from collaborative action, to lead and organize the great mass of humanity according to the tenets of transnational capitalism, especially individual consumption. The TNCC and its agents prefer to have cooperation from all, because the relations of force tilt to the working class and are not susceptible to permanent coercion by a handful against the many. Even selective coercion is expensive and risky, as it might unleash a backlash that cannot be easily contained – as de Lozado learned in Bolivia in 2003 and Mubarak discovered in Egypt in 2012. Far more effective is leadership by consent. Of course, if consent for capitalist leaderships cannot be won or negotiated with subordinate groups, violence from capitalist quarters will again rise up – as in Egypt in 2013.

For consent to be secured, powerful class allies and substantial numbers of subordinate groups must cooperate in the functioning of the hegemonic system. Hegemony appears as a consensual culture only so long as the leading group can meet the minimal needs of the majority (Sassoon, 1987, p. 94), or at least obstruct efforts for an alternative social arrangement. Thus, government, educational institutions, churches, political parties, and media work hard to advance practices and beliefs in individualism, market values, and deference to authority, while insisting that collective, social cooperation is misguided irrationality. Therborn (2008) observes that working men and women may consent to the social order because they may be disinterested in the form of rule to which they are subjected; they may be unaware of possible alternative social relations; they may feel individually isolated and powerless to affect change (p. 171). Lack of interest, information, and confidence are not personality traits or a permanent condition. Work rules, school curricula, media entertainment, and the entire panoply of behaviors and activities of daily life contribute to reproducing the existing social order, of building consent for the cultural hegemony of consumer capitalism. "The structure of the global capitalist system is maintained through the support of millions of citizens guided by charismatic personalities who routinely take control of the media and politics to manipulate emotions and logic" (Robinson, 2004, p. 159). To be successful, media localize and hybridize entertainment content with familiar, attractive, and culturally inclusive images.

Consumerist media entertainment has become culturally internalized and domesticated in nations around the world. In short, commercialized media producers everywhere emulate and consent to the tenets of transnational capitalist leadership, commodifying and marketing diverse and hybrid cultural products for global trade (e. g., world music, ethnic chic, fusion cuisine).

Zee TV broadcasts adaptations of global media content and style in Hindi-language serials, Hindi films, and Hindi music that massage transnational media themes into local variations (Derné, 2008, pp. 113–114), facilitating consumerism and self-gratification. As work life and social life become more commercialized and atomized and urban neighborhoods become more isolating, media narratives and images may displace the primary traditional sources of group identity, such as school, ethnicity, religion, even sport and political parties. Transnational media and their local partners promote consent for ruling social practices and cultural norms, particularly consumerism and individualism within whatever larger cultural package is on offer, such as European identities, pan-Asian identities, Islamic identities, and so on.

Shifting social positions wrought by the changes in production, work experience, daily life, immigration, and so on are accompanied by shifting media images that pleasantly confirm the legitimacy of the new social order. In the context of transnational media, individuals integrated into (and benefitting from) the new production relations, with more corporate and work socialization into norms, values, and styles, and with more education, will be more likely to adopt transnational political perspectives provided by TNMC narratives and images.

Media images emanating from a transnational capitalist cultural hegemony are not explicitly manipulative; nor do these images "make" viewers accept consumerism or individualism. Rather, "images weave together the symbolic fabric of a hegemonic political culture" (Fernandes, 2000, p. 612) in stories that confirm the familiar patterns of daily life under capitalism, mostly paralleling individual social class positions. In India, "advertising, television programming, and Hindi films all play a role in constructing [and confirming] the experiences of the elite consuming classes as the norm" (Derné, 2008, p. 93). The average citizen really is alienated and atomized, with little power over what will be produced, and with scant positive representation on television or in film (Alper & Lestyna, 2005). Women and non-dominant cultural groups actually do experience ethnic and gender inequality at work and on the street, enduring negative stereotypes on screen (Dines & Humez, 2010). Working class citizens who are isolated from their neighbors and co-workers scramble for individual survival, while depicted as little more than lovable buffoons on television (Butsch, 2003). The majority of citizens really are excluded from political policy, locally, nationally, and internationally and excluded from both media production and accurate representations.

The primary control we have is what we eat (within our budget), what we wear (within our budget), and what we do in our leisure time away from work (because we have no rights in the workplace). In mass, urban, anonymous society, we witness on a daily basis the disinterest of others, the faux friendliness of store clerks, and the impersonal bureaucratic behavior of those in charge – the common malaise of all of us in a social order that leaves consumption as the primary expression of self and creativity. In this environment, we relish entertaining images of selfless heroines, direct action superheroes, bumbling authorities, rewarding romantic personal relations, and the positive rewards of self-confidence and self-interest. Content provided by TNMCs satisfies our desires, reiterates social inequality as the norm, and builds its consumerist cultural hegemony in the process. TNMC media express content historically and psychologically appropriate for transnational capitalist relations.

Hybrid media models and localized stories confirm the compatibility between local cultures and the global order. Transnational media thus obtain validity, while their stories establish and explain the ground on which people move, providing appropriate meanings for behaviors and relations already active in daily life outside of media (Derné, 2008; Gramsci, 2011, Vol. 3, p. 170). In this transnational political and social configuration, governments do not police the neoliberal order alone. Transnational corporations (TNCs), advertising firms, and TNMCs employ marketing agents, publicists, scriptwriters, and programmers to create what is effectively a discipline for consumerism. As much as possible, mass desire is channeled into ritualized forms of consumption that provide profits to corporations and commonsense explanations to the rest of us (Galbraith & Karlin, 2012b, p. 19).

The cultural hegemony of transnational capitalism, often cast as globalization, appears as common sense to broad sections of all social classes across most nations. European businessmen, Dubai construction workers, French college students, teachers, journalists, and politicians from every land, and workers from Chinese factories and Bengali sweatshops to manufacturing plants in Mexico and the United States mostly accept the rule of the market and its insistence on individual competition, including an economically justified reduction in social welfare and public service. Working classes, ethnic diasporas, gendered labor forces, and disenfranchised youth may have individual goals and collective concerns, but for now individual consumption, the cultural norms of "work hard, play hard, keep your head down," and (absent any other reasonable possibility) convince most citizens that "there is no alternative" to the free market and global competition.

Cultural hegemony develops according to class relations and practices. Global media experiences are framed by social class, gender, and ethnicity. There are those who make decisions and those who do the work, while pleasing multicultural offerings assure viewers of the naturalness of it all. Media entertainment symbolically naturalizes the TNCC regime of market relations, codified as individualism, self-gratification, consumption, deference to authority, and the privileging of apolitical entertainment and spectatorship over citizenship and participatory democracy.

Consent begins on the factory floor and in the digitally computerized office, while media messages and cultural pastimes confirm with gratifying consistency that individual success derives from personal initiative cushioned with acquiescence to authority. Caught between a little coercion and a little benefit, labor abides by management's rules, consenting to wage relations that provide some modest security, reassured by pleasing cultural images and dominant political messages that legitimize the hegemonic leadership of the transnational capitalist class. One should be thankful for a job, an income, and recognize one's personal skill or luck in securing gainful employment – with tacit acceptance of supervision and corporate goals assuring continual reward. Co-workers and families by their actions seem to agree. The culture of daily work reinforces the social relations of wage labor and capitalist profit. Away from work, recreation and entertainment sustain the drudgery – TGIF! "Thank God, it's Friday!"

Given their immediate and ongoing economic and material benefit from the structure of transnational capital, an elite global middle class "shares a common aim of promoting a consuming ideology around the world" (Derné, 2008, p. 121). Such a complicit culture is the preferred mode of rule of transnational capitalism: contemporary cultural hegemony expresses the condition of widespread consent (or tacit acceptance) among diverse classes and ethnic groups for the capitalist structure and practices of wage labor production and consumerist dissemination of social and cultural life.

Relations of Production and Transnational Capitalist Cultural Hegemony

What is media power? The power to decide programming, the power to decide format and genre, the power to decide who has access to media production, to decide media content, its purpose, values, and ideology. Transnational media power derives from capitalist social relations based on private ownership and profit. The irrepressible necessity for commercial growth drives all media to adapt, merge, or disappear. This global trend adversely affects remaining public service media, which can be seen drifting towards advertising and entertainment (Hendy, 2013). According to the TNCC, media are private industries, and as such must abide by market rules. Decision-making power falls to those who own and finance media operations. Exceptions appear either as community media, in political and ethnic subcultures (like "outlaw" music genres in Indonesia; Bodden, 2005), or as part of revolutionary projects for social transformation, as in Nicaragua in the 1980s and contemporary Venezuela. In each case, media are both economic and cultural, and decisions over both are the result of power relations.

The structure and ideology of capitalist globalization have an indissoluble link with the structure and content of global media entertainment. Media "conform to the economic imperatives that affect other industries. Workers produce values that owners appropriate. One enterprise expands at the expense of another" (Schiller, 1976, p. 79). In the process, TNMCs

attract local partners who want in on the profits, increasing the predominance of commercial media everywhere – organizationally and ideologically disseminating the cultural values of individualism and consumerism
(Frith & Feng, 2009).

Rewards and sanctions organized by capitalist institutions, such as corporations and the legal system, enable as well as constrain (Bourdieu,
1992) – securing mass consent for existing social relations. Capitalism
"forces people into highly exploitative relations; and it does so regardless of
their culture, their background, [their nation]. All it is interested in is
profits" (Chibber, 2013). So, just as other transnational industries control
dispersed sites and processes of production, from design to manufacture, so
too TNMCs organize new relations of media production across borders.
TNMC television companies intersecting with Hollywood, Bollywood,
Chollywood, and even Nollywood's entrepreneurism reproduce and regulate a "new international division of cultural labor" through their "control
over cultural markets, international co-production, intellectual property,
marketing, distribution, and exhibition" (Miller et al., 2005, p. 52).

In each case, transnational capitalism rearranges the social relations of
production that transform class relations globally and locally. Again, this
has not been simply coerced: in Eastern Europe, foreign investment
followed economic and social restructuring to "reinforce the tendency to
organize the market and the economic organizations in ways similar to, or
transplanted from, more economically advanced countries" (Jakubowicz,
2007, p. 116). Transnational investment was "actively *solicited* by Eastern
European businesses, governments, and entrepreneurs" (Hollifield, 1993,
p. 2). The "commercial logic of the market" also influenced media reform in
post-Soviet Russia, which became one of the most rapidly growing advertising markets in the world (Vartanova, 2008, p. 20). In every locale, popular
consent seems to follow transnational production trends.

Global restructuring includes shifting production sites such that the
transnational media "labor economy is dispersed throughout the world"
(Govil, 2007, p. 92), increasingly in global media cities that attract eager
creative and production workers. Production of any particular film includes
multiple locales with multiple jobs (from filming and editing to costume
design and marketing) willingly performed by many nationally distinct
work forces, entrepreneurs, small businesses, and contractors.

Labor can take manifold forms in local media production, from "special
effects, sound recording, editing, film processing, music and dialogue
coaching, to acting, directing, filming, scouting locations, building sets,

catering, government relations, set publicity, watching and interpreting" (Miller et al., 2005, p. 113). With localized TNMC production, jobs are constantly ending and starting, further establishing capitalist control while winning consent from those workers who have jobs and diluting alternative possibilities by constantly dispersing temporary workers. In the TNMC system, workers are caught in "perennial uncertainty and lack anything beyond temporary wages" (Miller et al., 2005, p. 115). Enamored TNMC executives and postmodern theorists celebrate the autonomy of creative workers in this environment of decentralized production and the accumulation of wealth from the labor of those creative workers, arguing for consent to the new world order.

The New International Division of Cultural Labor

While it has always been true that that power differentials in social relations have dictated who can speak and when, the transition to transnational capitalism has radically altered how communication is produced and distributed. "The ability to transcend spatial limitations on commerce [with communication technology] has increased the variety, importance, and organization of various up-front and after-market windows worldwide when calculating potential sales revenue" (Havens, 2006, p. 38) – permitting transnationals to take advantage of differences in labor costs, tax policies, interest rates, and local services. Economists have noted that global flexible production schemes based on relocating production, increasingly in the developing countries, has accelerated measures to increase labor productivity everywhere. Folker Fröbel, Jürgen Heinrichs, and Otto Kreye (2004) designate this global condition the "new international division of labour," arguing that it has led to a manufacturing crisis in industrial countries and production in developing countries controlled by transnational capital merged with national (p. 15). To overcome the social power of organized labor in industrialized nations, capital exports production elsewhere.

> The development of the world economy has increasingly created conditions (forcing the development of the new international division of labour) in which the survival of more and more companies can only be assured through the relocation of production ... where labour-power is cheap to buy, abundant and well-disciplined; in short, through the transnational reorganization of production. (Fröbel, Heinrichs, & Kreye, 2004, p. 15)

Labor insecurity is the norm. Companies move production where lower wages, higher tax incentives, or other factors of production beckon.

Parallel developments in transnational media have created a "new international division of cultural labor" (NICL) (Miller et al., 2005, pp. 120–123). As TNMCs produce media commodities, ideologies, and profits, they also produce and reproduce the capital relation itself (Therborn, 2008, p. 137) – the underlying motivation for capitalist cultural hegemony.

There is no "de-centering" of power in this new global order. Global production does not disturb the TNMC "organizational hierarchy or the forms of specialization which stratify the working class and create a social layer of administrators and overseers who rule – in the name of capital – over the day to day operations in the workplace" (Harvey, 1999, p. 31), no matter what nationality, ethnicity, or gender supplies the workforce or management. Global media production creates local regional enterprises "with complex links between film, video, television, telecommunications, animation, publishing, advertising, and game design" (Davis & Yeh, 2008, p. 65) – all based on acquiring multinational talent and the cheapest creative labor possible. TNMC production recruits national governments, small media firms, and local workers to compete among themselves over wages, benefits, and working conditions.

Where jobs are few and wages are low, workers may willingly consent to their own exploitation as evidence of their own individual fortune or professional skill. In China, for instance, Mattel requires workers to be on the job 10–16 hours a day, seven days a week (Frost & Wong, 2007), yet most workers tolerate such conditions in exchange for regular wages. Media production is not "a simple reflection of the controlling interests of those who own or even control the broad range of capital plant and equipment which make up the means by which cultural goods are made and distributed. Within the media are men and women working within a range of codes and professional ideologies, and with an array of aspirations, both personal and social. The ambitions can be idealized; much cultural production is routine, mundane, and highly predictable" (Golding & Murdoch, 1991, pp. 25–26). The autonomy and creative contribution of media workers are curtailed within transnational production structures that prescribe who does what and who makes decisions. Over time, these practices encourage the internalization of capitalist norms as commonsense behavior.

Although individual access to media technology in the Internet age is unprecedented (nominally demonstrating the "openness" of the ruling social system), the capacity to reach others is severely limited and always subject to the "off" switch controlled by privately run servers, as Egyptian democracy activists discovered when their social media challenged the Mubarak regime in 2011. Incredibly, some researchers continue to popularize the democratic myth of media access, imagining that "new media technologies enable anyone to start their own culture industry" (Poster, 2008, p. 699). Unfortunately, the information age of transnational capitalism remains one of unbridled *reception* of TNMC messages. The power to tell stories drifts to global media networks that have excessive control over communication via satellites and other media technology (Artz, 2007; Schiller, 1999, pp. 66–68; Thussu, 2000).

The new international division of cultural labor (NICL) "facilitates the free movement of capital into cheap production locations, contains labor mobility and undermines labor solidarity" as a mobile elite exploits whichever country charges the least (Miller et al., 2005, p. 152). Ultimately, the cultural hegemony of transnational media brings economic and political rewards for elites and their middle class technocrats; rewards obtained from rapacious free market policies that encourage individual entrepreneurialism and undermine social solidarity among workers by repeatedly subcontracting abroad with smaller independent studios.

Training for Consent

An essential feature of transnational media's capacity for organizing and profiting from the division of cultural labor is the existence of shared business cultures sustained through extensive co-productions and joint ventures. In Russia, "business publications are among the first media enterprises when introducing international models and styles of practices" (Koikkalainen, 2007, p. 1326). Their production practices promote a market economy, while their journalistic practices communicate acceptable reporting, writing, and professional behavior. Indeed, the rapid growth of Russian business media provides a striking example of capitalist hegemonic leadership and its effective use of communication for training class allies (Vartanova, 2008).

Daily business practices demonstrate the legitimacy of TNMC leadership and build consent for its hegemony. In China, local publishers have formed joint ventures with several TNMCs, including Hachette (*Elle, Marie Claire, Woman's Day*), Hearst (*Cosmo*), Condé Nast (*Vogue*), and Shfunotomo (*Rayli, Mina*). The local editions receive text and photos. Staff from the head offices in Paris, New York, and Tokyo are sent to train Chinese staff and editors, directing and modeling the required business norms of communication, editorial decision-making, content tone and style, marketing, audience research, and managerial practices – cultivating local publishers in the ways of TNMC operations, including preferences more amenable to advertising, such as changing "magazines for reading to magazines for seeing" (Frith & Feng, 2009, p. 169).

Throughout the training, facilitators coach participants and model appropriate business behavior in social interaction, humor, and even affectations. In short, transnational capitalist class solidarity is cultivated and reproduced around shared commercial interests and these agreed-upon "best practices" for production, distribution, subcontracting, and labor relations. Aspiring local and national media look to successful transnational capitalists for economic, political, and cultural leadership.

Television producers and network executives see "light entertainment formats as insurance against uncertainty: they offer broadcasters more commercially efficient strategies of maximizing audiences" (Keane et al., 2007, p. 198). Genres such as game shows and reality TV attract viewers, limit costs for scriptwriting and acting, and take advantage of low-cost labor in all local adaptations. Around the world, governments agree on deregulation and commercialization, while TNMCs can expect standardized, equivalent media worker skills and pro-industry attitudes at lowered costs. The combination of work norms across national media labor markets and standardized formats with predominant images echoing individualism assures substantial media profit with minimal labor solidarity across gender, ethnicity, and national borders. Most importantly, production norms secure consent for the social relations of production and their ideological explanations. For now.

Without this global culture of production organized according to capitalist social relations, TNMCs could not successfully negotiate cultural hegemony in practice or in image. Whatever hybridity theorists might imagine, common dominant values, attitudes, norms, and behaviors are being cultivated in and by transnational media production. Hierarchies of professional skill and decision-making become "common sense" through enforcement and repetition on the job, backed by copyright laws and noncompete penalties that prevent workers from developing their creativity (Bettig, 1997). Because TNMCs are vertically and horizontally integrated and interlocked with other communication technology companies, transnational media business and programming standards are duplicated across media platforms and delivery systems, from television, film, satellite, broadband, and mobile technologies, facilitating a leadership position for TNMCs in new media uses, as well. Widespread consent has come with work norms and mass entertainment, but democracy and public access to production by the millions of workers and citizens are not part of the hegemonic equation.

Transnational consolidation and concentration assert the conditions for producing media, including aesthetics, style, form, and content. Reliance on formats, for instance, maximizes the adaptation of content and the distribution of standardized codes and conventions. Although national governments and cultural organizations, including religious groups, frequently attempt to block "foreign" imports of culturally "inappropriate" values, TNMCs have hegemonically adapted. TNMCs have "stripped away" those questionable elements and "substituted local flavour and values," so that the hybrid program "provides the DNA, the recipe, and the technology for invigorating local television" with commercially structured and commercially viable formats (Keane et al., 2007, p. 200). Commercial success for TNMCs includes localizing production for local languages and cultures, as well as producing content for segmented national audiences: the cosmopolitan elite who own and manage industries, speak English, and participate fully in world economics and politics; the affluent middle classes, including managers, technicians, academics, politicians, and small business people; the working classes, both skilled creative workers, contractors, builders, and less skilled service workers; the lower working class of manual and casual laborers. TNMC leadership provides something for everyone in a truly hegemonic flourish.

A New International Culture of Consumption

A new transnational culture of consumption has grown in tandem with the new international division of cultural labor. As transnational production temporarily undermines labor organization and identity through temporary labor regimes, consciousness of social class and shared circumstances is muted. The combination of a hegemonic pull to consent for some economic reward and institutional coercion against collective resistance seeps into everyday life. Lifestyle identities (in fashion, leisure activity, fandom) attract otherwise alienated men and women (Machin & Van Leeuwen, 2007, p. 55). In terms of cultural hegemony, absent other more democratically authentic identities, commercialized lifestyle norms are an appealing benefit provided by capitalist class leaders and their media.

The accumulation of wealth by the TNCC and its managerial and political elite has created an international market for the affluent and their interest and ability to purchase high-end consumer goods, consume large amounts of media and cultural commodities, including media technology, media content, live concerts, and travel. Taiwanese consumer culture, for instance, "hungers for diverse Japanese and Korean imports, including mobile phones, electronics, automobiles, cosmetics, clothing, and so on" (Huang, 2011, p. 8). Globally, cosmopolitan elites attract targeted media and advertising. Transnational marketing to this social class both reflects its consuming power and reinforces its prestige and ethos as cultural trendsetters. Media are produced, priced, and targeted for other social classes based on the lifestyle aesthetic established by elites, contributing to capitalist cultural hegemony both materially and symbolically which is actively consented to in consumer behavior. Media produce and distribute material products, which also always contain symbolic and social meanings. Media thus profit directly and facilitate profits for other TNCs.

TNMCs develop TV stations with languages and formats appropriate for advertisers targeting different audience segments. TNMCs have likewise produced audience-specific films, magazines, newspapers, and music genres. Chua (2006) discerns "consumer communities" from dedicated fans to occasional consumers that parallel the uneven flows among the targeted transnational East Asian media markets, including fan clubs that are established by the celebrities or production companies themselves as a "means of sustaining consumer interest" (p. 10). Importantly, across all the national accents and social class cultural preferences, themes of consumerism and individualism predominate: independence, freedom, career, romance, and self-gratification jump out from all the TNMC produced stories and narratives, serving the interests of transnational capitalism and its yearning for increased profits.

Of course, individual consumer choice is woefully inadequate for the democratization of work or culture. Fans electing their favorite member of the Japanese idol band AKB48 "vote" by purchasing a CD in a commercial distortion of democracy (Galbraith & Karlin, 2012b). Following the "Hello Kitty" craze in Taiwan that expressed youth resistance to regimented education and dress, candidates in the presidential election campaign in Taiwan generated support and profit by marketing stuffed animals as campaign icons to non-political youth. Political expression metaphorically available in a commodity is a weak substitute for a politically active citizenry. Passing off consumer choice as democracy (or pleasure as power in some variants) is a worn-out cliché and will not hold, although it seems accurate to note the denigration of the electoral process to a sales contest. More importantly, demonstrated regularly around the world, the contradictions between the production and content of global capitalist culture and the experiences and conditions of life for labor and its allies will continually fracture mass consent, erupting in organized political and social resistance – washing away pretensions of consumption as political power. For the moment, the shiny bubble of transnational entertainment predominates, attempting to cover the fragile, brittle social order with diversionary fun, games, and shopping.

Advertising in the Transnational Era

Production of media content for magazines, newspapers, film, television, radio, and the Internet has no consequence until the article, movie, or program reaches readers and viewers, which explains why TNMCs have horizontally integrated production with distribution across companies and borders. To streamline the distribution of media content, TNMCs have ramped up their use of marketing and advertising for their own products. Self-advertising and self-promotion increase the sales of magazines, DVDs, video games, mobile applications, and media-branded consumer products from cereal to clothing.

As noted in Chapter 3, media advertising is crucial to the overall capitalist economic cycle. Advertising expenditures topped $557 billion in 2012 (Nielsen, 2013), indicating a vibrant, profitable industry and illustrating its importance for all other industries. Globally, the advertising industry has consolidated like the rest of transnational capital.

A handful of transnational, interlocked corporations produce and distribute advertising in alliance and consultation with other TNMCs and other transnational corporations. The largest advertising firm in the world, Dentsu Japan, controls about 30% of the market in Japan and East Asia, owns McGarryBowen (US), and recently acquired the Aegis Group, parent to the Carat and Vizeum global media networks, expanding its presence in Europe. Dentsu's 2012 revenue topped $22 billion. Omnicom and Publicis Groupe talked of a $45 billion merger in 2013 that included DDB, BBDO, Leo Burnett, Saatchi, and other firms. Globally active, London-based WPP has annual revenues of $10 billion. Advertising is directly interlocked structurally and financially with transnational media, finance, and consumer goods producers.

The top four advertising firms also have members active in the Trilateral Commission, the World Economic Forum, Council of Foreign Relations, and the Center for Strategic and International Studies. Directors and shareholders of transnational advertising corporations are part of the transnational capitalist class and fulfill an important economic and political role in securing consent for consumerism, the free market, and the production of corporate profit.

Deregulation of the media, which is all but complete on a global scale, unleashed the friendly dogs of advertising. Tracking and hunting the terrain of neoliberalism and transnational production, advertising and entertainment media jockey for the speedy development of consumerism. From their review of dozens of studies, Hye-Jin Paek and Zhongdang Pan (2004) learned that "as the market economy develops Chinese consumers are acquiring a more positive attitude toward the quintessential capitalist message form – advertisements" (p. 492). They found sufficient evidence of the effects of capitalism and advertising to draw "causal inferences on media impact of consumerist values," with advertising being "a vanguard of the emerging consumer society" (Paek & Pan, 2004, pp. 492–493). Media advertising directly contributes to individualistic and consumerist values, such that exposure to advertisements relates to the acceptance of conspicuous consumption, self-fulfillment, individual indulgence, and the worshipping of affluent lifestyles (Paek & Pan, 2004, p. 495).

TNMC women's magazines in China are largely funded by fashion advertisers, including L'Oréal, Procter & Gamble, Estée Lauder, Shiseido, Kosé, Unilever, and Benetton (Frith & Feng, 2009, p. 166). Individual consumerism now drives Chinese popular culture. Across Eastern Europe and Russia, a similar commercial media process unfolds under the direction of TNMCs and their advertising allies. Following deregulation of the media, Russia became one of the most rapidly growing advertising markets in the world, leading to a search for niche audiences and diversity in entertainment for delivering advertisements (Vartanova, 2008), while public media disappeared and social and cultural needs went unfulfilled.

Like media content in general, transnational advertising does not always rely on globally standardized specific messages. In most locales, advertising strategies "use well-known nationalist songs, popular commercial film actors and the sponsorship of cultural and sporting events that evoke strong national support" (Fernandes, 2000, p. 615). In Japan, celebrity idols actually depend on advertising campaigns to market their own careers (Galbraith & Karlin, 2012a). In South Korea, K-pop music stars and their marketing managers use social media to speak to their fans about their personal lives and the products they use (Beattie, 2012). Advertising firms consciously attempt to align marketing strategies with specific national and local cultural conditions, making explicit linkages between products and targeted social classes (Fernandes, 2000) – increasing consumer activity and consent for market values.

Including the crucial role of media in capitalist cultural hegemony, the circulation of commodities in the "production → distribution → consumption" cycle that expresses the process of accumulation of wealth from labor should be amended as "production → advertising and media content → distribution → consumption." This cycle defines transnational capitalism and its media system: advertising is essential to winning mass consent for consumer capitalism and the worldwide distribution of commodities. Advertising comprises part of the economic logic of media production – audiences are produced for sale to advertisers who in turn feed audiences persuasive messages intended to increase sales of other products.

Advertising does more than move products; it provides a "magic system" that transforms commodities into potent social signifiers (Jhally, 1990; Williams, 1980, p. 170). High heels become a sign of femininity, a sports car becomes a sign of masculinity. Raymond Williams explained the history of advertising as a communication practice that moved from description of quality and pricing, to a communication industry that influences the market – a system for financing media and persuading consumers to change their behavior and follow the leadership of capitalist politicians and marketers. "Advertising developed to sell goods … but the material object being sold is never enough: this indeed is the crucial cultural quality of its modern forms" (Williams, 1980, pp. 182, 184). In this sense, advertising contributes mightily to capitalist cultural hegemony. Advertising whispers, asserts, and blares from far and wide that consumption brings happiness, that consumer choice demonstrates democracy, that living in a world of commodities is the best of all possible worlds. Advertising even offers financial aid to struggling economies: "Cash-strapped Spain towns [are now] a prime target for advertisers" who strike deals for landmarks, public buildings, and even iconic statues like Christopher Columbus draped in a Barcelona soccer shirt advertising Qatar Airlines (Kane, 2013). Participating in an advertised and advertising culture tacitly and actively exhibits and reproduces consent for the social order of production for consumption.

For transnational capitalism, the best working class consciousness is brand consciousness, which can organize individual social practices and define identity. Advertisers spend millions because they have determined that television images are the prompt, proximity to the star is the desire (Karlin, 2012, p. 79), and consumer behavior is the cultural outcome. Pleasurable moments and desires are facilitated and exploited by advertisers using entertainment, a vital part of the cultural hegemony of consumer capitalism. Celebrating men and women as consumers who think, feel, and act in "self-motivated, self-interested, and self-reflexive ways" (Dunn, 2008, p. 79) only shuffles individualism to the top of the deck; it does nothing to build democracy or universal cooperation necessary for a less commercial, more humane social order.

Advertising does not seek satisfaction; advertising promotes continuous dissatisfaction that can only momentarily be suspended by some immediate purchase of a commodity. If one purchase provided satisfaction, further purchases would not be necessary. But advertising, and the capitalist commodity system that relies on its persuasive appeals, must have continuous, never-ending, ever-expanding consumption. Desire as expressed in advertising can only be achieved in the imagination. The permanent lack of actual fulfillment contributes to alienation, which quickly returns after each purchase. In Japan, celebrity idols are "replaced regularly and endlessly, even destroyed only to be recreated, thereby fueling the continuous movement of capital (Galbraith, 2012, p. 194). Consumer behavior, predicated on a constant search for pleasurable rewards, propels the capitalist system.

The Hegemony of Advertising and Entertainment

The dehumanizing essence of capitalism could not be revealed more starkly: human needs and human desires are manipulated as a means to harvest consumer fodder for the never-ending demand for capitalist profits. Obviously, satisfying human needs and desires is anathema to such a system that offers only the continuous allure of satisfaction just out of our reach. Consumer behavior assures ongoing consensual dedication to the social system. Organizing production more rationally for human needs would provide goods that work well, last long, and have minimal environmental impact. Advertising that meets media-instigated consumer wants may win mass consent and participation, but it diverts us from more meaningful and rational public conversations about what kind of world we could devise for full human realization.

Advertising and media entertainment – the twin-headed monster of consumerism has roamed the world for decades searching for audiences and consumers, suffocating attempts at human-centered communication. In the twenty-first century, consumer capitalism dominates global culture. The appeal is the temporary gratification that needs repeated feeding. We enjoy the stories and images. We identify with the heroes and heroines. We desire the accoutrements of celebrity and star. We engage narratives that assure us that individual consumption brings satisfaction. We consent to the purveyors of entertainment and advertising, accepting their claims as guides to everyday life. Cultural hegemony by transnational capitalism requires as much.

Yet, we all sense the inadequacy of a system based on continuous consumption and environmental destruction. Whenever we break from diversionary entertainment, we recognize that humanity is missing from these fictions of consumption. Transnational capitalist cultural hegemony cannot continue to meet the needs of humanity. Inequality, overproduction, the depletion of natural resources portend unresolved antagonisms. Political and social crises recur as economic conditions deteriorate and collapse or cultural conditions unearth insurmountable inequalities. At those moments of rupture, alternative ways of being arise to confront the violence of nation-states defending capitalism. At those times, no sit-com, no action movie, and no commercial advertisement will win consent for a social system that offers nothing for humanity.

References

Alper, L., & Lestyna, P. (Producers). (2005). *Class dismissed: How TV frames the working class* [Videorecording]. United States. Media Education Foundation.

Artz, L. (2007). Review. Cultures in orbit: Satellites and the televisual. Lisa Parks. *International Journal of Media and Cultural Politics*, 3(1), 99–102.

Artz, L., & Murphy, B. O. (2000). *Cultural hegemony in the United States*. Thousand Oaks, CA: Sage.

Beattie, A. C. (2012, June 11). Marketing's next wave: The Korean pop star. *Advertising Age, 83*, 6.

Bettig, R. (1997). *Copyrighting culture: The political economy of intellectual property*. Boulder, CO: Westview Press.

Bodden, M. (2005). Rap in Indonesian youth music of the 1990s: Globalization, outlaw genres, and social protest. *Asian Music, 36*(2), 1–26.

Bourdieu, P. (1987). What makes a social class? On the theoretical and practical existence of groups. *Berkeley Journal of Sociology, 32*, 1–117.

Bourdieu, P. (1992). *An invitation to reflexive sociology*. Chicago: University of Chicago Press.

Butsch, R. (2003). Ralph, Fred, Archie, and Homer: Why television keeps re-creating the white male working-class buffoon. In G. Dines & J. M. Humez (Eds.), *Gender, race, and class in media: A text-reader* (pp. 575–585). Thousand Oaks, CA: Sage.

Chibber, V. (2013, May). Marxism, post-colonialism studies, and the tasks of radical theory. Interview by J. Farbman. *International Socialist Review, 89.* RetrievedJune27,2013,fromhttp://isreview.org/issue/89/marxism-postcolonial-studies-and-tasks-radical-theory

Chua, B. H. (2006, March 16). East Asian pop culture: Consumer communities and politics of the national. Presentation to Cultural Space and the Public Sphere in Asia Conference. Seoul, Korea.

Davis, D. W., & Yeh, E. Y. (2008). *East Asian screen industries*. London: British Film Institute.

Derné, S. D. (2008). *Globalization on the ground: New media and the transformation of culture, class, and gender in India*. Thousand Oaks, CA: Sage.

Dines, G., & Humez, J. M. (Eds.). (2010). *Gender, race, and class in the media: A critical reader*. 3rd edn. Thousand Oaks, CA: Sage.

Dunn, R. G. (2008). *Identifying consumption: Subjects and objects in consumer society*. Philadelphia: Temple University Press.

Fernandes, L. (2000). Nationalizing 'the global': media images, cultural politics, and the middle class in India. *Media, Culture & Society, 22*(5), 611–628.

Frith, K., & Feng, Y. (2009). Transnational cultural flows: An analysis of women's magazines in China. *Chinese Journal of Communication, 2*(2), 158–173.

Fröbel, F., Heinrichs, J., & Kreye, O. (2004). *The new international division of labour*. Cambridge, UK: Cambridge University Press.

Frost, S., & Wong, M. (2007, September). Monitoring Mattel in China. *Asian Monitor Resource Centre.* Retrieved from http://www.amrc.org.hk/alu_article/codes_of_conducts/monitoring_mattel_in_china

Galbraith, P. W. (2012). Idols: The image of desire in Japanese consumer capitalism. In P. W. Galbraith & J. G. Karlin (Eds), *Idols and celebrity in Japanese media culture* (pp. 185–206). New York: Palgrave Macmillan.

Galbraith, P. W., & Karlin, J. G. (Eds.) (2012a). *Idols and celebrity in Japanese media culture*. New York: Palgrave Macmillan.

Galbraith, P. W., & Karlin, J. G. (2012). Introduction: The mirror of idols and celebrity. In P. W. Galbraith & J. G. Karling (Eds.), *Idols and celebrity in Japanese media culture* (pp. 1–32). New York: Palgrave Macmillan.

Garnham, N. (1990). *Capitalism and communication: Global culture and the economics of information.* Thousand Oaks, CA: Sage.

Golding, P., & Murdock, G. (1991). Culture, communications, and political economy. In J. Curran & M. Gurevitch, (Eds.), *Mass media and society* (pp. 15–32). London: Edward Arnold.

Govil, N. (2007). Bollywood and the frictions of global mobility. In D. K. Thussu (Ed.), *Media on the move: Global flow and contra flow* (pp. 84–99). New York: Routledge.

Gramsci, A. (2000). *The Antonio Gramsci reader: Selected writings, 1916–1935.* D. Forgacs, (Ed.). New York: New York University Press.

Gramsci, A. (2011). *Antonio Gramsci: Prison notebooks. Vols. 1–3.* J. A. Buttigieg, Trans. New York: Columbia University Press.

Harvey, D. (1999). *The limits to capital.* 2nd edn. New York: London.

Havens, T. (2006). *Global television marketplace.* London: Palgrave Macmillan.

Hendy, D. (2013). *Public service broadcasting.* New York: Palgrave Macmillan.

Hollifield, A. (1993, August). The globalization of Eastern Europe's print media: German investment during the post-revolution era. Paper presented at Association for Education in Journalism and Mass Communication. Kansas City, Missouri.

Huang, S. (2011). Nation-branding and transnational consumption: Japan-mania and the Korean wave in Taiwan. *Media, Culture & Society, 33*(1), 3–18.

Jhally, S. (1990). *The codes of advertising: Fetishism and the political economy of meaning in the consumer society.* New York: Routledge.

Kane, C. (2013, June 28). Cash-strapped Spanish towns a prime target for advertisers. *Chicago Tribune,* p. D2.

Karlin, J. G. (2012). Through a looking glass darkly: Television advertising, idols, and the making of fan audiences. In P. W. Galbraith & J. G. Karlin, (Eds.), *Idols and celebrity in Japanese media culture* (pp. 72–93). New York: Palgrave Macmillan.

Keane, M., Fung, A. Y. H., & Moran, A. (2007). *New television, globalization, and the East Asian cultural imagination.* Hong Kong: Hong Kong University Press.

Koikkalainen, K. (2007). The local and the international in Russian business journalism: Structures and practices. *Europe-Asia Studies, 59*(8), 1315–1329.

Machin, D., & Van Leeuwen, T. (2007). *Global media discourse: A critical introduction.* New York: Routledge.

Marx, W. D. (2012). The jimusha system: Understanding the production logic of the Japanese entertainment industry. In P. W. Galbraith & J. G. Karlin (Eds.), *Idols and celebrity in Japanese media culture* (pp. 35–55)). New York: Palgrave Macmillan.

Miller, T., Govil, N., McMurria, J., Maxwell, R. , & Wang, T. (2005). *Global Hollywood 2.* London: British Film Institute.

Nielsen. (2013, April 11). Global ad spends grows 3.2% in 2012. Retrieved from http://www.nielsen.com/us/en/insights/news/2013/global-ad-spend-grows-3.2-percent-in-2012.html

Paek, H., & Pan, Z. (2004). Spreading global consumerism: Effects of mass media and marketing on consumerist values in China. *Mass Communication and Society, 7*(4), 491–515.

Poster, M. (2008). Global media and culture. *New Literary History, 39*(3), 685–703.

Robinson, W. I. (2004). *A theory of global capitalism: Production, class, and state in a transnational world.* Baltimore, MD: Johns Hopkins University Press.

Sassoon, A. S. (1987). *Gramsci's politics.* 2nd edn. Minneapolis: University of Minnesota Press.

Schiller, D. (1999). *Digital capitalism: Networking the global market system.* Cambridge, MA: MIT Press.

Schiller, H. (1976). *Communication and cultural domination.* White Plains, NY: International Arts and Sciences Press.

Therborn, G. (1983). Why some classes are more successful than others. *New Left Review, 138*, 37–55.

Therborn, G. (2008). *What does the ruling class do when it rules?: State apparatuses and state power under feudalism, capitalism and socialism.* London: Verso.

Thussu, D. K. (2000). *International communication: Continuity and change.* London: Arnold.

Vartanova, E. (2008). Russian media: Market and technology as driving forces of change. In E. Vartanova, H. Nieminen, & M. Salminen (Eds.), *Russian media 2007: Convergence and competition* (pp. 20–31). Helsinki: Communication Research Center, University of Helsinki. Retrieved from http://www.hssaatio.fi/images/stories/tiedostot/RUSSIAN%20MEDIA%202008%20-%20EXTRACTS%2020%20NOVEMBER%202008.pdf

Vujnovic, M. (2008). The political economy of Croatian television: Exploring the impact of Latin American telenovelas. *Communications, 33*(4), 431–454.

Williams, R. (1980). *Problems in materialism and culture.* London: Verso.

Further Reading

Artz, L., & Murphy, B. O. (2000). *Cultural hegemony in the United States.* Thousand Oaks, CA: Sage.

Miller, T., Govil, N., McMurria, J., Wang, T., & Maxwell, R. (2008). *Global Hollywood 2.* 2nd edn. London: British Film Institute.

Mosco, V. (2009). *The political economy of communication.* 2nd edn. Los Angeles: Sage.

6

Power Decentered
Dominant Diversity

As Europe and the United States adjusted to a post-colonial world in the 1950s and 1960s, multinational corporations invested heavily in the exploitation of natural resources in the developing world. Scholars and technicians believing that the Western model of consumerism and two-party elections was best, argued that media and advertising would contribute to national development in Latin America and elsewhere. Very quickly it became clear that capitalist development by multinational industries meant underdevelopment dependency. A small elite class in each nation benefitted from its alliance with US and European companies, but for most of the population Western "development" brought a market economy and all of its social inequalities.

While many communication scholars like Wilbur Schramm and Everett Rogers remained wedded to the development model, others recognized the social and cultural consequences of North American economic and cultural dominance. Herbert Schiller, Armand Mattelart, and Luis Beltrán, among others, revealed how US media exports to Latin America in particular appeared to be cultural imperialism.

Cultural Imperialism and Cultural Dominance

Cultural imperialism theory became prominent in Latin America (Beltrán, 1982; Matta, 1977) and informed many of the supporters of the New World and Information Order that arose in UNESCO. At the time, the West

Global Entertainment Media: A Critical Introduction, First Edition. Lee Artz.
© 2015 John Wiley & Sons, Inc. Published 2015 by John Wiley & Sons, Inc.

overwhelmed the media systems and cultural practices of developing nations that lacked the infrastructures for producing their own media. Leading media influenced the choices by indigenous commercial media and their governments that willingly adopted market norms and values (Schiller, 1976).

As if speaking about transnational media today, Armand Mattelart (1976) explained that cultural imperialism does not impose a uniform culture but "changes its form and content" and "adapts to different realities and national contexts" depending on its expansionist opportunities (p. 160). This cultural imperialism seeks social control through the "conquest of hearts and minds" by "taking into account the specific interests and needs of each age level, each social category" as the means for producing a universal culture that expands American influence (Mattelart, 1976, pp. 160–161). Cultural dominance is not imposed; it requires administration by the national dominant classes in the developing countries. Hollywood movies' market share runs 80%–90% in Latin American countries, but it dips below 50% in France and is broadly 60%–75% over Western Europe (Hopewell, 2013). However, cultural imperialism "cannot be summed up as the volume of imported products or cultural commodities (European Audiovisual Observatory, 2002, p. 161). The USA produces the models, but the national bourgeoisies (capitalist classes) may perfectly well 'nationalize' these models" through "operations of decentralization" and local reproduction (Mattelart, 1976, p. 161).

Herb Schiller's *Communication and Cultural Domination* (1976) sketched the contours of corporate dominance in the world economy of that time, arguing that media production and distribution conformed to the same economic imperatives and structural forms as other multinational industries of the 1970s. Schiller referred to educational institutions, scientific research, corporate training programs, tourism, and public diplomacy as key components in the cultural environment that existed alongside mass media products.

Despite caveats offered by cultural imperialism theorists, critics were quick to challenge the provocative terminology rather than the substance of the insights. Admittedly, the term "imperialism" does not capture the complex processes or relations of Western media and media produced in developing nations. In fact, imperialism does not reflect what Schiller, Mattelart, Boyd-Barrett, and others have accurately described as cultural domination through media, education, and business training protocols.

Imperialism is enforced exploitation of one nation by another for the benefit of nationally based capitalist profits. Multinational media do not exploit labor or resources in Latin America for export and manufacture in the United States. Paul Simon's appropriation of Ladysmith Black Mambazo to save his career on the harmony of traditional South African music and Disney's use of traditional European folklore or other national cultural narratives certainly suggests exploitation of the local by the global. However, more generally media corporations seek to export media for direct sales and to attract audiences that can be sold to advertisers. Increasingly, transnational media seek to establish local production for local consumption, leaving the "foreign" nation and culture out of the economic and cultural process altogether. Disney prefers that its productions and co-productions in and for Latin America reach a wide consuming audience; thus Disney works to obstruct competition from other transnational and national media.

What "cultural "imperialism" actually describes is domination, maybe even predominance, but it is not *imperialism*. This is not a semantic difference. It goes to the heart of the social process of production, distribution, and consumption. Unfortunately, the term provokes knee-jerk responses that may be valid, but off point. For instance, Tamar Liebes and Elihu Katz (1990) argue that US television wasn't "imperialistic," but was globally dominant due to the sheer availability of its programming, the relative "openness" of its narratives, and the "universal" appeal of its themes – identifying some of the structural mechanisms that all but guarantee cultural dominance. Of course, Liebes and Katz were at pains to demonstrate the polysemic nature of US programming, so they skirted the cultural consequence of their fairly accurate assessment of the actual global media flow. At any rate, what Schiller and Liebes and Katz (at least partially) unearth is closer to cultural hegemony than imperialism.

Although using a problematic vocabulary, Schiller reports early on how transnational capitalism and TNMCs lead the development of a global commercial culture. He accurately explains how the capitalist class uses global institutions to politically defend and reproduce its economic relations, while parallel institutions, particularly media entertainment, culturally and ideologically obscure control and domination by incorporating political and cultural alternatives wherever and however possible while still maintaining the social relations of transnational capitalism. The predominance of commercial consumerist forms and content interferes with potential cultural and political alternatives, as global television and film "push toward invigorating, intensifying, and legitimizing a focus on the individual over collectivity" (Derné, 2008, p. 164). Global entertainment media then and now promote individualism and undermine democratic practices and relations. TNMCs in their corporate relations and practices of production deny access to the public, organize labor away from decision-making, and assure content suitable for advertising and consumption, regardless of real human needs.

Much of what Schiller, Mattelart, and others observed are elements of cultural hegemony. Unfortunately, at the time few had access to Gramsci's writings, which were not widely available in English until the mid-1970s. Even then, because cultural studies quickly appropriated and dismantled Gramsci's materialist and class perspective, critical political economists did not approach his work until much later. It's quite remarkable that cultural imperialism theorems were not only accurate for the time, they expressed a portent of the transformations to come.

Not everyone responds to reality in the same way. Reality takes on meanings according to perspective, skill, interest, and social position. Skeptics seeking to avoid the realities of class have frantically run from the realities of capitalism, proferring several substitute explanations for global media activities. Although evidence has been sparse and arguments often convoluted, various attacks on cultural imperialism theories and attempts to deny cultural dominance based on political economy of the media have searched for evidence that would dispute or undercut claims of transnational capitalist dominance. Findings have been many; arguments flashy. Yet, power has been unpersuaded by theory.

While cultural hegemony recovers and adapts many of the insights from cultural imperialism theses, other approaches have discarded the entire perspective in futile attempts to dispute social class and the workings of capitalist power.

The Inertia of Contraflow: Dominance Undenied

The most direct refutation would be evidence that nations presumed to be subject to cultural dominance were actually producing and exporting their own content. Increased media exports from the developing nations to Western countries and decreased media exports from Western countries to developing nations would – by simple arithmetic – demonstrate that communication flow was more balanced, not unequal, and therefore not subject to domination. The argument is logical and simple: media "contraflow" from the developing world to the developed world refutes all charges of domination. Contraflow announces resistance and independence by formerly subordinate nations; contraflow reveals that there are alternatives to Western programming. In this view, media contraflow and media produced from subordinate and alternative perspectives (often called "subaltern") refute the claims of cultural imperialism. Unfortunately for its hopeful proponents, significant contraflow cannot readily be found.

In the twenty-first century, media flows are not flows between nations. Transnational media narrate culturally specific content mixed with global capitalist themes of consumerism and individual gratification without regard for national identity or influence. In fact, media cross borders most easily when they find international partners, erasing any claim to national identity in the process. As O Globo merges with Telemontecarlo in Italy, partners with SSE in Monaco, buys shares in SIC television in Portugal, or signs joint ventures with Televisa and News Corp (De Gouvea Neto, 1997), O Globo in structure and definition no longer is a Brazilian firm: it has merged and transformed into a medium-sized transnational media corporation (TNMC) with ownership, production, and distribution integrated across national borders by transnational capitalists seeking to share profits from a variety of countries. Transnational media send messages across all borders, messages that have a shared, singular, core purpose: advancing consumerism and capitalist social relations with entertaining narratives that win viewers and fans, building cultural hegemony for commercial culture and the market.

Imagining contraflow as an indicator of non-dominance of Western media remains only a quaint and outdated effort to explain the disappearing national markers in global media. Samba is Brazilian, curry is Indian, Italians play bocce, French eat brioche, Middle Eastern cuisine includes pita, and some Asians may enjoy eggrolls, but in no case do such elementary stereotypes mark meaningful cultural difference.

Likewise, to explain global media now, it is singularly insufficient to identify film, television, or other media productions by their country of origin. *Lincoln* (2012), Disney's Touchstone film nominated for 12 Academy Awards, was produced by DreamWorks, a Reliance Entertainment 50% joint venture. So, is the film Indian or North American? Do we decide by language? Then all films produced in Hindi are Indian, including Disney's UTV movies? The twisting analyses required by apolitical searches for contraflow create contradictory and peculiar observations: CNN's deal with

Network 18, a $300 million multimedia Indian company, accelerates Western media flows (Thussu, 2007, pp. 20–21), while Univision, the largest Spanish-language TV network in the United States, owned in the 1990s by Mexico's Televisa and Venezuela's Venevisión, represents contraflow? Korean telenovelas, Indian cinema, and Al-Jazeera news broadcasts are contraflow (Thussu, 2007, p. 23) – even when co-produced as joint ventures with "Western" companies? News Corp's joint venture, Phoenix TV, is contraflow because it broadcasts in Mandarin (Thussu, 2007, p. 24)?

By such contraflow accounts, Saudi Prince Al-Waleed bin Talal, one of the richest men in the world, participating overseer of a feudal regime and shareholder in Citibank, is a leading "subaltern" communicator resisting Western domination because his Rotana television network is based in a developing country. Democratically speaking, the all-female Saudi band Accolade – which cannot perform publicly under Saudi law – has more validity as subaltern than Al-Waleed, given the oppression of women in Saudi Arabia and their challenge to patriarchy (McElroy, 2008). Legitimizing private commercial media (Al-Waleed's, Ambani's, or the Huayi Brothers') as nationally representative of contraflow does a real disservice to the millions of citizens denied access to media who really would like to communicate their stories, experiences, and interests outside TNMC frames.

If contraflow and subaltern definitions were adjusted to designate communication of and for an alternative media hegemony, one born from social classes and allies developing a more democratic, non-commercial media system, subaltern contraflow would have explanatory value, because meaningful media contraflow appears only when working classes and their allies have media access, when they organize to produce and distribute independent messages and narratives. TeleSUR (Television of the South), the regionally based, democratically run transnational satellite channel of the Bolivarian revolutionary project, transmits voices from working class and indigenous communities across Latin America (Artz, 2006). Journalists from Venezuela, Argentina, Uruguay, Cuba, and Bolivia report on democratic and national-popular movements, allowing media to serve subordinate classes. TeleSUR is not national contraflow, but it does give voice to subordinate and alternative perspectives, providing a limited contraflow to TNMC entertainment. The community-based network of 1,000+ radio and television stations in Venezuela today (Artz, 2012) and the short-lived CORADEP (Public Radio Cooperative) in Nicaragua in the 1980s (Artz, 1993) are also examples of subaltern communication arising from movements of subordinate classes demanding media access and democratic power.

The change in media "flow" reveals the transformational outcome of changed social relations of production – from nationally based production for export to a transnational system of capitalist co-production of global products for local consumption and local products for global consumption. The appearance of diverse flows between nations indicates the success of capitalist cultural hegemony as local media are implicated in transnational media operations or employ practices and ideologies culled from TNMC business models. Cultural hegemony predicts that diverse privatized national media adopting TNMC practices will export programs, but the content will remain ad-driven entertainment. Cultural hegemony expects that national media contraflow and subaltern content will appear, but in the hands of TNMCs will exhibit ideological content amenable to dominant social relations and capitalist leadership.

Diverse local productions may offer alternatives, but they pose no oppositional challenge to capitalist cultural hegemony and its consumerist entertainment. Subaltern communication challenges capitalist cultural hegemony only to the extent it represents, organizes, and leads decisive social groups, especially the working class, to different, more democratic social practices and cultural norms: democratic decision-making; workers' control of industry; public access to media; affirmative equal rights for women, ethnic and religious groups, and indigenous nations. Any subaltern movement ultimately needs to assemble a new cultural hegemony of solidarity to realize its vision and its power (Gramsci, 2000; Sassoon, 1987; Artz & Murphy, 2000, 2012).

Cultural Proximity: Bringing Domination Home

Another answer discounting cultural domination from abroad is cultural proximity, the theoretical cousin of contraflow. Proximity theory notes the obvious: media audiences usually prefer media content that reflects their own cultural experience. Given a choice, domestic audiences prefer local media over media imports.

At one time, Joseph Straubhaar (1984, 1991) found that audiences preferred television programs in their own language, with scenery and historical icons from their own cultures, demonstrated by the relative popularity of local telenovelas compared to US imports in Brazil. Although the rediscovery that people tend to feel more comfortable speaking their own language in familiar surroundings is not particularly profound, as a component of audience choice it was repositioned as evidence of the limited ability of Western media to influence other cultures – a remarkable analytical leap. Positing that "ultimately people like to see something close to their lives" (Hong, 1998, p. 46) becomes a condition "limiting the influx of Western media products" (Chadha & Koovri, 2000, p. 425) presumes transnationals are incapable of producing culturally proximate content – a claim immediately refuted by the global success of *Millionaire*, a transnational production which obtained cultural proximity in every locale. Analytically, large audiences for one local television genre – Brazilian telenovelas, Japanese "trendy" dramas – were presumed to disprove media predominance and influence from abroad. Unfortunately, this approach to "cultural proximity" simply counts instances of non-dominant culture as evidence of non-domination, reducing cultural values and norms to percentages of television schedules.

Telenovelas' content reveals ample proof of the presence of dominant commercial culture (Oliviera, 1995; Beltrán, 1982). Steve Derné (2008) notes that the styles, images, and themes from American soaps have heavily influenced "the content and representational styles" of Hindi drama, including their unequivocal celebration of urban consumer lifestyles (pp. 33–35). Another Latin American example of cultural proximity (and contraflow) might be *Sábado Gigante*, the Chilean-based Galavisión-Univisión weekly variety show that is broadcast across Latin America and the United States. In an extensive content analysis of *Sábado Gigante*, Martha Sánchez, Janet Cramer, and Leonel Prieto (2003) concluded that internationally the show communicates "an escape from real material conditions and political engagement to a land where luck, riches, consumption, and the 'American way' may be seen as salvation" (p. 146) – a kind of hybridized, Disneyfied, "Latinized" variety show for all people. Cultural proximity may be the bait, but viewers are soon hooked on consumerism as a "local" cultural activity.

Cultural proximity theory relies on tautological surety: whenever and wherever audiences prefer a program, cultural proximity must exist. Proximity holds out weakly for any audience-generated common feeling or attraction, attaching proximity to shared consumerist pleasures – solid evidence of the cultural hegemony of transnational media and capital.

At some not-too-distant moment, Polish media (likely allied with a TNMC) will script and film their own telenovelas – resurrecting "cultural proximity" as a truism once again. Meanwhile, Disney's UTV in India, News Corp's STAR TV Asia, and Discovery Channel in Europe promote

Brazil in Poland

The popularity in Eastern Europe of O Globo's Portuguese-language telenovelas (the exemplar for cultural proximity) essentially scraps the concept of most of its explanatory power. Poles do not speak Portuguese, don't compose sambas, prefer feijoada over pierogis, experience the same seasons, or travel across the same climates and landscapes. Yet, telenovelas are "muy popular" in Poland. Yes, most Poles and many Latin Americans are Catholics, but Catholicism has never been a necessary convention in telenovela narratives. Arguing that Poles have more "cultural proximity" to Brazil than their own Polish heritage defies all reason. It seems that Poles, and Hungarians and Croatians, can decipher Brazilian cultural codes enough to enjoy stories of obstructed romance, underdog success, and generational plots that frequent telenovelas. More to the point: the political economy of media infrastructures in Poland is not as prepared for production and export as in Brazil or Mexico, and telenovelas are a cheap option for filling TV schedules (Jakubowicz, 2007, pp. 368–371). Cultural proximity is not the primary variable in media content in Poland.

TNMC "cultural proximity" with programming that is both produced locally and feels familiar to local audiences. In certain instances, a firm may even aspire to "cultural proximity" with one distinct locale as a means to improve its global reach. As part of its branding strategy, Guinness needs to be as Irish as possible, especially now that it has merged with Grand Metropolitan, a European transnational hotel operator. Likewise, operating as part of a transnationally consolidated media network, MTV Polska aspires to be "culturally proximate" to its Polish audience although production occurs elsewhere. In a different context, South Korean transnational television, film, and music producers work to mask their cultural and national identities with an appearance and feeling of Asianness constructed through content collaboration with two or more cultural corporations in the region, creating a multi-lingual, multicultural, market-based proximity to reach East Asian consumers. Korean singer BoA sings in Korean, Japanese, and English; singer Rain learned English, Chinese, and Thai to "demonstrate his cultural proximity to his fans" (Siriyuvasak, 2010).

In these commercial variants, cultural proximity loses all connection to any actual local culture.

A more substantial and consistent understanding of global media structures and practices recognizes the centrality of capitalist social relations, including globally "flexible" labor, transnational/local co-productions, and the predominance of localized media entertainment content. Cultural hegemony places the proximity of cultural preferences and norms in the context of implemented and accepted dominant practices in diverse local cultures, all following the neoliberal economic and political leadership of the transnational capitalist class (TNCC) and TNMCs.

Transnationally exchanged formats build on local preferences and simultaneously spread local preferences across borders, creating a global culture that is "proximate" to many viewers. Whatever audiences watch, in whatever language, with whatever cultural gloss, culturally proximate content is produced transnationally using multiple, diverse cultural contributions to nourish global consumption. "Consumerism has become an Indian value," says a top magazine editor (Fernandes, 2010, p. 614) – and a Brazilian value, and a Nigerian value, and a global value for most locales. Indeed, we are all becoming cosmopolitan as expressed by transnational media and advertising exuding cultural proximity for consumers in every nation.

Hybridity: Domination through Diversity

Of all the claims about the limits of media dominance, the recurring promotion of the power of audience is most prevalent. Skeptics of global media influence and fans of active audiences believe that audiences and cultures do not accept imported media content as is, but creatively decode and repurpose meanings to construct hybridized forms and meanings for local uses. In some versions, hybridity means that dominance is not possible because local populations create their own meanings by decoding media images for their own pleasures. Presumably, local media create their own hybrid forms that also undercut dominant influence. Thus, in terms of global media effects, hybridity is "local resilience in the face of cultural invasion and global homogenization" (Huang, 2011, p. 4).

Anthropological studies and textual analyses of cultural development reveal that all practices, rituals, and media content are hybrids of previous cultural cross-pollination. For anthropologists, hybridization means "the ways in which forms become separated from existing practices and recombine with new forms and new practices" (Rowe & Schilling, 1991, p. 231). Of course, recognizing that cultures are hybrid offspring with multiple ancestors is really quite mundane, although the results of that phenomenon often have profound significance. In the hands of pluralist apologists for capitalism and its commercial media, the validity of observations about hybrid media messages becomes an invitation to ignore media industry power.

Somehow the mere existence of hybridity in culture has been transformed into a theory that dismisses cultural dominance from any source and discounts the structural and institutional effects on meaning (Fiske, 1988; Bhabha, 1994) so that consumers "indigenize products to serve their own cultural purposes" (Beynon & Dunkerley, 2000, p. 29). Michael Keane, Anthony Fung, and Albert Moran (2007) contend that TNMC power has been displaced because "producers and consumers meet as co-creators of hybrid programming" such that "self-identification with tasty food" is evidence of political agency and "non-governmental organization activity" (pp. 15, 139). For liberal pluralists, hybridity has "refurbished the view ... [that] the customer, though perhaps a little bruised, is still ultimately sovereign ... heroic resistance fighters in the war against cultural deception" (Golding & Murdock, 1991, p. 28).

Cultural borrowing, hybridization, and indigenization are common processes in global cultural flow and international media. "Without the breakthroughs of blacks, Jews, Italians, Irish and others would [North American] music even exist?" (Reich, 2013, p. D1). "Where did Walt Disney find the stories for his films Cinderella and Pinocchio? Who inspired Garcia Márquez to make Remedios la Bella rise to heaven, body and soul? From what northeastern mouths did Vargas Llosa take his captivating narration? In the cultural universe we are all debtors and creditors" (López Vigil, 2007). All cultures are the culmination of diverse contributions awaiting further alteration. Audience-initiated decodings of received media content and the repurposing of dominant meanings by local media creators that hybridize cultural artifacts are contradictory assemblages of TNMC productions and local revisions.

The real controversy over hybridity regards its content and meaningful effect. Hybridity may be "mutually constituted" (Kraidy, 2002); one might even note the inordinate contribution of creative content by local cultures in a particular TNMC product, or how some cultures strategically hybridize and "domesticate" imports as a means of "innovation by emulation" (Huang,

2011, p. 4). A much more important question than hybridity *per se* is the content. Some hybrids promote consumerism and market power. Some hybrids undermine consumerism and authority. The resistance or power of any image can only be measured by the social consequence of the message itself, not its author or its viewer.

The question is to ascertain which hybrids do what and how. What proportion of meaning emanates from TNMC producers? What part of the content reflects influences or interpretations contributed by local cultures? What values appear in hybrid media and do they reinforce or challenge the status quo? "How are these programs refashioned, resignified, modified – and how are they subsequently read and evaluated? (Keane et al., 2007, p. 9). What's new? What's different? Is it a platypus or just another duck of a different color? How much of the hybrid expresses local independence or creativity and how much of the hybrid appropriates local creativity for commercial purposes?

Even for content as unique as Pokémon, "children do not produce meaning alone; instead they interact with the meanings constructed by others" (Brougère, 2004, p. 206). Meanings constructed by animators, scriptwriters, and peers prompt responses. Indeed, the larger social order and its social relations of production, its political norms, and yes, its dominant cultural practices, including 3–5 hours of television viewing every day, frame both child and adult experiences and reactions. Our circumstances within the larger culture, including access to and preference for particular media images and narratives, are shaped by our social location. "A shared culture arises more from a shared structural situation than from shared cultural inculcation" (Derné, 2008, p. 208). Thus, not surprisingly, affluent fan audiences for hybrid "idols" in Japan translate their "sense of familiarity and intimacy with the idol into action" as consumers (Galbraith & Karlin, 2012, p. 25). Indian working class men reject Hollywood and Bollywood film celebrations of conspicuous consumption and romantic marriage as unrealistic guides to action, but are attracted to movies with dominant male heroes. Structures carry meanings as much as media disseminate meanings.

In a TNMC-mediated world, social interaction between communicators occurs largely in a restricted environment for symbolic interaction, privileging the media producer and distributor of messages. Global cultural flow is TNMC directed, despite the appearance of local cultural eddies and dams. Moreover, TNMCs astutely respond to new currents as opportunities to prosper through local adaptation. TNMCs are both megaphone and social messaging service for neoliberal ideology and policy of the

Americana as Local

Over time, "images and commodities [may] tend to lose their cultural identity" (Iwabuchi, 2004, p. 73). In many places "American" icons are conceived as national. "McDonald's is now so much a part of their world that to Japanese or Taiwanese young consumers it no longer represents an American way of life," because "meaning construction is never free from the command of transnational media industries" with their localization strategies that may "naturally" appear local (Iwabuchi, 2004, p. 73).

Consuming McDonald's and listening to K-pop music does not seem foreign, because the local-national culture has morphed into the same practices, attitudes, and tastes of what was previously viewed as foreign. Hybrids have value for local cultures to the extent that media fit their cultural experience. Media content that appeals most to local audiences works from those political and social relations that frame their cultural world (Derné, 2008, p. 210). As transnational capitalism comes to dominate domestic social relations of production, TNMC-local hybrids reflect and reproduce cultural relations for individual consumerism and private accumulation of wealth with little concern for democracy and equality. The hegemony of market relations thus appears as common sense in TNMC narratives and images.

American icons become local. Hybrid local culture serves global capitalism.

transnational capitalist class: extolling the "myth of consumer agency to convince consumers that they are empowered to choose what they consume" (Galbraith & Karlin, 2012, p. 25).

The constitutive power of TNMCs is not absolute, but only politically informed and active groups can effectively turn oppositional decodings into actual political change. Differential "readings" of dominant media are informed by one's social location that provides access to cultural repertoires and symbolic resources that sustain different interpretations (Golding & Murdock, 1991, p. 30). Besides, whatever our understanding, however we make meaning, the media can continue to broadcast its coded, preferred narratives and images to thousands and millions of others that individually we can not reach without media access.

The issue then is not one of polysemic, alternative readings of messages received, or even one of how to produce new hybrid meanings. It's a question of having the power and capacity to participate in the communication process as an interactive producer and distributor of messages. Entertainment media can provide diversity aplenty – something for everyone. The information super-highway can reach millions of receivers, but democratic communication requires the full participation in the construction of messages and meaning. The "fetishism of the consumer" as power broker is only a "mask for the real seat of agency," which is the producer" (Appadurai, 1996, p. 42). Actively decoding or not, relegated to only being a receiver limits one's ability to communicate with others, but that is precisely how privatized commercial media structure the communication process.

In Turkey, commercially run Arabesk and Turkish pop radio offer "*gazino* tavern-like entertainment" for the working class, while Western pop radio creates a "party atmosphere for an upscale audience" (Algan, 2003, p. 185) – demonstrating the hegemonic pull of transnational capitalist values. Using hybrid musical styles – nationalist "green" pop, Islamic pop, and a top-40 Turkish version of mainstream pop – local radio companies provide diverse venues for attracting audiences and advertisers, in line with the models provided by the transnational music industry and European commercial media. Likewise, "having accommodated foreign culture for a long period of time" Korea media excel at "refining imported culture" (You, 2006, p. 4). "Korean scholars credit cultural hybridity with simultaneously promoting globalization and localization of Korean pop culture" (Jang & Paik, 2012, p. 201), with traditional, even conservative, local inflections carrying homogenous themes of individual consumption and affluent lifestyle. Local Indian filmmakers introduce hybrid media content heavily influenced by TNMC programming and advertising such that even traditional Indian family values are combined with female cosmopolitan fashion and consumer independence (Derné, 2008, pp. 113, 147). Transnational media promote and profit from these hybrid local cultures which are "largely depoliticized, commercialized, and excluded from public deliberation" (Splichal, 2002, p. 6), so we will likely see spin-offs of these elements in local hybrids from East Europe to East Asia. In fact, transnational production incessantly promotes recycling, hybrid adaptation, and local repurposing of narrative and content to increase market share and hedge financial risk. Narratives and images of preferred cultural norms are thus produced, broadcast, and continually repeated in hybrid entertainment media, laying the groundwork and decorating the walls of popular culture.

Cloaking Power in the Hybrid

The cloak of hybridization does not disguise much to the discerning. Most examples of hybridity demonstrating popular power or resistance demonstrate new content but fail to include new forms or practices. Ironically, critics who champion the power of the audience seem unfazed by the apartheid media system that precludes audiences from becoming communicators. Marwan Kraidy (2005) argues that TV Azteca's *Tele Chobis*, a hybrid copycat of BBC's *Teletubbies* children's program, is a "complex embodiment of hybridity" featuring a "radical intertextuality" of cultural diversity (pp. 103–115). Yet, beyond *Tele Chobis*'s setting in Mexico, its "carnivalesque" style, and the addition of product advertising, it's hard to find any ground-breaking challenges to educational children's television. Hybridity of this kind represents difference not unlike that of McDonald's' global hybrids. "McDonald's may sell 'sushi burgers' in Japan and 'curry burgers' in India, but burgers remain burgers, and it is their 'burger-ness' that is the essence of their cultural significance" (Machin & Van Leeuwen, 2007, p. 107). One could argue that even if McDonald's sells shwarmas in Greece, the structure of production and consumption of the fast food maintains its significance for organizing social practices according to individualism, immediate gratification, impersonal social interaction, and other preferred practices of capitalist cultural hegemony. McDonald's has been successful in part because of its adaptability: franchisees have been careful to shape their products in ways that meet the needs and expectations of the local community, providing kosher in Israel and halal in Palestine (Crothers, 2010, p. 133).

Media formats incorporate hybrids, but they are not subject to just any reworking; they are not value-free. Hybrid formats have structures that disseminate ideologies, values, and preferred norms for transnational capitalist hegemony. Just as Christianity polished off pagan icons and rituals for better recruitment, the outcome of "mutually constitutive" processes depends on social and political power structured by institutions and communicative forms (MacMullen, 1997). Cultural mixing under a transnational capitalist order does not have equality in ingredients. There is scant global South influence in the global North, with the exception of massive sales of the condiment salsa and Shakira's music. As the United Nations Development Project concluded, "the unequal economic and political powers of countries, industries and corporations cause some cultures to spread, others to wither" (UNDP, 2004, p. 90).

Here is the point: not just any hybrid can undermine dominance. Like hegemony, hybridity has no political mantle of progress or reaction – it is a process and form that can be used for any number of political and cultural ends. Dominance does not depend on a single, universal culture. "The invention of a hybridized form of globality, one produced through the national imagination in liberalizing India, has been centrally linked to the production of images of the urban middles classes" (Fernandes, 2000, p. 620). Hybridity for the consuming middle class. On another continent: "The whole idea that France is being destroyed by global popular culture misunderstands the modern media, which increasingly create separate products for each national market rather than peddling a single imperial product" (Miller et al., 2008, p. 198). Hybridity for promoting a national market. In the United States, Robin Thicke's 2013 R&B/Hip-hop hybrid song, "Blurred Lines," is "nothing more than a montage of female sexual degradation, complete with hair-pulling by the singer and his rapping buddies" despite director Diane Martel claiming that because women look into the camera, "they are in the power position" (Villareal, 2013, p. 21). Hybridity for misogyny. In each case, hybrid media were produced by TNMCs appealing to targeted markets for commercial purposes.

Dominance works quite well, indeed much better hegemonically speaking, if local preferences are served transnational media offerings that articulate language, locations, and local cultural icons into the entertainment mix. TNMCs consciously advance hybridization through their efforts to indigenize local media programming and commodities. Hybridization by itself does not interfere with the commercialization of anything. In Turkey, "what undercut and strangled the diversity, creativity, and independence of the new media was its commercialization by monopolies willing to broadcast any style attractive to advertisers seeking particular audiences. Turkish audiences have tolerated, even sought out, this capitalist commodification of culture because it permits positive representations of their ethnicity and class culture" (Algan, 2003, p. 188). Cultural hegemony actively promotes hybrid media and culture in Turkey and elsewhere because they advance TNMC economic goals, understanding that "purely cultural changes have little effect on social arrangements" so pose little challenge to capitalist cultural and political leaderships, as Steve Derné (2008) found in his multi-year study of global media in urban India (p. 17).

Homogenizing Hybridity

Hybridity nestles comfortably in the larger homogenous culture. Individual content components fit nicely within global formats and effectively carry global themes. We might pause to recall that the quintessential entertainer, Disney, is the fairest hybrid in the land as it "plunders all folklore, fairy tales, and nineteenth- and twentieth-century children's literature," and recently African and Chinese stories, to reshape them (Dorfman, 1983, p. 24) for maximum commercial value and global distribution. The regeneration of hybrid genres underlines the intrinsic economic needs of Asian filmmakers as cultural producers, who effectively "act as initiators and gatekeepers of major's collaboration and involvement, as intermediaries balancing tensions and conflicts, and as catalysts triggering competition and consolidation at both national and regional levels" (Chung, 2011, p. 203). Active consent and participation by TNMC local and national partners makes the appeal of capitalist cultural hegemony more palatable for local audiences who willingly consume the creative hybrid genres that exhibit local cultural traits. The pan-Latin American variety show *Sábado Gigante* broadcasts hybrid content that stands on decades of Latin American cultural homogeneity.

> Politically, [national] homogenization was a condition that, in turbulent times, helped shield national elites from internal dissension and external invasion. Economically, homogenization bolstered and protected certain elite strategies, presented as beneficial for all Brazilians, Chileans, etc. but invariably serving the elite's notion of nation in trade, production, and social norms. (Sánchez, Cramer, & Prieto, 2003, p. 133)

With a tradition of exchanging global and regional programming across Latin America, regional and TNMC television has been an active agent in homogenizing culture for decades – hybrid variations notwithstanding.

Line up all the distinct hybrid media content produced by contraflow media and other diverse nation-based media alongside hybridized resistive decodings that have no political manifestation. List the myriad cultural differences among them. Add the other possible pleasurable uses and gratifications available to audiences who make their own meanings from received media content. Then, step back and take a broader look. Several recognizable and common themes appear across the multitude of hybrids.

There – among all the hybrids – clear tones and meanings stand out as shared similarities.

Cultural hegemony, as the manifestation of transnational capitalism's political economy, highlights hybridity as a process of homogenization. "Competition for the most lucrative audience segments leads to more sophisticated and costlier productions that require worldwide circulation" to be profitable (Havens, 2006, p. 159). Havens (2006) discerns the "development of distinct transnational taste-cultures, which are roughly akin to social classes" (p. 159), suggesting that transnational social class audiences share cultural preferences and norms which must appear in homogenized media content to be well-received. Capitalist leaderships provide something for everyone within their hegemonic universe, to ensure the reproduction of social relations and practices necessary for transnational capitalism. Thus, in addition to the homogeneous transnational forms of media (telenovelas, competitive game shows, reality TV, factual entertainment, and Hollywood/Bollywood/Chollywood action-adventures), homogeneous themes of individualism, consumerism, spectacle entertainment, and deference to authority inhabit all localized, hybridized commercial media content according to the social class proclivities of each audience segment.

Even scholars like Marwan Kraidy, Michael Keane, Dayan Thussu, and Shuling Huang, who are keen on distancing their work from political economy and an overtly materialist cultural hegemony, supply ample evidence that local media employ "strategic hybridization to promote cultural products, entertainers," and other images that are "exploited by various businesses to gratify consumer desires for novel commodities" (Huang, 2011, p. 15). In her dissection of the local culture in Leixlip, Ireland, Martha Van Der Bly (2007) pens a more elegant obfuscation, claiming "heterogeneity, but within the context of one world culture" (p. 234). However one might couch it semantically, even according to the hesitant, we must concede that commercialized local hybrids (produced for diverse cultural and social class audiences) uniformly conform to transnational capitalist cultural hegemony. This is not just one possible description of media transnationalism. The themes (however locally composed) are exceedingly transparent: individual consumerism, celebrity entertainment, and acceptance of the power and authority of the capitalist market.

Transnational media and their local expressions depend on capitalist labor relations and undemocratic political practices comprising a cultural hegemony that promotes consumerism – to promote sales – to promote the

Cosmo in China

The global expansion of women's magazines reflects a somewhat different trajectory than that anticipated by hybridity theorists. In Holland, "the global already impinged on magazine readers, but they were not yet aware of it" because *Cosmo* and *Elle* were presented as fully Dutch (Machin & Van Leeuwen, 2007, p. 35). However, within a few years, the global was "outed" and accepted: "Mostly American songs, magazines, and websites are directly accessed by local young women, in English, and without any mediation from Dutch cultural elites" (Machin & Van Leeuwen, 2007, p. 36).

In the same two magazines in China, "featuring indigenous models," they take on the look and feel of "local" magazines but "they are hardly 'hybrids' because they reflect and transmit consumer values that clearly serve the interests of the global brands" (Frith & Feng, 2009, p. 170). If Beyoncé's "girl power" tour appears as liberating for women, then Chinese models in *Cosmo* must indicate liberalization of women's rights, as well? Frith and Feng (2009) insist "the over emphasis on women as consumers … may actually limit women's understanding" of their potential roles in society (p. 172).

Likewise, South Korea's "stylish entertainment industry, driven by pop music and TV dramas, not only amuses but also serves as a potent and willing vehicle for marketing messages" (Beattie, 2012). In the Netherlands, China, Korea, and elsewhere, the culture of entertainment and consumerism predominates – most often through local hybrid variations on a theme.

social system that is based on wage labor that exists solely to produce and sell commodities. This capitalist cultural hegemony provides individual pleasures, but it does not aspire to meet human needs, to use knowledge for a sustainable, non-consumptive ecology, or to consider democratic collective solutions to global problems. Political economy and cultural hegemony are better guides to understanding transnational media, local cultural practices, and the possibilities for meaningful "hybrid" cultures that nurture humanity in all of its variations.

The hybrid content of contemporary entertainment media produced and disseminated by TNMCs meet the commercial, cultural, and ideological needs of the developing transnational capitalist system. Under the current transnational media regime, hybridity contributes to winning consent for a transnational capitalist order. TNMC media content does not create a new social order, but consistent, repetitive, and comforting themes and narratives explain, reinforce, and legitimate social relations of class inequality that insist on atomized individuals fending for themselves in the marketplace. Hybridity gives one more recognition that TNMC media and cultural flows have "decentered the nation-based power structure and vitalized local practices of appropriation and consumption of transnational capitalist cultural products and meanings" (Iwabuchi, 2002, p. 35) as a means to consolidate global capitalist power.

Hybridized media content parallels and bolsters social practices necessary for transnational capitalism, particularly individual consumerism and its corollary cross-beam of support, a politically disenfranchised transnational working class. In this matrix, global power has been dispersed, not reduced. Media and culture have erupted with diverse hybrid entertainment forms and content, but democracy has suffered. US dominance may have declined (excepting its military power), but the TNCC has consolidated its leadership over the global economy. We face a new hybridized corporate structure, as well: DreamWorks struggles as a US-based film studio, but after Indian capital injects $325 million, DreamWorks survives to profit anew in transnational alliances with TNMCs nominally housed in Korea, China, Japan, Britain, India, and the United States.

Content by and for Transnational Capitalist Cultural Hegemony

Cultural hegemony explains that TNMCs actively create their own preferred hybridity. Through mergers, joint ventures, and co-productions, TNMCs build structures of consent among capitalist classes and their managers. The social relations of TNMC production provide minimal benefits to creative workers, securing consent among dispersed labor forces. And from these two hegemonic processes, TNMCs harvest an abundance of diverse, hybrid, local creative offerings for re-use in all media content. The resulting hybrid hegemonic content shares its attractive narratives and expressions replete with apolitical perspectives and lived experiences familiar to all and enjoyable for many. As the respected leaders of global entertainment and culture, TNMCs find and appropriate creative contributions of diverse cultures to better package their stories, images, and products for winning widespread consent.

The dialectical process of merging and synthesizing diverse and often contradictory perspectives and communication into meaningful entertainment packages occurs within the context of transnational media business goals and practices. Programming content emerging from these relations of production aims to meet the cultural preferences of diverse audiences while encouraging consumerism and other cultural practices that will reproduce those same capitalist social relations. To bolster capitalist cultural hegemony, TNMC entertainment omits or expunges messages of class solidarity (beyond family or small group), anti-capitalist societal critique (beyond individual corruption), and participatory democratic decision-making (beyond product purchase).

Diversity in the Familiar

Popular entertainment has become homogenized in form, if not completely in content, in standardized theme, if not completely in narrative. "Global markets, mass consumption, mass communication, and mass tourism disseminate the standardized products of a mass culture ... the same [kinds of] consumer goods and fashions, the same films, television programmes, and bestselling music and books spread across the globe" (Habermas, 2001, p. 75) in all their local variations. Once standardization becomes internalized there is no need for policing, as participants consent to the hegemony of form, which can be seen in entertainment genres around the world.

Particular forms, from telenovelas to children's cartoons, privilege dominant representations within prescribed conventions of form and genre. Transnational co-production agreements, format contracts in particular, impose a variety of constraints that local contractors and producers must accept as they search for hybrid local content and narratives. "Cultural forms are mechanisms for regulating public discourse" (Golding & Murdock, 1991, p. 27), but men and women view media entertainment without necessarily discerning the similarities of conventions across genres. Indeed, the form and theme conventions provide each specific genre and each unique program with a familiar and comforting invitation to audiences to imbibe in the content.

Codes and conventions work to acclimate viewers to prompts and responses. Certain formulaic buttons trigger certain expected reactions:

laugh-tracks cue humor; dark and rainy settings portend danger; deep adagio music cues sadness; and so on. In a television, film, and Internet society, our tastes are inundated by TNMC messages and images. This world influences our conception of others and ourselves. We may be individuals, but we're often doing the same things and buying the same stuff, and mostly doing it passively as spectators and consumers of advertised products. Our lives have become atomized, as we turn to personalized blogs, twitter feeds, and Amazon preferences. The world of choice is indeed multiple, various, and dynamic. But it is the result of advertising and networks targeting audiences so that "something is provided for all so that none can escape" (Adorno & Horkheimer, in Bowman, 2012, p. 41). Still, "the culture industry perpetually cheats its consumers of what it perpetually promises. The promissory note which, with its plots and staging, draws on pleasure is endlessly prolonged; the promise, which is actually all the spectacle consists of, is illusory: all it actually confirms is that the real point will never be reached, that the diner must be satisfied with the menu" (Horkheimer & Adorno, 2002, p. 139).

The conditions of media production and distribution place limits on the form and content of media, and consequently a thorough political economy of cultural hegemony must consider what the conditions and relations of production have wrought. Moreover, the conditions of production, the current structures, and general practices of transnational media outlined in previous chapters should suffice to enable us to make the great leap forward to media content.

Content for Consent

A brief foray into media entertainment content seems more than appropriate if the claims about "ownership → programming → social use" that were presented earlier are to be demonstrated. Political economy attempts to discern the structural constraints on human action; cultural hegemony attempts to discover the practices and understandings arising from those structural constraints that can be used to win consent for that same structure. The details provided on transnational corporate interlocks, transnational capitalist class political organizations, and the structure of transnational media, including its use of transnational social relations that profit from social class hierarchies in production, lead to content appropriate and necessary for building political and cultural consent.

John Fiske (1988) once recognized that television genres are instruments of power that "form the network of industrial, ideological, and institutional conventions that are common to both producers and audiences out of which arise both the producer's programs and the audience's readings" (p. 111). The codes and conventions that cling to specific genres also constrain the possibilities for the viewer's understanding, increasing the possible effects of media over time and across national boundaries.

Action movies, the most prevalent global film genre, dramatically illustrate the content TNMCs serve audiences everywhere. The next chapter provides examples of action movies from around the world. None of the examples are fully decoded semiotically; nor are they assessed with a rigorous content analysis. Recurring prominent themes are presented as the most likely intended meanings. Observations indicate the connections between ownership, programming, and cultural consequence that can be generated from a cultural hegemony perspective that attends to the political economy of global media at this historical conjuncture. With little doubt, the content and themes of action movies confirm the connections between media structure and programming, indicating the emerging contours of transnational capitalist hegemony.

References

Algan, E. (2003). Privatization of radio and media hegemony in Turkey. In L. Artz & Y. Kamalipour, (Eds.), *The globalization of corporate media hegemony* (pp. 169–192). Albany, NY: New York University Press.

Appadurai, A. (1996). *Modernity at large: Cultural dimensions of globalization.* Minneapolis: University of Minnesota Press.

Artz, B. L. (1993). Communication and power: Popular radio in Nicaragua. *Journal of Radio Studies, 2*(1), 205–227.

Artz, L. (2006). TeleSUR (Television of the South): Discarding contraflow for horizontal communication. *International Journal of Media and Cultural Politics, 2*(2), 225–232.

Artz, L. (2012). 21st century socialism: Making a state for revolution. *Triple C: Cognition, Communication, Co-operation, 10*(2), 537–554.

Artz, L., & Murphy, B. O. (2000). *Cultural hegemony in the United States.* Thousand Oaks, CA: Sage.

Bhabha, H. (1994). *The location of culture.* New York: Routledge.

Beattie, A. C. (2012, June 11). Marketing's next wave: The Korean pop star. *Advertising Age, 83*, 6.

Beltrán, L. R (1982). *Comunicacä o dominada (Communication and domination).* Rio de Janeiro, Brazil: Paz & Terra.

Beynon, J., & Dunkersley, D. (2000). Introduction. In J. Beynon & D. Dunkersley (Eds.), *Globalization: The reader* (pp. 1–38). New York: Routledge.

Bowman, P. (2012). *Culture and the media.* New York: Palgrave Macmillan.

Brougère, G. (2004). How much is a Pokémon worth? Pokémon in France. In J. Tobin (Ed.), *Pikachu's global adventure: The rise and fall of Pokémon* (pp. 187–208). Durham, NC: Duke University Press.

Chadha, K., & Kavoori, A. (2000). Media imperialism revisited: Some findings from the Asian case. *Media, Culture & Society, 22*(4), 415–432.

Chung, H. (2011). Book review. *Cultural Trends, 20*(2), 201–204.

Crothers, L. (2010). Globalization and American popular culture. 2nd edn. Lanham, MD: Rowman & Littlefield.

de Gouvea Neto, R. (1997). Case Study: TV Globo: The Brazilian media giant. *International Executive, 39*(2), 255–270.

Derné, S. D. (2008). *Globalization on the ground: New media and the transformation of culture, class, and gender in India.* Thousand Oaks, CA: Sage.

Dorfman, A. (1983). *The empire's old clothes: What the Lone Ranger, Babar, and other innocent heroes do to our minds.* New York: Pantheon.

European Audiovisual Observatory. (2002). The imbalance of trade in films and television programmes between North America and Europe continues to deteriorate. Strasbourg, France. Retrieved July 8, 2013, from http://www.obs.coe.int/about/oea/pr/desequilibre.html

Fernandes, L. (2000). Nationalizing 'the global': media images, cultural politics, and the middle class in India. *Media, Culture & Society, 22*(5), 611–628.

Fernandes, S. (2010). *Who can stop the drums? Urban social movements in Chávez's Venezuela.* Greensboro, NC: Duke University Press.

Fiske, J. (1988). *Television culture.* London: Methuen.

Frith, K., & Feng, Y. (2009). Transnational cultural flows: An analysis of women's magazines in China. *Chinese Journal of Communication, 2*(2), 158–173.

Galbraith, P. W., & Karlin, J. G. (2012). Introduction: The mirror of idols and celebrity. In P. W. Galbraith & J. G. Karling (Eds.), *Idols and celebrity in Japanese media culture* (pp. 1–32). New York: Palgrave Macmillan.

Golding, P., & Murdock, G. (1991). Culture, communications, and political economy. In J. Curran & M. Gurevitch (Eds.), *Mass media and society* (pp. 15–32). London: Edward Arnold.

Gramsci, A. (2000). *The Antonio Gramsci reader: Selected writings, 1916–1935.* D. Forgacs, Ed. New York: New York University Press.

Habermas, J. (2001). *The postnational constellation: Political essays.* Cambridge, UK: Polity Press.

Havens, T. (2006). *Global television marketplace.* London: Palgrave Macmillan.

Hong, J. (1998). *The internationalization of television in China: The evolution of ideology, society, and media since the reform*. Westport, CN: Praeger.

Hopewell, J. (2013, June 18). Hollywood stymied as Europe sticks with its limits on film and TV. Variety. Retrieved October 12, 2014, from http://variety. com/2013/film/global/hollywood-stymied-as-europe-sticks-with-its-limits-on-film-and-tv-1200497446/

Horkheimer, M., & Adorno, T. (2002). *Dialectic of enlightenment (Cultural memory in the present)*. E. Jephcott, Trans. (Originally published 1944). Palo Alto, CA: Stanford University Press.

Huang, S. (2011). Nation-branding and transnational consumption: Japan-mania and the Korean wave in Taiwan. *Media, Culture & Society, 33*(1), 3–18.

Iwabuchi, K. (2002). *Recentering globalization: Popular culture and Japanese transnationalism*. Durham, NC: Duke University Press.

Iwabuchi, K. (2004). How Japanese is Pokémon? In J. Tobin (Ed.), *Pikachu's global adventure: The rise and fall of Pokémon* (pp. 53–79). Durham, NC: Duke University Press.

Jakubowicz, K. (2007). *Rude awakening: Social and media change in Central and Eastern Europe*. Cresskill, NJ: Hampton Press.

Jang, G., & Paik, W. K. (2012). Korean wave as tool for Korea's new cultural diplomacy. *Advances in Applied Sociology, 2*(3), 196–202.

Keane, M., Fung, A. Y. H., & Moran, A. (2007). *New television, globalization, and the East Asian cultural imagination*. Hong Kong: Hong Kong University Press.

Kraidy, M. M. (2002). Hybridity in cultural globalization. *Communication Theory, 12*(3), 316–339.

Kraidy, M. M. (2005). *Hybridity: The cultural logic of globalization*. Philadephia, PA: Temple University Press.

Liebes, T., & Katz, F. (1990). *The export of meaning: Cross-cultural readings of "Dallas."* New York: Oxford University Press.

López Vigil, J. I. (2007, June). Media content as social property. *Revista Envio, 311*. Retrieved from http://www.envio.org.ni/articulo/3580

Machin, D., & Van Leeuwen, T. (2007). *Global media discourse: A critical introduction*. New York: Routledge.

MacMullen, R. (1997). *Christianity and paganism in the fourth to eighth centuries*. New Haven, CT: Yale University Press.

Matta, F. M. (1977). *La información en el nuevo orden internacional (Information in the new world order)*. Geneva: United Nations Research Institute for Social Development, LIET, Instituto Latinoamericano de Estudios Transnacionales.

Mattelart, A. (1976). Cultural imperialism in the multinational's age. *Research on Peace and Violence, 6*(4), 160–174.

McElroy, D. (2008, November 25). Saudi girl band challenges the rules limiting women. *Daily Telegraph*. Retrieved from http://www.telegraph.co.uk/news/worldnews/middleeast/saudiarabia/3518077/Saudi-girl-band-challenges-the-rules-limiting-women.html

Oliveira, O. S. (1995). Brazilian soaps outshine Hollywood: Is cultural imperialism fading out? In K. Nordenstreng & H. Schiller (Eds.), *Beyond national sovereignty: International communication in the 1990s* (pp. 116–131). Norwood, NJ: Ablex.

Reich, H. (2013, July 14). America's mix tape. *Chicago Tribune*, pp. D1–2.

Rowe, W., & Schilling, V. (1991). *Memory and modernity: Popular culture in Latin America*. New York: Verso.

Sánchez, M. I., Cramer, J. M., & Prieto, L. (2003). "Sabado Gigante (Giant Saturday)" and the cultural homogenization of Spanish-speaking people. In L. Artz & Y. Kamalipoour (Eds.), *The globalization of corporate media hegemony* (pp. 130–150). Albany: State University of New York Press.

Sassoon, A. S. (1987). *Gramsci's politics*. 2nd edn. Minneapolis: University of Minnesota Press.

Schiller, H. (1976). *Communication and cultural domination*. White Plains, NY: International Arts and Sciences Press.

Siriyuvasak, U. (2010). Cultural industry and Asianization: The new "imagined" inter-Asia economy. Retrieved from http://bookrepublic.org/wpcontent/uploads/2012/10/UBONRAT-Asianization-Jan-2010-FINAL1.pdf

Splichal, S. (2002). The principle of publicity, the public use of reason and social control. *Media, Culture and Society*, *24*(1), 5–26.

Straubhaar, J. D. (1984). Brazilian television: The decline of American influence. *Communication Research*, *11*(2), 221–240.

Straubhaar, J. D. (1991). Beyond media imperialism: Asymmetrical interdependence and cultural proximity. *Critical Studies in Mass Communication*, 8, 39–59.

Thussu, D. K. (2007b). Mapping global media flow and contra flow. In D. K. Thussu (Ed.), *Media on the move: Global flow and contra flow* (pp. 11–32). New York: Routledge.

UNDP. (2004). *Human Development Report 2004*. New York: Oxford University Press.

Van Der Bly, M. C. E. (2007). Globalization and the rise of one heterogeneous world culture: A microperspective of a global village. *International Journal of Comparative Sociology*, *48*(2–3), 234–256.

Villareal, T. (2013, July 26). No blurred lines in Thicke's huge hit: Ubiquitous song, video are degrading to women. *Chicago Tribune*, p. 21.

You, H. (2006, June). The origin and future of "Hallyu." *Korea Focus*. Retrieved from http://www.koreafocus.or.kr/design1/Essays/view.asp?volume_id=48&content_id=101213&category=G

Further Reading

Derné, S. D. (2008). *Globalization on the ground: New media and the transformation of culture, class, and gender in India.* Thousand Oaks, CA: Sage.
Galbraith, P. W., & Karlin, J. G. (Eds). (2012). *Idols and celebrity in Japanese media culture.* New York: Palgrave Macmillan.
Kraidy, M. M. (2005). *Hybridity: The cultural logic of globalization.* Philadephia, PA: Temple University Press.
Thussu, D. K. (Ed.). (2007). *Media on the move: Global flow and contra flow.* New York: Routledge.

7

Superheroes to the Rescue

Bam! Pow! Screech! Bang! Action movies seem to happen just as fast, with just as much substance as these expletives. Actions movies get our adrenalin pumping. These also provide an "imaginative escape from the safe and boring world of modern institutions" (Cantor, 2013, p. 26). From the small screen to the cinema screen, transnational media have settled on action movies as a top money-making genre (Table 7.1).

To maximize profits, transnational media corporations (TNMCs) attempt to produce and disseminate content that will attract and please large audiences. For movies that can transcend or at least translate well across nation and culture, content must not be too localized. Due to the high cost of movie production, transnational media seek uniformity in their media commodities and audiences. Potentially many genres are available to diverse audiences, but TNMCs and their collaborators have found two genres that travel well: animation and action-adventure. Animation works for the obvious reason that character voices and music can easily be composed for any language audience. Action movies rely on the predominance of easily understandable action scenes: car chases, fistfights, gunfights, special effects, and violence and action in general. George Gerbner explains that action movies thus are a "good commodity for the global market since violence travels well and one does not need to translate it" (quoted in Jhally, 1994). Additionally, conventions of action-adventure movies include fairly direct, recognizable codes and narratives – officials, heroes and vigilantes, criminals and villains, direct action, rising narrative action and simplistic resolution through the defeat of the antagonists

Global Entertainment Media: A Critical Introduction, First Edition. Lee Artz.
© 2015 John Wiley & Sons, Inc. Published 2015 by John Wiley & Sons, Inc.

Table 7.1 Selected action movies

Selected action movies	Gross revenue ($ millions)
The Raid: Redemption (2011)	15 (top Indonesia film)
Tropa de Elite (*Elite Squad: The Enemy Within*) (2011)	27 (top Brazil film)
Taepung (*Typhoon*) (2005)	30
Dhoom (*Blast*) (2004, 2006)	35
Dabangg 2 (2012)	38
Ra.One (2011)	38
Ek Tha Tiger (*Once There was a Tiger*) (2012)	50
Krrish 3 (2013)	51
Chennai Express (2013)	63
D-War (*Dragon Wars*) (2007)	79 (top Korea film)
Dhoom 3 (2013)	80 (top India film)
Gwoemul (*The Host*) (2006)	92
House of Flying Daggers (2004)	92
The Girl with the Dragon Tattoo (Swedish) (2009)	104 (top Sweden film)
Asterix & Obelix: Mission Cleopatra (2002)	111 (top France action film)
Hero (China) (2002)	177 (top China film)
Taken (2008)	226
The Girl with the Dragon Tattoo (English) (2011)	262
Pacific Rim (2013)	406
Transformers: Revenge of the Fallen (2009)	836
Spider-Man 3 (2007)	890
The Dark Knight (2008)	1,004
The Dark Knight Rises (2012)	1,084
Skyfall (2012)	1,108 (top UK film)
Transformers: Dark of the Moon (2011)	1,123
Iron Man 3 (2013)	1,214
The Avengers (2012)	1,511

Note: Gross revenues do not reflect distribution. Ticket prices in the United States average about $8, in India about $1.20.

by the hero. Of course, there are multiple variations on the theme: martial arts action, quests, historical action, suspense, thrillers, revenge action, fantasy, military, comedy action, buddy films, and many more.

Action movies have no unanimous definition. Indeed, action movies exhibit a "generic hybridity" (Purse, 2011, p. 2), adopting tropes and forms from other "genres" such as romance, comedy, science fiction, and drama – constructed from diverse sources and impulses like all other media content and cultural practice. Erik Lichtenfeld (2007) finds "physical action" in "fistfights, gunfights, swordfights," and other physical conflicts to be the defining characteristic of the genre (p. 5). In a genealogy of action movies going back to 1910 swashbucklers, Steve Neale (2000) suggests that action movies have a "propensity for spectacular physical action, a narrative structure involving fights, chases, and explosions, and in addition to the deployment of state-of-the-art special effects, an emphasis in performance on physical feats and stunts" (p. 52). Lisa Purse (2011) emphasizes individualized action. Any of these definitions suffice for roughly categorizing the films identified as action-adventures: movies with significant physical action that informs the narrative, the plot, and the resolution.

The question here is: what is the relation between transnational media structures and practices and the content of their media productions? Specifically, what themes in action-adventure content conform to and promote the interests of transnational media production? No extended content analysis will be offered here; rather, apparent themes from recent popular action-adventure movies from around the world will be considered characteristic ingredients for TNMC action movies.

Top-grossing action films produced by transnational media and joint ventures premiering in India, Korea, Indonesia, South Africa, France, Brazil, and the United States are accepted as representative of the hybrid action genre. Top-grossing films indicate large viewing audiences, thus suggesting favorable reception to the film content across nations and cultures. In each case, the films referred to here were produced, co-produced, or distributed by transnational media in joint ventures. Not coincidentally, action movies in general attract more audiences in every nation, region, and internationally compared to other genres. For instance, eight of the ten highest-grossing films of all time that premiered in India are action movies, including *Chennai Express* (2013), *Dabangg* (*Audacious*) (2012), and *Don* (2006, 2011), which are included in the sample here, along with *Ra.One* (2011) and the *Dhoom* (*Blast*) (2004, 2006, 2013) movies. Likewise, TNMC action movies have attracted the largest audiences in Korea, including *D-War*, *Host*, and *IRIS*. Since *Crouching Tiger, Hidden Dragon* (2000), attempts at constructing a pan-Asian cinema have relied heavily on action movies, especially wuxia martial arts films. The "whole point is to popularize a new transnational genre" (Chan, 2005, p. 77). Not unexpectedly, given the reach of established transnational media such as Disney and Time Warner, the global leaders in box office revenue are action movies such as *Avatar* and superhero series including the *Avengers*, *Iron Man*, and *Batman*. In all, from East to West and North to South, action movies in many languages bring audiences to the theaters by the millions, generating billions in revenues for TNMCs.

The universal attraction of action movies confirms the substance of cultural hegemony – consent for dominant social relations can be constructed in media images attractive to diverse subordinate groups. Because a fully functioning hegemony allows an active role for viewers, the most successful film narratives acknowledge the contradictory social and cultural experiences of the working class majority, in all of its ethnic, gender, cultural, and experiential difference. Yet, action movies do not generally elicit thoughtful reflection or engagement with complex social problems. "Objects – cameras, listening devices, computers, cell phones, automobiles, trains, etc. – are given vitality in the film, but life is largely drained from the people" (Walsh, 2007).

Action movies consistently provide direct actions and fantasies that in part challenge the status quo in the abstract and villainy in general, providing entertaining stories that include opposition and resistance to unacceptable social conditions. The aesthetics of these films capture both social contradictions and political resistance as part of the rhythm and narrative of conformity to action codes and conventions. "Smack, bam, take that!" confirms the righteousness of certainty and clarity in dispatching the undesirable. Unfortunately, the themes and ideologies of transnational media content creatively rework legitimate challenges by diverse social groups and classes towards conclusions and relations that reinforce status quo social relations. In the contemporary world this means action films help imbue an ideology that corresponds to rationale for military interventions, economic inequality, and environmental destruction. Only the "techno glamour" of first-person shooter video games exceeds the level of visceral involvement in violence that action movies deal out (Keeton & Scheckner, 2013, p. 6). This hegemonic construction of action and ideology is not a US phenomenon. It is an international condition of TNMC production and distribution.

Movie producers reflect and address contemporary issues, even when telling stories about the past. Authors, scriptwriters, directors, and producers construct and distribute representations that present images and narratives according to their worldview and the expectations of their transnational media managers and funders. Superheroes flourish at times of adversity: world wars, atomic bomb scares, terrorist fears. Iron Man is the human drone of the twenty-first century. The Batman *Dark Knight* trilogy recounts responses to terrorist threats. An increasingly transnational capitalist world may mute previous nationalist stereotypes (or not), depending on the joint venture and target market. For example, Hong Kong-based MediaAsia, which has joint ventures with Fox Sports and China Film Group, and a distribution agreement with Disney's Miramax, cast a popular Chinese star as lead actor and changed the narrative of its third *Infernal Affairs* movie to "please [Chinese] authorities and audiences" (Davis & Yeh, 2008, p. 34). Pakistani and Indian operatives mute their nationalism in *Ek Tha Tiger*, thereby appealing to both national audiences with universal action romance themes. In the process of muting heavy nationalist overtones to expand market share across regions, TNMC producers privilege market relations and abstract law and order as the norm. Accordingly, representations of challenges to capitalist society and diverse state authorities are visualized and written as threatening, irrational, and dangerous to humanity itself. Working class interests and experiences that might suggest democratic critiques of inequality, poverty, disease, and other societal dysfunctions are subsumed by grotesque caricatures like Bane in *Batman*, stereotypical urban thugs as in *Elite Squad* (Brazil), vengeful drug gangs in *Taken* (France), or irrational terrorists in *Tube* and *IRIS* (Korea).

Transnational media action films popularize images, representations, and ideas that – when repeated and accepted – become part of a global common sense for how the world is and how it should be. The recurrent image of special forces and secret missions in action movies suggests that unaccountable government programs are legitimate. Or at least very cool. Irony, satire, and clever banter contribute to action movie claims that "only one, morally righteous side exists" – that of the government operative using extraordinary measures (Keeton & Scheckner, 2013, p. 56). The dominant themes of action thrillers, with all of their variations, promote and reinforce the lived experience of transnational capitalism. Action-adventures work to close down change by revealing social injustice, cultural bias, government incompetence and corruption in de-politicized narratives that champion the movie star character and debase democracy, the public, and humanity itself as ineffectual and unimportant. We may identify with the direct action of the hero or superhero, but thereby we deny our own power, our own efficacy in righting wrongs, in changing and making history. Robin Hood may rob from the rich and give to the poor, but his heroism depends on a continuing social inequality – the rich stay rich, the poor depend on heroic charity. In contrast, democracy and social equality demand an end to wealth inequality and dispose of the need for individual Robin Hoods as the Merry Band of humanity becomes the collective agency of social change.

Transnational media have influence by their sheer ubiquity and dominance over public communication and culture. Consumption of media and culture is certainly not a passive proposition, but the spectacle of action-adventure films invites willing participation and engagement by viewers. Visual effects and a variety of escapist fantasies package consistent ideological themes advancing cultural norms. Krrish (India), IRIS operatives (Korea), and Don (India), all of which are on a par with "the best mindless entertainment the American film industry can crank out" (Alter, 2011), join Wolverine, Batman, the Avengers, and other superheroes in acting out the desires of global audiences in spectacle-driven escapism. As we enter, witness, and respond to the world of the thriller, starring Bruce Willis, Matt Damon, Jet Li, Salman Khan, and other action actors, we consume narratives and ideologies favorable to capitalist social relations. In the rush of the action, we hurtle towards frames legitimizing hyper-individualism and political passivity dependent on heroic authority – not always fully conscious of the push and pull of the technical and narrative devices at work. The inequality of life, the tacit acceptance of authority, and our presumed powerlessness in the face of overwhelming structural practices are reinforced as common sense through the entertaining spectacle of direct action against evildoers.

Organizing Action for Cultural Hegemony

Once we have recovered our breath and our heart rates return to normal after viewing the action spectacle, we might reflect on some of the more obvious themes. Like other movie genres, action movies have "a concoction of elements – some a matter of plot, some mythological, some purely cinematic – that create for the audience a sense of ritual and a host of expectations" (Lichtenfeld, 2007, p. 1). Erik Lichtenfeld (2007) catalogs action tropes, including: loner hero, vengeance with violence, corrupt government officials, chase and crash scenes, neat weapons, one-liners, and a depraved enemy, among others. Lane Crothers (2010) lists happy endings, status quo norms, individual action, legitimate violence by the hero, and enhanced sexuality in female images as characteristic of action movies. David Wong (2013), on his popular blog, cracked.com, aggressively asserts that superhero action movies exhibit "five ugly lessons" paraphrased as: common folk are helpless, raw talent and wealth legitimate authority, due process interferes with justice, violence is good, and finally, the wealthy deserve our adulation, emulation, and support.

While each movie (whether based in India, Brazil, France, or elsewhere) may not exhibit every characteristic of TNMC-produced action movies, there appear to be five consistently dominant themes: (1) danger, evil, calamity is everywhere, including corruption within official institutions; (2) the average citizen is either uninterested or incapable of resisting villainous attacks; most officials are incompetent or incapable, as well; (3) individual heroes (and superheroes) must come to the rescue of all good people and our way of life; (4) violence can and must be used with impunity by heroes; civil rights, due process, and legal niceties get in the way of real justice; (5) wealth and power are legitimate and part of a good society; ultimately the status quo – minus the bad officials – is restored. Each TNMC action movie exhibits some of these elements.

Hopefully, the workings of the transnational media political economy and its cultural hegemony may be more fully recognized as each of the identified dominant themes are presented, with illustrations from selected popular action movies from around the world.

1. Danger and evil are everywhere; calamity is imminent

Society seems to be deteriorating in contemporary action movies, or at least under serious threat from corruption, invasion, crime lords, terrorists, crazed powerful villains, and even natural disasters. In Korea, there is terror in the subway (*Tube*, 2003), attacks from monsters (*Gwoemul* [*Host*], 2006; *D-War*, 2007), terror on the high seas (*Taepung* [*Typhoon*], 2005), and on the Korean peninsula from the North (*IRIS*, 2010). In Brazil, urban youth gangs threaten middle class security (*Tropa de Elite* [*Elite Squad*], 2007, 2011); in Japan, gangs brutalize townspeople (*Zatoichi* [*Swordsman*], 2003). In Paris, drug lords kidnap children (*Taken*, 2008); in the United States, drug syndicates are rampant (*2 Guns*, 2013). London thugs accost the elderly in *Harry Brown* (2011). Drugs, crime, and violence have become so normalized that some action movies introduce compassionate anti-heroes (*Ocean's*, 2001, 2004, 2007; *Don*, 2006, 2011; *Dabangg*, 2010, 2012), who act out fantasies of anti-social power. Meanwhile, assassins threaten kings, treacherous rebels threaten emperors in China (*Hero*, 2002; *Myth*, 2005). Evil Russians attack righteous Americans, while other villains threaten chaos (*X-Men: First Class*, 2011; *X-Men: Last Stand*, 2006). Screaming hordes of indistinct Somalians attack civilians and Marines in *Black Hawk Down* (2002). Increasingly, aliens threaten human life (*Green Lantern*, 2011; *Transformers*, 2011; *Avengers*, 2012; *Pacific Rim*, 2013; *Krrish 3*, 2013). The entire Batman series rests on various villains threatening Gotham, from Scarecrow's toxin to Bane's bomb threat and various Joker plots. Nazis and neo-Nazis lurk in the Swedish government (*Girl with the Dragon Tattoo*, 2009, 2011). In an ironic bow to political reality, even the US government and military are rife with corruption in action movies (*Shooter*, 2007; *Jack Reacher*, 2013). Even going to the circus can end in disaster with children caught in a fire (*Krrish*, 2006). Citizens and families must face unexpected calamity at any moment, from any quarter – from fires, floods, and quakes to corrupt government officials, urban gangs, terrorists, and aliens. *Variety* depicted the world of *Batman Returns* (1992) as "an utterly consistent universe full of nasty notions about societal deterioration, greed and other base impulses" (Staff, 1992). These few examples can be supplemented by scores of others produced in recent years. Action movies unite in their thematic mantra to all: Be afraid, be very afraid!

2. The average citizen is powerless

Mass democratic social movements have characterized the twenty-first century, from Bolivia, Argentina, Brazil, and Venezuela to Tunisia, Egypt, and Bahrain as well as Indonesia, Burma, and Thailand. One might think scriptwriters would find some inspiration from the heroic struggles for democracy around the world. Resistance against dictators, monarchs, and military juntas would seem rife with dramatic possibilities. Even looking from a narrow Hollywood lens, it would seem that someone could imagine an action movie of the people, by the people, for the people. Yet, whatever the national or cultural impulse, TNMC action movies avoid all considerations of citizen power. At best, citizen actions prove futile when faced with the powerful forces of corrupt officials, violent criminals, terrorists, and super villains. All but the hero die at the hands of terrorists or in the raging sea of *Typhoon*. Most often citizens flee or cower when attacked or confronted with unjust demands. Even trained personnel can't prevent corruption or defeat attackers: in *Shooter*, government officials tolerate a US senator guilty of war crimes, in *Machete* (2010), hard-working Mexican immigrants cannot prevent attacks from politicians and vigilante groups; *Captain America* (2011) has to issue orders to confused local police; Gotham's finest seem incapable of thwarting even the most obvious street crime.

Moreover, the average citizen is not only helpless, but expendable – count the number of background characters destroyed as collateral damage in fight scenes and battles, as in *Taken* or *Pacific Rim* – reminiscent of a Disney-like mass of Huns, savages, or helpless street urchins. Action movies counsel that citizens would best concentrate on family, home, and work, and otherwise stay out of the way. After saving the city or the planet, even the action hero, the purveyor of the narrative arc, returns home, where he belongs and wants to be (Crothers, 2010, p. 43). Politics and decisions about the world are for experts, officials, the elite. Women may be feisty (Catwoman, Raven, and Zoya in *Tiger*) but more often they are wife or love interest, such as Lois Lane (*Superman*), Mary Jane (*Spider-Man*), or the romantic beauties in Korean and Indian action movies, all with the necessarily coded cleavage so the audience does not misinterpret their narrative role.

Given the universal dedication to producing action movies for global consumption, TNMC content often depicts considerable diversity among citizens, reflecting and accepting a multicultural world – if for no other reason than cultural diversity improves market reach. Recent action movies feature identities and locals with considerable geographic and cultural diversity. Yash Raj Film's *Ek Tha Tiger* (2012) relates the action romance of an Indian and a Pakistani spy, with stock characters from both nations. Reliance filmed *Don 2* in Germany with German support. In the movie, Don is imprisoned in Malaysia with a wide range of ethnic characters. MediaAsia recruited popular Chinese actor Chen Daoming to assure better reception by Chinese audiences, while still featuring Taiwanese and Hong Kong actors and locales. Global cultural hegemony mixes in diverse cultures from a multitude of nations; but diversity disguises its lack of democracy. TNMCs implicitly recognize this in their orchestrated inclusion of the great unwashed as background and secondary characters in action movies, presenting a visual richness and narrative backdrop for the action of heroes – elites who really matter in the story and in capitalist life.

The ideological message bubbles up in every action-adventure: collective, cooperative organization and mass democratic action by citizens rarely appear in TNMC stories. Feeble attempts by unlicensed heroes to take action are quickly dispatched with violence and further defeat. Citizens acting in solidarity with integrity and for their own democratic interests may be broached in a few movies, as when villagers help Rahul escape capture in *Chennai Express*, a tenant hides an honest Indonesian cop from gangsters in *Raid: Redemption* (2011), or citizens and inmates refuse to blow up the other in *Batman: Dark Knight* (2008). Still, in these and other instances, citizen action is always limited and indeed quite symbolic of their limited capacity for affecting change or defending themselves. Moreover, the aftermath of any citizen action is always replete with the more powerful and spectacular actions of the heroes. Although rape and sexual abuse have prompted significant public outrage, including public protest and legislation, in *Girl with the Dragon Tattoo*, and its sequels, it takes the individual research skills and physical prowess of Salander (and her journalist ally) to mete out justice – the rest of society is mere bystander.

An important component of capitalist cultural leadership is the TNMC's ability to restrict or marginalize alternative explanations and proposals for more democratic social relations. Collective action for the common good is an anathema, a threat to capitalist cultural hegemony that seeks to separate all of humanity to its most diverse, atomized core, thereby preventing the coalescing of forces capable of democratic social change – which after all is based on participation and decision by the majority. If working classes and other subordinate groups can be dissuaded from considering their collective interests, if dominant messages and entertainment in general promote a belief that "there is no alternative," "there is nothing we can do," and "what I do won't matter," possibilities for a new cultural hegemony of democratic participation and citizen action are curtailed. Action-packed spectacles demonstrate the futility of citizen action. Either class and community solidarity do not appear, or attempts at cooperative efforts by average citizens are summarily dispatched with malice, silently or loudly communicating the unreasonableness of democratic agency by us, the viewers.

Yet, at the same time, effective capitalist cultural hegemony cannot ignore gross social inequality or the social contradictions of capitalism, so critiques must appear in popular entertainment. However, social critiques and political challenges must be creatively pushed aside as unfathomable or even detrimental. In *Batman: Dark Knight Rises* (2012), the possibility of a fair distribution of wealth – a concept appealing to many of the world's poor, including the American working class – becomes an evil act. Bane's crude enforcement of the expropriation of wealth includes forcibly dragging families from their homes and sham show trials sentencing them to exile or death. So much for challenging the 1%! Any consideration of a progressive income tax, democratic control and sharing of national wealth, or a humanitarian concern for the world's collective social well-being does not enter the narrative. Instead, a crazed madman physically attacks and humiliates nice well-off families as part of his plan to destroy Gotham: any discussion of a more democratic redistribution of wealth is detonated over the bay along with Bane's bomb, saving Gotham from villains and villainous thoughts once again.

3. Individual heroes must come to our rescue

We need protection by the lone, righteous hero. In an earlier action movie, *Blade Runner* (1982), a police officer saves humans from android replicants. Bruce Willis reprises lone heroic action in the *Die Hard* (1988, 1990, 1995, 2005, 2013) franchise, battling evil with extreme vengeance and catchy one-liner jokes. Contemporary action heroes such as Batman, Spider-Man, and members of S.H.I.E.L.D., the Avengers para-legal agency, rescue all. Batman stops individual muggings and the poisoning of Gotham. Local Indian cop Chulbul beats up robbers in *Dabangg* and then single-handedly destroys a corrupt criminal operation. Loner subway cop sacrifices himself to save his love and his Korean city in *Tube*. Only Bob Lee Swagger (*Shooter*) can stop a corrupt senator and his international criminal operations. When nature and terror threaten Korea in *Typhoon*, the actions of determined hero Sejong overcome both attacks. Amoral thugs, drug lords, and terrorists are so ruthless that citizen action is unthinkable – covert operations by the BOPE (Special Police Operations Battalion) squad in Brazil (*Elite Squad*) and the NSS in Korea must use extra-legal tactics and violence. Shen Cheng goes undercover as a gangster in *Infernal Affairs III* to clean up crime in the city. A blind swordsman rescues intimidated Japanese townspeople from extortion by Yakuza gangsters in *Zatoichi*. Without the X-Men the Cuban Missile Crisis would have ended in nuclear disaster and perhaps the end of the world. A Celestial Dragon superhero saves Los Angeles in Korea's *D-War*, because even the US Air Force, US Army, and LAPD's finest cannot withstand the monster, Bulcos. In India and Pakistan, citizens can count on Tiger and Zoya, good kung fu street fighters and spies, to protect them from foreign attacks. War veteran Harry Brown metes out vigilante justice to rid his neighborhood of anti-social thugs. Almost without exception, citizens and their official protectors are ineffectual against attacks from enemies, supernatural or human.

In Mumbai, Chicago, and Zurich no one can stop motorcycle gangs or catch master thieves until radically tough cop Dixit (and his sidekick) set traps, conduct elaborate street chases, and kill gang members in Yash Raj's *Dhoom* stories, distributed globally by the Chinese Dalia Wanda Media group. On occasion, individuals may provide logistical assistance to the hero, as in *Iron Man, Shooter, Once There Was a Tiger* – just as the Lone Ranger has Tonto, Batman has Robin and Arthur, Tiger has Gobi, and

Bruce Willis has a series of buddies in his action movies. In the end, though, the heroes stand alone to save the community and civilization.

Hyper-individualism as Action Requirement

In action-adventures, individualism wears a superhero suit. There should be a big "I" sewn on the front of their costumes. Superman lives in a "Fortress of Solitude." Tony Stark, the Iron Man, lives alone except for his secretary. Batman lives in his mansion and cave, with no one but Arthur. Peter Parker is friendless with no one to share his superpowers. The X-Men have each other, but they are isolated from humanity and other mutants. Wolverine is the extreme loner ... even working alone on his own movie franchise. The centrality of individualism in action movies serves capitalist cultural hegemony.

The myth of individualism has been prevalent in American culture for centuries, but the ways in which this myth has been translated into popular culture (and now appears increasingly in global culture) reveal much about changing social relations buffeted by pressures from transnational capitalism. In consumer societies, "individualism means individual character, or independent action as opposed to cooperation ... opposes interference of the state in the affairs of individuals as opposed to socialism or collectivism" (Adi, 2008, p. 4). The promotion of such politically infused individualism disguises social restrictions placed on individual citizens by corporate work norms and government regulations, framing individualism as choice in the consumer market. Black superheroes (e.g., *Blade*,1998, 2002, 2004) dramatically embody the individual disconnect from society. Individualism appears in popular discourse as the dramatic opposition between freedom and constraint, between individual and government or society. "The themes found in action movies usually deal with these two oppositions between individual and society ... the hero is depicted as a loner, an individual not compatible with society" or at least authority (Adi, 2008, p. 5). American heroic mythology "is the image of the cowboy riding alone" (Robertson, 1980, p. 6) or the superhero in the single-occupancy Batmobile. The embodiment of individualism must depend on one's own capability – the hero must confront evil, alone against a hostile world. In the twenty-first century, TNMC action heroes come in two varieties: shy billionaire or average man transformed by science fiction.

The singular loner appears in TNMC action movies everywhere, even in societies where individualism has not historically been prevalent, including Korea, India, Japan, and Indonesia. In the Indonesian hit *Raid*, an elite forces officer appears as a lone hero, subduing dozens of thugs in a violence-laden siege of an Indonesian slum building. Given the incredible Indonesian audience response (more than 250,000 viewers in a country with only 600 screens) and a planned three-film series, it appears that spectacles and themes of action movies uncover some not-so-latent desire for individual direct action against social ills in Indonesia. In *Raid*, Rama the hero cop confronts criminal gangs and official corruption and incompetence, two conditions of life for most Indonesians. Rama's effectiveness in dispatching with extreme prejudice both gangs and authority resonates with Indonesian audiences, effectively displacing collective social critiques of Indonesian society within the dramatic conflict between individual evildoers and individual heroes – no dialogue and no reflection on society and its unequal social relations appear within the spectacle of the raid.

We are stimulated. We are pleased. The hero wins. We win. We have vicariously experienced fantastic feelings of direct action and success. What can be more effective for cultural hegemony? TNMC action movies provide a simulacrum of righting wrong, evening the score, having control over the outcome of a 90-minute segment of fictional life. Along the way, we learn, we viscerally know, that we need individual heroes, individual elite leaders, to dispense justice and defend our way of life. Considerations about our way of life are secondary to the thrill of victory, the catharsis of spectacle, and the collective sharing of individualism in action. Audiences may actively construct their own cultural meanings from movie narratives, but from any perspective, action movies do not call us to action, but nurture us as politically passive audiences.

Reliance on the codes and conventions of action movies severely restricts possible alternative story lines. Writer and director Guillermo del Toro's stated intent to raise human empathy with his production of *Pacific Rim* falls short because he cannot escape the demands of the genre and its format. In del Toro's story, single pilots cannot handle the neural load of operating the sophisticated weapons needed to combat invading Kaijus. To defend humanity, individual pilots must "drift" their minds together. But "drifting" two pilot's psyches only tangentially makes del Toro's political point that "we're all together in the same robot [in life] … we can only be complete when we work together" (Russo, 2013). Unfortunately, for audiences used to clearer messages in action movies, the defense of humanity still ultimately depends on the heroic efforts of two collaborating pilots emotionally and psychically joined as one (one of whom is female). Not counting the incompetent and duplicitous government officials, the immense majority of humanity, represented by extras in the movie, does not work together. In *Pacific Rim*, most humans are at best spectators and at worst casualties in the epic battle against alien invasion. The individual hero appears here as a pair of combat pilots, technically doubling the power of one, but falling short of the more numerous teams of X-Men, Avengers, Justice League, and even the animated Teen Titans. Del Toro's attempt at freedom from elitism cannot overcome the conventional action movie formula of incredible spectacle in defense of status quo expectations. The idea that cooperative, collective action by determined and organized citizens is possible is more alien to action movies than the invaders that TNMCs imagine and design. For transnational capitalism organized citizen action is probably much scarier.

4. Hero violence is always good

To warrant self-reliance and individualism, the action hero must be deemed good and righteous. Hero violence is always warranted. Roger Ebert (2012) complained that *Raid* shows there is a "fanboy audience for [the] formula, in which special effects amp up the mayhem in senseless carnage" of "'hard-driving, butt-kicking, pulse-pounding, bone-crunching, skull-smashing, bloodcurdling' (in *Hollywood Reporter*) and 'largely a hand-to-hand, fist-to-face, foot-to-groin battle, with a few machetes and guns tossed in for good measure' (in *Variety*)." Yes, the film is about violence. Violence rules. But more importantly, only violence by the hero resolves. Perhaps that is the point: capitalist cultural hegemony asserts that power can legitimately mete out punishment in pursuit of its ends – and action heroes enthusiastically perform violent acts without regard to laws, civil rights, human rights, or on occasion even human decency. As the promo poster for *Jack Reacher* (2012) proclaims: "The law has limits. He does not."

While he was still part of the good mutant bunch in the X-Men universe, Erik shackles a female villain to a bed frame and chokes her until she reveals information he wants. Bob Lee Swagger tortures an FBI agent for information and closes the *Shooter* story with a brutal assassination of a US senator and military officer who had evaded justice through legal loopholes. Salander was victimized in *Girl with the Dragon Tattoo*, her abusers are wretched, so each extrajudicial act of violence is justified, indeed relished, by the narrative and its conditioned audience. In *Dabangg, Elite Squad, IRIS, Jack Reacher, Rowdy Rathore*, and many other action movies, hero

208 *Superheroes to the Rescue*

cops beat, torture, and kill whoever gets in the way of their mission. As cop hero Nascimento says in *Elite Squad*: "There are three kinds of policemen in Rio. Those who are corrupt, those who look the other way, and those who go to war" – a war that takes no prisoners and obeys no civilian laws. Civil rights just get in the way of cops doing the right thing and beating thugs – or in the case of the Special Police Operations Battalion in Brazil, beating corrupt government officials.

Rowdy Rathore beats up goons in India, hangs two from a bridge, and then cuts the rope so they fall to their death. Like James Bond in the United Kingdom, the National Security Service agents in *IRIS* have license to cold-blooded assassination and other extra-legal action in the pursuit of Korean security. In *Taken*, a former CIA agent kills many and assaults more in his relentless vigilante rescue of his daughter; casual violence is part of the script. The anti-hero in the *Don* movies poisons the food of dozens of guards and inmates alike in his prison escape. In *2 Guns*, a formulaic black–white buddy movie (Artz, 1998), bantering undercover operatives dispense sadistically random violence. *House of Flying Daggers* (2004) creatively employs visual effects and dramatic color imparting artistic appreciation for a spectacle of blood. Audiences at Cannes may have given *Flying Daggers* a standing ovation, but Zhang Yimou's masterful presentation of violence still anesthetizes and normalizes violence by authority. Good is stretched to its limits in *Watchman* (2009): hands are hacked, heads are split, and a child's body is torn apart, while insipid humor soothes the visceral reaction to justified hero violence. Using less graphic violence, Batman, Iron Man, Superman, Spider-Man, and the agents of S.H.I.E.L.D. dispense their own justice with little regard for the rule of law. In *Dark Knight*, Batman even beats up cops and then "dangles them out of the window of the skyscraper (where one frayed rope means five police officers plummet to their deaths)" (Wong, 2013).

Any hero or superhero is free to use violence with impunity in action movies. Vigilantes are deemed worthy of dispensing violence if they have had prior legitimate military service, as in *Gran Torino* (2000) and *Harry Brown* (2011). Due process and presumption of innocence are circumvented in narratives that alert the audience to the unquestionable guilt of the antagonists. Audiences witness murder, burglary, corruption, and other criminal acts in scenes that leave little doubt as to guilt or innocence. When the hero arrives to mete out justice, the niceties of due process, habeas corpus, trial by peers, and innocent until proven guilty in a court of law seem unnecessary – and would interfere with the action sequence. We are asked to believe fictional police integrity despite actual rampant police corruption – such as the systematic use of torture to frame innocent black men (e.g., Sergeant Burge in Chicago), corrupt gangster-police (e.g., the Ramparts unit in Los Angeles), and police abusers and murderers from the West to East Coast (e.g., Rodney King, Amadou Diallo) – and hundreds more cases of official police misconduct (Packman, 2011) common in most nations.

Action heroes can ignore laws and due process with the absolute certainty of guilt and evil of their targeted victims. Any question about civil rights would disrupt the certainty of action and the quick resolution of justice by individual heroes. Heroes may be brave, patriotic, loyal, and righteous, but heroes do not answer to, or ultimately respect, any law or institution. They all have their own laws that represent a higher moral authority – the authority of righteousness in direct action against evil. Indeed, in action movies violence by the hero is always the most responsible choice. How far is it from there to justifying collateral damage from bombing Iraqi or Syrian cities? Or condoning hundreds of civilian deaths from Obama's drone attacks on terrorist targets that are always known with "certainty"?

5. The status quo of wealth with power is best

Long before transnational capitalism, and before transnational media began producing movies for world audiences, action movies featured lone action heroes who defended law and order. Often those heroes were misunderstood underdogs, marginalized souls pulled from their everyday lives to perform heroic deeds in defense of polite society. Luke Skywalker faces down the Empire. The skinny Karate Kid overcomes bigger bullies. Little hobbits walk barefoot to Mount Doom. Irascible movie critic David Wong (2013) suggests that today's superheroes tend to depend on wealth and power, not courage and hard work. Wong asserts that the new Sherlock Holmes movies, James Bond, and even the *Fast and Furious* movies feature "invincible badasses who answer to no one," not the common underdog of yesteryear courageously rising to brave deeds. Even if Wong overstates his case, in any superhero movie there is no question who wins: the Avengers, X-Men, Superman, Iron Man, Krrish, the elite special teams of BOPE, IRIS, and the Pakistani or India special forces. "It's fun to watch the Hulk punch monsters out of the sky," says Wong (2013). In action movies, when the action is done threats and individual villains have been conquered and the status quo remains comfortably intact. In some cases, the entire story presumes wealth is evidence of goodness due to character traits and plot line – Batman, Ironman, and the Avengers have almost limitless wealth and unlimited resources. In the romance action *Chennai Express* Rahul's bravery and heart earn him marriage to his love and her rich family.

Within this mix, action movies recognize social problems, but effectively distort any potential social conflict over wealth, quality of life, the environment, or the human condition in general. Criticisms or fault lines in contemporary society are shaped into irrational disruptions to an otherwise pleasant social order. Even when the wretchedness, greed, and selfishness of civil society are exposed, the Justice League prefers the status quo to the Joker's anarchy.

Within these conventions, social criticisms shared or recognized by audiences are framed as outrageous attacks on normalcy. Only the worst of villains express the most sensible challenges: in Disney's *Lion King*, the most despicable characters, the hyenas, ask the simple question, "Why do we even need a king?," only to be slapped silly by Scar, the evil pretender to the throne. Disney's narrative ensures our cheering for the new king of the jungle. Even the grass won't grow until the rightful king returns. In *Dark Knight Rises*, Bane demeans a commonsensical proposal for social democracy and democratic economic relations with his ruthless expropriation of Gotham's elite. Sin and his sister survive brutality, starvation, and rape in *Typhoon*, but their justified embitterment at Korean social injustice becomes twisted into a plan for a nuclear cloud over the entire Korean peninsula. Social injustice disappears amid the greater threat of mass destruction by a crazed individual with a personal vendetta.

Disney, Reliance, CJ Entertainment, Warner Bros., and other TNMCs prevent any clear discourse about wealth inequality in the world. Although 30,000 children starve to death every day and some 870 million hungry people in the world live on less than $2 a day, Reliance/CJ Entertainment casts crazed mass murderer Sin and Warner Bros. selects arch-villain Bane as the spokespeople for social justice. Granted, any movie-goer can decode the messages to construct alternative, even oppositional meanings. But the encoding of action movies underlines the ideological preferences of TNMCs.

Accordingly, the narrative, dialogue, character development, and stylistic techniques express and improve the likelihood of hegemonically preferred interpretations. Scar, Bane, Loki, Joker, Sin, and various corrupt officials and drug lords are physically cast as menacing by familiar markers through costume, make-up, dialogue, lighting, music, narrative action, and other technical devices that combine to nurture character development and action according to the story plot. Audiences are cued to character traits and expectations, lending opportunities for surprise endings or plot twists, but seldom open enough in their coding to allow widespread interpretations at odds with the writers' and producers' intent. Superhero movies are so obvious in their depictions of evil, little comment is needed.

Action movies with human heroes rely more on the narrative: flashbacks provide background to character traits; vignettes allow characters to act out morals, values, inner feelings for audience review; settings, music, lighting, and other techniques promote preferred meanings; and finally, the conventionally expected conclusion of action movies rewards the good and punishes the bad. Heroes may injure a few bystanders in their pursuit of justice; villains threaten to take down entire cities or species. Almost anything the hero does in the pursuit of justice must be tolerated, if not emulated. Everything said or touched by the villain must be evil and mistrusted.

What better way to recognize social contradictions and inequality than forthrightly bring it into the narrative arc of the movie, then discredit and discard all challenges as the musings of madmen or villains? Whatever resistive meanings may be possible from audience alternatives, interpretations apparently are largely short-circuited. *Lion King* merchandizing profits come from sales of Simba, Nala, and all things Akunamata. The hyenas, not so much. It would be quite difficult for parents to bring home cuddly hyena stuffed animals for their children as a means to encourage anti-feudal, anti-monarchy perspectives and educate their youngsters about democracy and equality. Likewise, advertisers know to place products with the unquestioned stars of action movies – the James Bonds, Batmans, Dons, and the French Asterix superheroes – not the antagonist Goldfingers, Jokers, or other villains.

In the end, existing social structures and familiar institutions of power are legitimated and preferred. Challengers are extreme, dangerous, ultimately unsuccessful, and have no narrative or political legitimacy. Importantly, while challengers are volatile and protecting heroes are vibrantly active, domination itself is passive, neutral, almost invisible in its common sense. The aim of all policing, including hero-driven action, "is to maintain the status quo; and from such a perspective, the ends might often easily seem to justify the means … it can easily make sense to demonize and try to deter protests and protestors. Media images are crucial here. They help to make sure that protests are regarded (because represented) as scary, violent affairs, associated with criminality, irrationality, and danger. Such a representation [in news or action movies] is likely to help deter potential challenges in future and also to pre-empt and undermine future protests by strengthening the hold of a 'pre-digested' interpretation of protests as bad, criminal, and/or futile" that appears in all action movies (Bowman, 2012, p. 56).

The power and legitimacy behind the individual action hero is faceless, nameless, and culturally understood as insurmountable, while action heroes always defend the existing state power of diverse national capitalisms. One should not be distracted by the hero's rejection of authority. The hero rejects authority to defend authority. Batman operates outside society, battling to protect that society. Bourne exposes a secret spy unit so a "legitimate" spy unit can do its job. Harry Brown acts to re-establish the rule of law. Dixit, Rowdy, Cheng, and the entire elite squad BOPE break the law to save the law. In essence, legitimate rejection of authority is only available to the hero; for all others, laws, rules, and norms must be followed. TNMC action heroes are allowed leeway in their own actions, because in the end action heroes and movies defend the status quo.

The X-Men join together to save humanity (from villainy and communism). Batman and Superman work with and for law and order. Bob Lee Swagger may assassinate a US senator, but the attorney general and Congress are protected. The Special Police Operations Battalion glamorizes police brutality in defense of Brazilian wealth and power. Tiger works for India's Research and Analysis Wing (RAW), spying and killing in the name of patriotism; his romantic other does the same for Pakistan's Inter-Services Intelligence (ISS). Each *Infernal Affairs* installment explicitly supports the Hong Kong or Chinese governments. The same symbiotic relationship exists between heroes and institutions in action movies set in Korea, Indonesia, Australia, Scandinavia, Europe, and the rest of the world. Stuart Hall (1994) once put it bluntly: "the meaning of a cultural symbol [like action hero] is given in part by the social field into which it is incorporated, the practices with which it articulates and is made to resonate ... what counts is the class struggle in and over culture" (p. 449). In this case, the social field is the transnational expansion of capitalism with TNMCs producing and marketing action movies that provide the spectacle of battle on behalf of transnational capitalism personified through heroes and villains.

Action movies as a body of cultural work are a means for sustained symbolic media violence and seduction in defense of transnational capitalism, against democratic human-centered resistance on behalf of the working class, the global impoverished, and their allies. Action movies present protest, challenge, and political critique of capitalism and its governing norms and institutions as misguided, naïve, disruptive, and unworthy of consideration, shielding capitalist hegemony from critique and challenge.

These themes cannot be missed by audiences of any culture: (1) we must be afraid, danger is everywhere; (2) as citizens, we are powerless; (3) individual heroes are our best hope; (4) heroes must use violence; (5) wealth and power prove the legitimacy of the status quo. Of course, no one goes to the action movies to learn these tenets of capitalist cultural hegemony. We go for entertainment, for enjoyment, even a visceral release from daily life, with a "willing suspension of disbelief" as Samuel Coleridge once said about fiction. Yet, we absorb the repetitive messages and their cultural meanings. "Watching [an action] movie is not simply an escape from drudgery into dreaming: it is a place of desperate dreaming, of hope for transformation" (Walkerdine, 1990, p. 354). Within the narrative provided by TNMCs, transformation cannot occur; only individual adjustments are possible. In the end, action heroes rescue the whole rotten social order. As Emrakeb Assefa (2005) reports about Ethiopian viewers of American action movies, action heroes (who don't need to talk) are role models because they behave like "men," using guns and violence, controlling and changing their lives (pp. 84, 77). Again, this "transformation" is not of society, but within the youth's "conviction that taking action through the power of the gun and the mind can change one's life" (Assefa, 2005, p. 77) without any transformation of society or its gross inequality and injustice. S.H.I.E.L.D. is fictional; the alliance of transnational media corporations is real and powerful. This stands in contrast to the Arab Spring revolts of 2012, when Superman t-shirts were a common sight on youth acting with real political power that toppled governments.

Transnational Production

None of the movies cited here is primarily a local or national media product. Their global box office success is matched by the cross-cultural pollination of the script, the multinationalism of their actors and settings, and their interlocked transnational collaboration, production, and distribution. Reliance and DreamWorks produced the *Dabangg* (2010, 2012) films in Hindi, Tamil, and Telugu with subtitles for international release. Reliance and DreamWorks collaborated with German officials and studios and the Malaysian government in producing the *Don* (2006, 2011) movies. *Chennai Express* (2013) is the work of Red Chilies Entertainment, Discovery, Disney, and UTV, Disney's Indian division. *Rowdy Rathore* (2012) was produced by SLB Films which collaborates with UTV Disney. *Taken* (2008), with Liam Neeson, is a French production by Europa Corporation (which is part of Euro Media Group with studios in Germany, Italy, Belgium, and the Netherlands), Canal +, and five other studios, including distribution by 20th Century Fox. Europa has joint ventures in Japan with Sumitomo, Kadokama, and Asmik Ace as well as co-productions with China Fundamental Films. As a transnational joint venture, *Taken* grossed over $225 million globally. Distributor Finecut sold *IRIS* to Mega Film in mainland China and MFA + to German-speaking Europe, with a joint venture distribution in Japan with Kadokawa. The Marvel superhero movie franchises are as complex as the array of Marvel comicbook characters: currently Spider-Man lives at Columbia/Sony for three more movies, Iron Man and other Avengers belong to Viacom/Paramount (for at least five more movies), and Wolverine and the X-Men are the property of 20th Century Fox. In 2012, Disney purchased Marvel Entertainment for $4 billion along with the rights to its characters, pending the end of existing agreements. New franchises, and franchises continuing beyond existing deals, will likely be under the Disney/Marvel name.

As Chapter 4 disclosed, these studios are part of a transnational media network that has multiple joint ventures and co-productions around the world. For instance, the American–Australian *Wolverine* (2013) was a collaborative project of 20th Century Fox, Donner Films, Seed Productions, Hutch Parker Entertainment, Dune Entertainment, Ingenious Media, and Big Screen productions, filmed in Japan, Australia, and New Zealand with post-production by New Zealand's Weta Digital and Australian Rising Sun Pictures.

Most other widely distributed action movies also have transnational roots. Nordisk Film and Zodiak Media produced the 2009 Swedish thriller *Girl with the Dragon Tattoo*, which grossed $104 million with subtitled distribution. These two firms also co-produced the film versions of Stieg Larsson's other two novels, *The Girl Who Played with Fire* (2010) and *The Girl Who Kicks the Hornet's Nest* (2010). Nordisk is a division of the Danish transnational, the Egmont Group, which publishes magazines and books with Disney, Viacom, and Nickelodeon characters for all of Europe and China. Nordisk/Egmont has joint ventures with LionsGate Films, Summit, and DreamWorks/Reliance. Zodiak Media has joint ventures in the United States (*Secret Millionaire*), Brazil (*Cante se Puder*), France (*Totally Spies!*), the Middle East and Australia/Asia (*Koffee with Karan*), Scandinavia, and Southern Europe. MGM, Sony/Colombia, and Zodiak's Yellow Bird Studios co-produced and distributed the English-version remake of *Girl with the Dragon Tattoo*, grossing another $262 million. *Elite Squad* (2007, 2011) was originally produced by an independent Brazilian studio and distributed by Comcast's NBC Universal and IFC. Following *Elite*'s domestic success, the transnational O Globo produced the second movie and purchased the rights for a television series. *Hero* (2002), the first officially sanctioned action movie in China, featured a pan-Asian cast and crew, US cinematographers, and Japanese costume designers; *Hero* was financed by Edko Hong Kong and the Chinese government, and internationally distributed by Disney's Miramax. Indonesian-based XYZ Films' *Raid: Redemption* (2011) was distributed by Sony, which purchased the rights to a US version and has pre-bought US, Latin American, and Spanish rights to the sequel, *Raid: Retaliation*. Alliance/Momentum has pre-bought for the United Kingdom and Canada; Koch Media has acquired the film for German-speaking territories; Korea Screen has pre-bought Korea; and HGC has pre-bought China. Deals for other major territories are also in negotiations. Additional Korean, Indian, Chinese, Indonesia, South African, and other action moviemakers regularly and increasingly collaborate with TNMCs, sharing scripts, investments, costs, and marketing strategies, as well as profits. Their shared economic and political perspective inspired (and partially funded) by a global capitalist leadership further encourages such transnational collaboration.

Action for Cultural Hegemony

Action movies are commodities produced for profit by transnational media corporations. As such, action movies seek to maximize audiences by nurturing and feeding their entertainment needs and desires, while simultaneously building consent for the world according to transnational capitalism. In addition to the five apparent narrative themes described above, TNMCs further advance transnational capitalism (and their own profits) by inviting participation by other transnational producers in the form of product placement, joint advertising campaigns, and product tie-ins. Movie-goers are familiar with *Batman*, *X-Men*, and *Avengers* product placements of Mountain Dew, Dr. Pepper, NASCAR, Visa, Harley-Davidson, Acura (the official car of S.H.I.E.L.D.), lunchmeats, perfume, hotels, and other products. The United Kingdom's Eon Productions, the studio behind James Bond movies, are well known for maximizing product placement. In *Die Another Day*, Revlon, Samsonite, Kodak, Omega, and British Airways were but a few of the placements. *Skyfall*, the 2012 Bond film, collected over $45 million in product placement funds. Audi was the car of choice and investor of record for the *Transporter* films (2002, 2005, 2008), a French action movie series produced by Europa, Canal+, and distributed by 20th Century Fox. *Green Lantern* used Mattel's Hot Wheels; the *Transformers* featured GM; *Shooter* found its way using Google; Sony helped Bond in *Casino Royale*; and the *I, Robot* hero wore Converse sneakers – all with ample funding from the brand producers. TNMCs are diverse in production and product placement: *Don 2*, for example, struck promotional deals with Google and YouTube to market the film; coordinated a campaign and product placement with McDonald's, collaborated on an on-line game with Sony and Android, published a comic book, and released a *Don* action figure toy line. Disney's UTV and SLB films marketed *Rowdy Rathore* in partnership with YouTube, UTV's Red FM radio, Safari Cinemas, and Zee TV. Clothing from Dollar, an Indian retailer, was featured prominently in the film. Korean films (and TV dramas) have prominently featured Apple, Samsung, Toshiba, and Mini Cooper, among other products. The list is long and growing: Sony's 2007 *Spider-Man* had nine product sponsors, *Iron Man 2* had eleven with more than $100 million in placement fees and marketing tie-ins (Hammp, 2010). In China, *Iron Man 3* (2013) included four extra minutes to include scenes with Tony Stark getting nourishment from Gu Li Duo, a Chinese milk drink (Chilton, 2013). Beyond the high cost of production, the need to share risk and benefit, and the ingratiation of advertising into all things cultural, the inclusion of brand names in action movies underscores the intimate relations between media and other commodities. A few superheroes like Batman have become both icon and profitable commodity beyond their movie presence: comics, video games, apparel, television, and metaphor for justice and vigilance: the perfect cultural representative for twenty-first century capitalism. Additionally, consumer goods symbolically linked to action heroes solidify the extreme individualism of the genre and allows viewers to vicariously identify with their hero, at least through consumption (Fiske, 1989; Lowenthal, 1979). Neither the marketing strategy nor the script is unintended: at Disney/Yash Raj Films, "We are very clear about every character in every script and what's required of the actors," says *Dhoom* producer Aditya Chopra, and Yash Raj briefs the actors "about the look and attitude" they need to cultivate so viewers will get the story and its meaning (Jha, 2005).

From Spectacle to Consent

While production, distribution, audiences, and profits from action movies and film in general remain dominated by US-based transnationals, the cultural impact cannot be measured solely by gross revenue. Action movies make up the largest portion of movie attendance in most countries. In India, for example, ticket prices are much lower so gross film income is much less, while audiences also have less disposable income for cinema and other culture industry commodities. Yet, action movies as culture and entertainment in India attract the largest audiences. Action movies also attract the largest audiences in Korea, Latin America, Europe, Scandinavia, and North America. And action movies are no longer just the purview of Hollywood-based producers. For instance, *Dabangg 2* opened to record weekend audiences in the United Arab Emirates, United Kingdom, Australia, South Africa, and even Mauritius and Fiji. The French-joint venture *Taken* had an even more remarkable reception around the world. Action movies no longer can be termed American or even Western, because the genre has been adopted and adapted by TNMCs globally.

The best action movies have ample spectacle, from the *Transformers* and *Batman* movies to *Sherlock Holmes, Rowdy Rathore, Dhoom*, and *Typhoon*. *Avengers* had more than 2,200 visual effects (Seymour, 2012). Action sequences (amplified with special effects) raise our adrenaline, lower our reflection, provide intense visceral stimulation, and considerable entertainment. Action movies make few demands on the audience, but deliver significant pleasure and titillation. *Taken* is "largely a brainless exercise" (Rotten Tomatoes, 2010). Action movies like *Dabangg* "camouflage a deficiency of substance with an abundance" of style and action (Malani, 2010), while *Avengers* may come off as "escapism of a sophisticated order" (Chang, 2012). Either way, in general, action movies create a fantastical "vision of a different social order while at the same time denying [any] resistance and containing it within the same fantasy" (Marchetti, 1989, p. 184).

Action movies depend on "unresolved contradictions" requiring individual hero direct action and allowing the viewer "to find within them structural similarities to his or her own social relations and identity" (Fiske,

1986, p. 392). Audiences live within the contradictions of capitalism, experiencing unfairness, inequality, duplicity, and even abuse by officials and supervisors. Quick, decisive, and successful action by an uncomplicated powerful hero against representatives of injustice obviously brings much vicarious enjoyment, as verified by the huge audiences for action movies. Numbing the mind, exciting the senses, and resolving social discontent with fictional action, action movies please audiences and make profits for TNMCs.

Although narrative is secondary to spectacle, action movies are perfect communication vehicles for carrying cultural hegemony. In action movies, spectacle is "coupled with the contradictory nature of plots and characters" (Marchetti, 1989, p. 197), some of whom are anti-heroes or morally ambiguous. Transnational action movies frequently include multi-racial, multi-ethnic, and alien buddies, and on occasion even provide more action roles for women. Still, although open to many different interpretations, action movies collectively advance transnational capitalism and its social relations with the themes categorized above. Importantly for capitalist global cultural hegemony, these themes are prevalent in TNMC action movies in any language from any nation. Action movies are transnationally produced and distributed by TNMCs to billions of citizens around the world – repetitively disseminating the same enjoyable and culturally hegemonic messages of individual self-interest, the necessity of official violence, and the legitimacy of the status quo.

References

Adi, I R. (2008). Remythologizing individualism in American action movies. *Humaniora, 20*(1), 1–10.

Alter, E. (2011, December 27). Film review: Don 2. *Film Journal International.* Retrieved March 25, 2014, from http://www.filmjournal.com/filmjournal/content_display/reviews/specialty-releases/e3i7e5723ab9161df8db72072902b2ade1c

Artz, L. (1998). Hegemony in black and white: Interracial buddy movies and the new racism. In Y. Kamalipour & T. Carilli (Eds.), *Multicultural perspectives in the media* (pp. 67–78). Albany, NY: SUNY Press.

Assefa, E. (2005). An investigation into the popularity of American action movies shown in informal video houses in Addis Ababa, Ethiopia. Manuscript. *Rhodes University Eprints.* Retrieved from http://contentpro.seals.ac.za/iii/cpro/app?id=7836229085844392&itemId=1002871&lang=eng&service=blob&suite=def

Bowman, P. (2012). *Culture and the media.* New York: Palgrave Macmillan.

Cantor, P. A. (2013, Summer). The apocalyptic strain in popular culture: The American nightmare becomes the American dream. *Hedgehog Review, 15*(2), 23–32.

Chan, C. S. (2005). The fighting condition in Hong Kong cinema: Local icons and cultural antidotes for the global popular. In M. Morris, S. I. Li, & C. S. Ching-Kiu (Eds.), *Hong Kong connections: Transnational imagination in action cinema* (pp. 63–80). Durham, NC: Duke University Press.

Chang, J. (2012, April 19). Review: "Marvel's the Avengers." *Variety*. Retrieved October 3, 2013, from http://www.telegraph.co.uk/culture/film/film-news/10041924/Chinas-Iron-Man-3-milks-its-product-placement.html

Chilton, M. (2013, May 7). Iron Man 3 milks its product placement. *Telegraph*. Retrieved October 3, 2013, from http://www.telegraph.co.uk/culture/film/film-news/10041924/Chinas-Iron-Man-3-milks-its-product-placement.html

Crothers, L. (2010). *Globalization and American popular culture*. 2nd edn. Lanham, MD: Rowman & Littlefield.

Davis, D. W., & Yeh, E. Y. (2008). *East Asian screen industries*. London: British Film Institute.

Ebert, R. (2012, March 21). Review: The Raid: Redemption. *Roger Ebert.com*. Retrieved from http://www.rogerebert.com/reviews/the-raid-redemption-2012

Fiske, J. (1986). Television: Polysemy and popularity. *Critical Studies in Mass Communication 3*(4), 391–408.

Fiske, J. (1989). *Understanding popular culture*. London: Unwin Hyman.

Hall, S. (1994). Notes on deconstructing "the popular." In J. Storey (Ed.), *Cultural theory and popular culture: A reader* (pp. 442–453). London: Harvester Wheatsheaf.

Hammp, A. (2010, April 19). "Iron Man 2" sparks $100 million marketing bonanza. *Advertising Age*. Retrieved from http://adage.com/article/madisonvine-news/iron-man-2-sparks-100m-marketing-bonanza/143349/

Jha, S. K. (2005, February 26). Dhoom 2 goes on the floor. *Rediff India Abroad*. Retrieved from http://www.rediff.com/entertai/2005/sep/26dhoom.htm

Jhally, S. (Producer). (1994). *The killing screens: Media and the culture of violence.* [Transcript]. Retrieved from http://www.mediaed.org/assets/products/111/transcript_111.pdf

Keeton, P., & Scheckner, P. (2013). *American war cinema and media since Vietnam*. New York: Palgrave Macmillan.

Lichtenfeld, E. (2007). *Action speaks louder: Violence, spectacle, and the American action movie*. Middletown, CN: Wesleyan University Press.

Lowenthal, L. (1979). Biographies in popular magazines. In P. F. Lazarsfeld & F. Stanton (Eds.), *Radio research, 1942–1943* (pp. 507–520). (Originally published 1943). New York: Arno Press.

Malani, G. (2010, September 10). Dabangg: Movie review. *Economic Times/India Times*. Retrieved from http://articles.economictimes.indiatimes.com/2010-09-10/news/27619510_1_salman-khan-dabangg-chulbul-pandey

Marchetti, G. (1989). Action-adventure as ideology. In I. Angus & S. Jhally (Eds.), *Cultural politics in contemporary America* (pp. 182–197). New York: Routledge.

Neale, S. (2000). *Genre and Hollywood: Melodrama and the woman's film.* Oxford: Psychology Press/Taylor & Francis.

Packman, D. (2011, April 5). 2010 NPMSRP police misconduct statistical report – draft. The Cato Institute. Retrieved from http://www.policemisconduct. net/2010-npmsrp-police-misconduct-statistical-report/#_Summary

Purse, L. (2011). *Contemporary action cinema.* Edinburgh: Edinburgh University Press.

Robertson, J. (1980). *American myth, American reality.* New York: Hill & Wang.

Rotten Tomatoes. (2010). Taken (2009). Movie review. Retrieved from http://www. rottentomatoes.com/m/taken/

Russo, T. (2013, July 6). "Pacific Rim" is latest heartfelt project from Del Toro. *Boston Globe.* Retrieved from http://www.bostonglobe.com/arts/ movies/2013/07/06/pacific-rim-latest-heartfelt-project-from-guillermo-del-toro/aTU5X0wLpNaUe1GpbHqDUO/story.html

Seymour, M. (2012, May 6). VFX roll call for The Avengers (updated). *FX Guide.* Retrieved from http://www.fxguide.com/featured/vfx-roll-call-for-the-avengers/

Staff. (1992, June 15). Review: "Batman Returns." *Variety.* Retrieved from http:// variety.com/1992/film/reviews/batman-returns-1200430018/

Walkerdine, V. (1990). *Schoolgirl fictions.* London: Verso.

Walsh, D. (2007, August 24). The Bourne Ultimatum – Action-packed, and it pays the price. *World Socialist Web Site.* Retrieved from http://www.wsws.org/en/ articles/2007/08/bour-a24.html?view=print

Wong, D. (2013). The 5 ugly lessons hiding in every superhero movie. *David Wong's End Times Report.* Retrieved from http://www.cracked.com/blog/the-5-ugly-lessons-hiding-in-every-superhero-movie/

Further Reading

Hassler-Forest, D. (2012). *Capitalist super-heroes: Caped crusaders in the neoliberal age.* Alresford, UK: John Hunt Publishing.

Marchetti, G. (1989). Action-adventure as ideology. In I. Angus & S. Jhally (Eds.), *Cultural politics in contemporary America* (pp. 182–197). New York: Routledge.

8

Media, Democracy, and Political Power

"Don't watch TV, make TV!" proclaims the banner on the front of Catia Television's studio in central Caracas, Venezuela. The slogan expresses, even demands, the essence of media and democracy. Communication isn't just about listening or watching. Communication means citizens have voice. And not just voice, but access to media that can broadcast and disseminate messages to the entire society. Democracy in media includes the right to receive information, the right to expression, and the right to distribute messages through all available media. As should be clear from previous chapters, the structure of media ownership "denies individuals from the lower strata the right to be heard and, more generally, denies the public the right to information pluralism that is required for democracy to function (Lupien, 2013, p. 238). In fact, a core assumption of radical democracy is that commercial media are, "despite their claims of neutrality, powerful social actors linked to the upper classes, social elites, or powerful corporations ... characterizations [that] call for the democratization of access and voice in the media sphere, for reforms to the media structure, or even for Gramscian counter-hegemonic strategies" of mass mobilization and societal reorganization (Kitzberger, 2010, p. 8). Myriad examples of "moments of rupture" in social relations and media practices from Chile, Portugal, Cape Verde, Peru, Bolivia, Nicaragua, Ecuador, Venezuela, and other countries in transition indicate that media technology may indeed advance democratic communication when given a radical resolution of social and political contradictions arising from transnational capitalism. Evidence demonstrates that a more democratic political economy of the media, arising within a politically transforming social order, allows space for public media access, social interaction, and participatory, democratic communication. But there is no change without power. Wherever working class organizations or indigenous communities have captured their right to communication, they have simultaneously grasped political power to one degree or another. The old adage of speaking truth to power has little purchase in history. Revolutions no longer speak truth to power; they speak the power of a new truth. "Don't witness history … Make history!" might be the watchword for a more politically active transnational working class desiring democratic decision-making in society and full access and control over its own media.

The relationship between technology and communication is political and economic. It is only through the expropriation of technology by commercial interests that media have been developed as a means of distribution rather than communication. The producers of early radio sets in the United States built only receivers, reducing their production costs and relegating millions to a lifetime of radio listeners. With commercial technology and commercial licensing, the public lost its right to be radio speakers (Brecht, 1983; McChesney, 1995). With high entry and production costs, cinema and television have been off limits to the public from the start. Video recorders and computer technology offer some opportunity for democratizing production, but distribution channels remain "mediated" by transnational media corporation (TNMC) ownership of satellites, cable, and Internet servers.

Transnational media corporations make what millions watch. We live in a world of Pokémon, Shakira, Pink, the Avengers, the Winx Club, WWE, la fea Betty, and dancing cats on YouTube. A world of celebrity, entertainment spectacles, and special effects brutality. The political economy of capitalist transnational entertainment media seamlessly communicates the cultural hegemony of consumerism and individualism. The cultural hegemony of entertainment media helps legitimate the international division of cultural labor. In this dystopic world, each consumer and each producer chooses jobs and TV programs from a menu printed by TNMCs. The cultural hegemony of consumerism becomes the practice and ideology through which transnational capitalism reproduces itself (Sklair, 2001, p. 6). The standardization of diverse local expressions of individualism, consumerism, and spectacular entertainment encourages the acceptance of institutional authority and market values. To the extent that TNMC images and narratives conform to domestic icons, localized scenes, and the diverse languages and cultures of local audiences, cultural hegemony may become internalized as the common sense of everyday life and its social relations. Global consumer culture results from TNMC efforts to "shape desires and create needs, opening up new areas for capital accumulation" (Derné, 2008, p. 25). The more local media align with TNMCs and "aim for the mass market ... the more likely they are to collaborate with the powers that be" (Bourdieu, 1998, p. 62). The fewer opportunities for democratic media practices, the more likely TNMC entertainment will flourish. Given the global blanketing of cultural expression with TNMC mass entertainment offerings, space for creative voices of citizens expressing more democratic humanist narratives is severely limited. The extent of public media access and control depends on which social relations, political conditions, and economic realities frame media practices.

Most efforts at media reform are naïve. All are limited. Indeed, media reform that accommodates market dictates and accepts neoliberal parameters for democracy is doomed to fail. In Eastern Europe, transnational media and local partners assured the dominance of market relations in Poland, while transnational political managers undercut the Solidarity movement's vision for a "Self-Governing Commonwealth" (Jakubowicz, 2007, pp. 93–96) and reinforced the disintegration of public media and the disenfranchisement of the working classes in the Baltic states, Czechoslovakia, Romania, and all of central Europe (Kalb, 2011). The new capitalist relations of power set the parameters for media operations, rejecting direct democracy in every Eastern European nation (Jakubowicz, 2007, pp. 143–152). The ferment of democracy was stifled with the entrance of transnational neoliberalism. Post-apartheid media reform in South Africa was trumpeted as a key contributor to democratization in the region. Yet, the International Monetary Fund (IMF) and World Bank structural adjustment programs emphasized deregulation and the privatization of public media, which were in line with the national political and economic objectives of the South African capitalist class in alliance with TNMCs (Ndlela, 2007, p. 72). Media history in most Latin American countries confirms that capitalist interests abetted by government policies and actions continually prevent public access to media (Fox, 1988; Fox & Waisbord, 2002). Media "reform" in Turkey (Yesil, 2013; Algan, 2003), India (Derné, 2008; Thussu, 2005), the Philippines (Coronel, 2001), and China (Zhao, 2003, 2008) follows similar trajectories. Shangyuan Wu (2010) finds that the authoritarian Singaporean government and the capitalist class it protects prevent public media from "generating debate on a wide range of issues" because the "desire for economic growth and its deep faith in global capitalism" hinders democratic media reform and advances media content which "voluntarily acts as a conduit" for transnational capitalism (pp. 114–117). Everywhere TNMCs operate, democracy and public media access are contained (and diminished) within media privatization regimes.

In light of the above assessments of media reform around the world, the three components of media introduced in Chapter 3 seem exceedingly central and interrelated: media ownership and control → production practices and programming content → social role of media. Each of these ingredients can be applied descriptively to any media institution, form, or system. These dimensions of media are dialectically interrelated: fundamental changes in media institutions and practices cannot be expected to be separate and apart from changes in the social order; changes in media roughly coincide with significant changes in social relations and cultural norms. Conversely, ownership and control of media, normative media practices, and the conservatizing social role of entertainment media are unlikely to change independent of dramatic political events leading to disruptions in the status quo.

Pairing the insights from political economy and cultural hegemony better explains entertainment media content than the oft-overstated existence of cultural proximity, contraflow, and resistant media hybrids. The extended examples of political economy and cultural hegemony appearing in action movies are replicated in animation, telenovelas, and other entertainment genres, each of which has similar transnational media production practices echoing transnational capitalist cultural hegemony. The production norms and practices of TNMCs have been standardized across the media entertainment industry. Conventions of broadcasting and cinema seem natural to audiences almost everywhere. Public access to media disappears; media spectacles drown out concerns for human solidarity, democracy, and a sustainable planet. Meanwhile, public "service" media are largely relegated to providing nature documentaries and educational programming.

TNMC leadership appears as undisputed in technology, marketing, profits, and the dominance of English – demonstrated not just in local studios and lines of local actors interviewing for jobs as extras, but also in the acceptance of TNMC prestige by the IMF, the International Telecommunications Union, the United Nations, and the European Union. As part of the transnational fraction of global capitalism, TNMC managers, technicians, and shareholders "control the levers of global policymaking" and media production (Robinson, 2004, p. 48). Transnational media power is hegemonic. TNMC entertainment "absorbs" words, images, and cultures in developing new hybrid forms as local media and culture acquire new transnational images and narratives (Gramsci, 1971; Ives, 2004, p. 88). Transnational entertainment media nurture local cultures, mixing the familiar with the exotic, the national with the cosmopolitan, in a soothing blend of consumer self-interest and market authority.

We shop at their stores. We vote for their parties. We watch TV. Life goes on, for now. In the short term, the overproduction of everything, including media products, along with the continued economic dispossession of millions of workers (who cannot afford enough consumer goods to maintain capitalist growth) push social contradictions towards crisis and resistance. On the verge of global economic and environmental catastrophe, the need for democratic media and working class access is critical.

Another media is necessary. Another media is possible. Another media is coming. But new, democratic media with widespread citizen participation in the creation and distribution of messages requires a different set of social relations. Media produced by and for advertising and transnational corporations will willingly accept our creative ideas and stories as fodder for consumerist entertainment – to encourage "the vast majority of passive spectators" to remain disinterested in political affairs (Herrera Miller & Ramos Martín, 2013, p. 11). TNMCs cannot tolerate social justice impulses, thoughtful reflection, or alternative social relations. TNMCs will not distribute narratives or cultural practices that reject the consumer market. For a democratic, interactive, participatory media with public access for all, another world is necessary – a world based on cooperation, collaboration, solidarity, cultural diversity, and a sustainable economy that ends capitalist growth. As teams of community journalists at Catia TV insist, we need to make our own media.

Ultimately, any media transformation requires a political economy in line with democratic public access and social ownership. No one owns the rainbow. No one has title to the oceans. No one owns the air. And, no one owns the airwaves – even according to capitalist-friendly US media regulations established by the Federal Communications Commission in 1934. Preferential licensing of commercial media curtails public access. To avoid commercial influence and government dominance, democratic media must be socially owned by communities that create their own communication.

The structure and practices of democratic media (i.e., ownership → production practices → social use) must correspond to democratic, participatory production, including democratic decision-making, cultural diversity of producers, open access to technology, training, and a maximum distribution of content with an emphasis on social development. With socially owned media, media content can be produced by citizens, young and old, men, women, ethnic majority, minority, and indigenous. Media will then meet community needs, socializing, educating, entertaining, and informing citizens with content enhancing and sharing humanity's diversity with humor, drama, and meaning. We can move beyond the debasing and humiliating drivel that TNMCs so often slough off today.

What do we lose without self-important pundits, fake wrestlers, real housewives, and demeaning advertisements on TNMC network television? What do we miss if bloody news, misogynistic music, and primal violence of men fighting in cages recede into an embarrassing media history? What would democratic media look like? What media would be made by ethnic "lumpen" looking for a "lump of bread and bottle of rum," as the working class is described by Venezuelan opposition paper *El Nacional* (as cited in Lupien, 2013, p. 231)? What will humanity do if it has access to media production and distribution? What will we say? The Bolivarian socialist project in contemporary Venezuela alerts us to one possibility.

Venezuela and Twenty-First Century Socialism: A Model for Democratic Media

Change is disruptive. Change can be scary. Ariel Dorfman (1983) tells of a poor Chilean woman who confronted him after the democratic election of Salvador Allende in 1970. She was a reader of fotonovelas, romantic love stories in picture book form. Dorfman and other media workers were publicly crusading against comics, soap operas, westerns, love songs, violent films, and other commercial entertainment like the fotonovelas. The woman was solemn and tender as she said, "Don't do that to us, compañero. Don't take my dreams away." Dorfman met the woman again a few years later, at the inauguration of a new community center. She came up to him again and announced that he was right; she didn't read "trash" anymore. She added, "Now, compañero, we are dreaming reality." She was writing her own stories. Dorfman explains the transformation:

> She had experienced, in those years, something truly different. She had outdistanced her old self, and was no longer entertained by those images,

which had been her own true love. She could now oppose her experiences of liberation, and that of her community, to the fraudulent visions of the media, run and owned by the same people who ran and owned Chile's economy and political system. She no longer perceived those media experiences as real, as eternal, as natural. (Dorfman, 1983, p. 5)

What had happened to that woman is what happens when "a people attempts to liquidate centuries' worth of economic and social injustice, when they begin to gain a sense of their dignity … what really inspires them is an alternative vision of humanity, a different way of feeling and thinking and projecting and loving and keeping faith. And a different future" (Dorfman, 1983, p. 5). Chile had nationalized its natural resources and minerals, reallocated land to those who till it, allowed workers to participate in the management of factories, and democratized institutions. But that was not enough. Simultaneously, a more difficult task was necessary: democratizing the media.

That woman from the slums was being shoved, poked, awakened. And while she was in that turbulent, searching stage, what she needed was a parallel interpretation at all levels of what her situation, of what the world, was … channels for expressing the joys, the doubts, the anxieties that come when people who were previously powerless begin to have some say in their existence. What she needed was a new language. (Dorfman, 1983, p. 5)

I witnessed similar awakenings in Nicaragua in the 1980s, when hundreds of workers, especially youth, were afforded the opportunity to broadcast on CORADEP (Corporación de Radio Difusión del Pueblo, the People's Radio Broadcasting Corporation, a network of 21 public, community radio stations) (Artz, 1993). I also caught glimpses of the much more profound social transformation in Venezuela, based on citizen participation, social ownership, and community media production and broadcast (Artz, 2012). Viewers and readers of TNMC news reports do not know about Venezuela. We only see and hear distortions of the Bolivarian movement, especially vitriolic attacks on the past president, Hugo Chávez. The US and European media uniformly misinform – from the *New York Times* and the *Guardian* to *Le Monde* and *El Pais*, from CNN and the BBC to Fox and Deutsch Welle. Short of visiting Venezuela, one must search websites like venezuelanalysis. com; journals such as *Latin American Perspectives, NACLA Reporter,* or *Green Left Weekly;* or discover insightful books (Ellner, 2010; Fernandez, 2010; Martinez, Fox, & Farrell, 2010; Wilpert, 2007) to find more accurate reports.

The dramatic democratic transformations taking place in Venezuela are largely hidden from the North behind clumsily constructed misrepresentations from TNMC news.

Community media in Venezuela represent one profound change indicative of a larger social process, offering a model for democratic, participatory communication where citizens can represent themselves. New community ownership structures, production practices, and programming content in media in Venezuela roughly parallel changing social relations in the country. A broad national debate preceded a referendum on a new constitution in 1999, which was ratified by 70% of the voters. The constitution explicitly makes a commitment to participatory democracy in all spheres of social activity, including the economy and the media. Participation is a key ingredient in the Bolivarian process, because "only participatory democracy – the people's ongoing, daily involvement in the political and economic affairs of the country – assures democracy" (August, 2013, p. 4). Participatory democracy strengthens citizen access, encouraging direct action and decision-making, frequent elections and popular referenda, opening politics to working classes, indigenous, and other majority sectors of the society. Mass mobilizations and self-organization are key components of participatory, radical democracy (Ellner, 2010). With government support and citizen participation, public educational and social programs were initiated beginning in 2000. Mission Robinson and Mission Rivas provide community-based secondary and continuing education, Barrio Adentro Mission brings health clinics to neighborhoods, Mission Mercal opens community grocery stores with subsidized food, and other programs in education, health, and culture across the country with "real citizen participation in the organization of communities to assure benefits, not as a gift, but as a right" of citizens (Parra, 2009).

No social missions were established for communication, but Articles 57 and 58 of the 1999 Constitution establish the right to "true and objective information" and the right of all citizens "to freely express their thoughts, ideas, or opinions" and to have access to "any means of communication and dissemination." Article 62 states that "the participation of the people in the formation, execution and control of public matters is the means necessary to accomplish the protagonism [social agency; the active subject of history is the "protagonist"] that will guarantee their complete development, both as individuals and collectively." The implementation of these rights was not dictated by the government, but was led by organized community groups around the country, as neighborhood committees and communal councils initiated their own radio and television broadcasts with popular support and citizen participation. Community media are popularizing a new cultural hegemony – offering a working class leadership that delivers economic security, political representation, and a creatively radical culture of participation.

This amorphous cultural hegemony has emerged based on socialist impulses articulated by Chávez that resonate among the popular classes. It remains for organized labor, social movements, and the PSUV to develop a collective leadership with adequate internal debates that can maintain a broad democratic movement for twenty-first century socialism.

With 19 successful elections in 15 years, the leadership of the Bolivarian revolution, organized in the Venezuelan Socialist Party (PSUV), represents and relies on mass support for its programs and policies, which must always be implemented by involved, participating citizen "protagonists." Although individuals and currents exist within the PSUV, the missions, and government agencies that tend towards bureaucratic control, the more prevalent process is one of political interaction and debate among class and community organizations. A prime instance of social movement connection with governing is the parliamentary process of "Legislator Pueblo," where citizens propose laws directly to the National Assembly. In 2011, legislators approved a tenant's movement initiative, the Law on Renting, protecting tenants and small landlords from speculators and poor housing conditions (Robertson, 2011). The National Assembly passed a draft of a media workers' proposal on "Communications for People's Power" in 2012, intended to support 1,200 community media operations through increased networking, funding, licensing, and community control (Embassy, 2012).

The Right to Speak and Be Heard

International law has long recognized the importance of freedom of expression as a fundamental right in a democracy. The Universal Declaration of Human Rights asserts in Article 19: "Everyone has the right to freedom of opinion and expression; this right includes freedom to ... seek, receive and impart information and ideas throughout any media and regardless of frontiers." In other words, freedom of expression is an inalienable right of all citizens, not just those who own commercial media. Access to media production and distribution are the only guarantees of a democratic plurality of voices and channels. In Venezuela, the right to communicate means you have access to the means of communication.

At the insistence of media workers and organized community groups, media laws were modified following the 2002 coup. In 36 short articles, the 2004 Law on Social Responsibility for Radio and Television establishes the right of active participation and oversight of citizens in all the processes of production, distribution, and consumption of media messages. As 2004 MINCI (Ministry of Communication and Information) Director Jesse Chacon explains: "If communication is a social and an individual right, people must be able to practice it … We must privilege the right of communities over private interest. The private media are exerting their right to make a profit, while the organized communities use it as a mechanism for social development" (Iacobelli & Grioni, 2004). Citizens and communities now have the right *and* the means for media production and distribution.

The National Assembly has written laws to curb TNMCs, expand working class media access, limit private ownership, and privilege community social ownership, providing more public space for popularizing democracy, participation, and new social relations not based on advertising, profits, and audience markets. Essentially the socialist-leaning government has used its power to nurture another site of democratic power by establishing non-government media under workers' control for communicating a more humanist culture.

Transnational Media at Home

Historically, media in Venezuela have been commercial, private, and highly concentrated (Golinger, 2004). Commercial media still comprise more than 70% of all media operations. A small group of business families own a dozen television stations, including the large national broadcasters: Venevisión (the Cisneros Group), Teleleven, RCTV (the Phelps-Granier group), and until selling in 2013, Globovisión (Ravell's virulently anti-Chávez station); and more than three dozen regional stations (Fox & Waisbord, 2002). (This media landscape mirrors that of Argentina, where the Clarin group dominates, Brazil, with O Globo dominant, Mexico, where most major media belong to Televisa and TV Azteca, and other Latin American nations, all of which have consolidated TNMC and/or national media predominance). Supportive of successive conservative and neoliberal governments, these major media have been highly profitable, selling mass audiences to advertisers through mass entertainment from soaps to game shows. Venevisión has become a significant second-tier TNMC, with more than 70 media outlets in 39 countries, including shares in Univisión, the largest Spanish network in the United States, DirecTV Latin America, AOL Latin America, Playboy Latin America, as well as beverage and food distribution (e.g., Coca-Cola and Pizza Hut in Venezuela), and other cultural productions, including the Los Leones baseball team and the Miss Venezuela Pageant. Venevisión produces some 184,000 hours of telenovelas each year that are broadcast in 38 countries – more than exported by Argentina, Mexico, or even famed Brazilian soap opera distributors. Eight or nine telenovelas appear in each weekly schedule (see http://www.venevision.net/programas for current productions).

Commercial media and entertainment remain dominant and robust, exceeding paper, auto, and all agricultural production in net profits. With the exception of Venevisión and occasionally the news daily *Últimas Noticias*, commercial media are sensationalistic, oppositional, and at times even rabid in their attacks on the Bolivarian movement. In addition to the large commercial stations, there are a few specialty broadcasters such as Vale TV, a Catholic, educational channel, Meridiano, a sports channel, La Puma, a music channel, and LaTele, an entertainment channel (Wilpert, 2007). Six families own the six largest daily papers.

The government-run VTV has a national footprint, primarily broadcasting educational and public service programming, in addition to Chàvez's (now Maduro's) weekly *Alo Presidente!* show. On *Alo Presidente!* Chàvez answered calls from citizens, listened to their problems, advised, and provided solutions. The program also tours the country, with the president and local officials questioned live on issues and topics of the day (Kitzberger, 2010, p. 17). VTV also produces the occasional cultural program such as telenovela *Amores en Barrio Adentro* (*Love in the Neighborhood*), a love story with politics set in a changing Venezuela (Márquez, 2004). The narrative had romance, but rather than centering on individual self-interest the story expresses a sense of community and humanity. Love in a time of solidarity.

The summary for media political economy in Venezuela at the end of the twentieth century: consolidated private ownership of media; hierarchical production for profit through advertising-funded entertainment; programs created and distributed to target audiences of consumers, replete with narratives and themes advancing capitalist social relations, reinforcing passivity, authority, and individual consumption; a small corner for public broadcasting and a handful of community media.

A Media Coup, a Democratic Response

These conditions were dramatically challenged following the April 2002 coup, which was orchestrated under the leadership of major media, in particular the owners of RCTV, along with the Chamber of Commerce, the Catholic Church hierarchy, with current opposition figures Leopoldo Lopez and Maria Corina Machado (all in consultation with the United States) (Golinger, 2004, 2006). The coup leaders kidnapped Chávez, immediately "abolished" civil rights and the constitution, dissolved the National Assembly, occupied VTV, shut down Catia TV, the only independent television station in the country, and broadcast cartoons on their own national networks for the duration of the coup. Urban workers soon discovered the plot, however. The coup was short-lived – interrupted and blocked by mass civic action instigated in part by nascent community media in the hands of the more conscious working class sections of Caracas (Francia, 2002). Hundreds of thousands came into the streets and surrounded Miraflores, the presidential headquarters, where the coup occurred. After President Chávez was rescued the people celebrated their success.

More conscious leaders had a more sober post-coup assessment of the relations of power, however. Perhaps they recognized that a Chávez government had not overcome the power of the capitalist state. Seventy-eight Caracas-area media workers met with Chávez and other government representatives demanding more public independent media – media for revolution – not only in policy but in practice.

Although VTV was nationally broadcast, community media workers pointed out the fragility of a singular outlet. They wanted more than public service broadcasting. I witnessed this in Nicaragua in the 1980s: newly awakened citizens want to be more than listeners and viewers; they want their own media. Accounts of independent radio run by Bolivian miners in the 1960s and indigenous media in Bolivia and Ecuador today reveal the same attitudes among workers and community groups: community media workers want to run their own stations, to control the means for their own freedom of expression. In Venezuela, media workers insisted on expanding community media outside the state, on building community media directed by workers in communities. Government response was immediate. Within the year, Venezuela had a new mission for communication: the Ministry of Communication and Information (MINCI) launched a "strategic goal" to return the right of communication to the population, favoring independent, socially owned community media while increasing regulation and monitoring of commercial media. MINCI was the state apparatus response to working class demands.

The government acted to curtail capitalist relations in the media and to advance democratic, participatory relations of production. Media ownership diversified. Public ownership, as social ownership, was expanded, conceived as participatory and collaborative under direct popular control by citizens in their working class communities.

Meetings with community media activists in 2002 led to a much clearer understanding, and more pronounced emphasis on participatory community media production, codified in new media laws. In 2004, the National Assembly passed the Law on Social Responsibility of Radio and Television, establishing the rights of community media and public access to media production and broadcast. Within a few years, more than 300 FM radio and TV broadcasters were organized and licensed. By 2011, Venezuela was approaching 1,200 community media outlets (Venezuela en Noticias, 2012). The government provided equipment, technical resources and training using the Social Fund (a public resource drawing on revenues from the nationalized oil industry) – simultaneously impinging on capitalist prerogatives over resources and turning those resources toward participatory democracy. With licensing, the government provided space for public media – not just with low-wattage normally available to community media in most countries, but with wide access to FM channels, adequate broadcasting power wattage, and populated geographic locations so that "community" radio broadcasts reach 3 million in Caracas, for example.

With a government supporting social movements for democracy and equality, media production practices and control changed. Laws and licensing legitimized and empowered working class and community voices by ensuring direct access and control. In law and in licensing, commercial, state, party (including the PSUV), and religious officials are excluded from community media, while 70% of the production must be directly from community councils themselves.

Community, Public, and Participatory: Media Reform for Democracy

What is community media? In Europe they call themselves associative radio. In the United States, low power or alternative radio. In Africa, rural media. In Australia, public radio. In Latin America: educational in Bolivia, free in Brazil, participatory in El Salvador, popular in Ecuador, indigenous in Mexico, and community or citizens' radio in other places. Many names, one essence. The goal in each case is the same: to improve media access for all. Unfortunately, in most cases, the political economy of commercial media and TNMCs means that community media barely survive on contributions of listeners and volunteer media workers. With the exception of Pacifica Radio and KPFA in the United States, seldom do community radio signals reach mass audiences. Exceptional conditions prevail in Venezuela where working class citizens have exercised their power: community media cover most of the broadcast spectrum, reaching millions, with thousands of community-based programmers. The difference is power. Political power.

The development and expansion of national public broadcasting is the most easily recognizable change in the Venezuelan media landscape. The programs and processes of program production underscore how a more democratic political economy frames cultural practice. In addition to teleSUR, the cooperative satellite television venture of Venezuela, Argentina, Uruguay, Cuba, and Bolivia with 12 Latin American bureaus that establish an independent public media space for Latin America (www.telesurtv.net; Artz, 2006; McElroy & Wynter, 2006), and ANTV, the television channel of the National Assembly, three major public broadcasting stations (TVes, ViVe, and Ávila TV) have been established, along with the YVKE Radio Network with 10 stations. These public stations are primarily funded by subsidies from the Social Fund and "advertisements" for national social services. They are each independently run outside government direction, oversight, or even approval – highlighted by several shows highly critical of the government.

Participatory production practices demonstrate how social being affects social consciousness. As producers, editors, narrators, and videographers deepen their social awareness, they change professionally and personally. Their lives are transformed by small explosions in consciousness as they develop their own creativity, power, and experience social contradictions collectively. In conversations and interviews with producers, directors, and technicians (conducted in person in 2005 and 2008, and electronically 2010–2011) expressions of determination and desire for a new society were reminiscent of the Chilean woman who rejoiced in her new humanity. Individual media workers reflected on the cumulative experience of democratic participation and decision-making that emphasizes community, workers, women, indigenous, and the average citizen. In Venezuela, public media broadcast several community-based 15-minute documentaries every day, prompting hundreds of other personal self-realizations and transformations.

Celebrities and politicians obsess about airtime, fearing that if they aren't on the screen or the microphone they may lose their recognition and appeal. Transnational media feed the demons of celebrity and melodrama as a means to stimulate audience attention, framing drivel and sensation as worthy of report. Advertising and PR agencies (and university classes) around the world all accept that "media are the new merchants of reality ... what the media affirm remains affirmed. What they ignore does not exist" (López Vigil, 1998).

Therein is the problem: the majority of the world has no direct means of voicing its existence in its own words. It is no coincidence that dictators demand silence from their subjects – it is the best way to divide people and dehumanize them. TNMC entertainment brings pleasurable spectacles and dramatic stories to spur consent for a consumerist world. In contrast, community media are the means for the public to affirm its existence. "The first challenge of a station with social responsibility: to amplify the people's voice and thereby socially legitimize it" (López Vigil, 1998). Community media offer communication power.

Government Support for Public Broadcasting

In 2007, TVes (Televisora Venezolana Social) became the first national public broadcaster. A publicly run station with a board of directors elected by unions and community organizations, TVes receives $11 million from the National Assembly. TVes relies heavily on "productores independiente" (independent producers, or PINs), community-based journalists and program producers. Seventy-eight PINs provide some 229 programs on TVes' yearly schedule. Meant to be "a conduit through which independent cultural production reaches the airwaves" (William Lara in Ciccariello-Maher, 2007), for the first time in Venezuela, the working class, women, and indigenous people are featured prominently. TVes airs the first ever soap opera with a black lead. Documentaries of popular history are regular fare on TVes.

ViVe TV

Vision Venezuela TV (ViVe) was founded four years earlier as a Caracas-based local public station with a similar organizational public control. ViVe (or vives, "you live," as it is called) is dedicated to community productions as part of its "Sueño Bolivariano" (Bolivarian Dream) message, which values cooperation, solidarity, and collective work in place of individual profit and consumerism. Independent, public, and cooperatively run, ViVe is funded by the Social Fund and prohibits advertising. Only 10% of programming is produced in-house; the remaining 90% of shows come from community videographers and documentarians (with specials on traditional peasant planting practices, indigenous musical performances, local community cultural activities, and investigative pieces on housing, utilities, and even religious events). ViVe programming includes: *Secretos de Familila* (historical traditions across generations), *Querencia Andean* (Andean cultural traditions), *Historias de Vida* (narratives of community organizing), *Cultural de Dia* (arts and crafts expressing contemporary Venezuelan cultural diversity), *Espacio Musical* (national and international music with artist interviews), *Real o Medio* (critiques of media from Zulia), and many more (see http://www.vive.gob.ve/programacion for current programs). Programming constantly changes to air different experiences and interests, always with participation and production assistance by public videographers. More than 14,000 communities have been featured over the last 10 years, about 30 half-hour shows per week on average.

For the first time, women, Afro-Venezuelans, and indigenous people were prominent on local television. To ensure quality productions, ViVe organized community-based training for video production through community councils and some workers' councils. The Bolivarian socialist project created social missions in health care, housing, and education; ViVe represents a mission for communication, where television production is available to communities (Wynter, 2010). ViVe is not public service broadcasting as advocated by liberal pluralists or the media reform movement in the United States; it does not strive for impartiality (Hendy, 2013). Rather, ViVe is public access broadcasting, with public control and partisan public production of communication for social justice and social change. ViVe has mobile transmitting stations in working class and peasant communities in each region of the country, along with courses to teach citizens broadcasting skills.

A new social power has emerged as working class communities and individuals – directly participating and collectively collaborating – produce solidarity media and democratic cultural experiences. These creative producers consciously work for respect, support, and cooperation among working people and their allies.

Ávila TV: Hip-hop and the Politics of Participation

Ávila TV launched in 2006 as part of a socialist communication initiative by the Bolivarian mayor of Caracas, Juan Barretto. Close to 400 producers, most in their twenties, write, edit, film, and broadcast edgy, creative programming aimed at urban youth. Ávila has been described as a station with hip-hop sensibility and socialist lyrics (Cassel, 2009). A typical Ávila broadcast day includes news, political talk shows, features on international and community issues, and telenovelas about Caracas working class families – but no commercials. Their programming decisions are guided by an explicit commitment to a new social order, as expressed by one of the many articulate young producers: "We aren't trying to sell shampoo or name brand clothes, or any capitalist products for that matter. We are trying to stay true to our principles and combat consumerism" (Mellado, personal communication, June 2008). Watching Ávila TV, viewers quickly notice the style, the tone, the structure of programming. Even the music often feels argumentative, strident. Ávila is "not like ViVe, they privilege discourse, we privilege the aesthetic" (Mellado, personal communication, June 2008). In 2008, Ávila aired a weekly series called *El Entrompe de Falopio*, about women and gender issues in the revolution. A year-long live program, *Voice, Face, and Struggle of the People*, included one titled "Impunity," in which hosts, guests, and audience members sharply criticized the government for granting amnesty to the 2002 coup leaders. Telenovelas from Ávila have political overtones with not-so-subtle barbs at the opposition for undemocratic obstruction and the government for not championing working class interests and advancing socialism more quickly. High-quality documentaries, professionally and creatively produced, have included the widely acclaimed 2008 *El Golpe (The Coup)* and the 2008 feature *200 Years of Caracas: The Insurgent Capital of the Continent.*

Young producers at Ávila have aired shows on Afro-Venezuelans, indigenous cultures, and homosexuality – all topics ignored or taboo on commercial television. In 2013, Ávila launched new programming, including: live tours of Caracas' cultural and recreational life, *Caracas Misión*; video shorts by community videographers, cycling through self-management projects of community councils and missions; *Political*, with accounts of social movement democracy in action; *Desportes Caracas*, reporting on professional, amateur, and community sports activities, and many more (Ávila, 2013; see blog http://avilapendiente.blogspot.com/ for commentary and critique).

Ávila has been an integral part of RED TV (Education for the Revolution and Development of Venezuela), a city-wide educational project to bring classes in screenwriting, playwriting, and video production to the working class communities of Caracas. By 2010, 55 community councils in Caracas had media committees, where community members receive extensive training, mentoring, and equipment – cameras, computers, and editing software for video production and post-production. Community media committees then have regularly scheduled spots on Ávila's daily schedule for airing 15-minute video productions.

The Bolivarian government, nationally and locally, has created laws, provided resources, and prepared space for non-commercial, non-capitalist public media production. In the vocabulary of the Bolivarian project, new "protagonists" can now fully participate in creating their own culture, their own stories, expressing their own interests. While they are making video, making television, making communication, they are also making new human beings. In 2013, two new public stations were announced, one by and for youth, the other TV Obrera (Workers' TV) directed by labor, both to appear on the new Open Digital Television system (Presidente, 2013). Lives and experiences of working class communities and community activists are valuable, valued, and shared – informing the nation of how and what new creative human beings can and will be with the revolutionary transformation of society from capitalism to socialism.

Community Media: Independent and Democratic

Complementing public broadcasting, community radio and television in Venezuela have a rich tradition of participatory communication. By the 1990s, community media already had appeared: Radio Treat, TV Michelena, Radio Perola, Radio 23 de Enero, Active Radio La Vega, and many more paralleled social movements that used street media such as murals, flyers, megaphone "radio," film clubs, and websites like aporrea.org (ANMCLA, 2012; Fernandes, 2010, pp. 168–182). With some 300 radio stations, 60 television stations, and over 200 community-based newspapers, today millions of Venezuelans have and use community media.

These stations are not organized like community media elsewhere that have studios disconnected from their audience. Community media news reporters in Venezuela see themselves as "popular communicators" rather than journalists (Fernandes, 2010, p. 169). They rely on the direct capacity of each local community "to analyze, decide, implement, and evaluate what is relevant to its life" (Azzellini, 2013, p. 26). Communal councils, which operate most community media, are structures of direct democracy by residents, workers, and citizens self-organized at the local level. Communal councils encompass 150–400 families in urban areas and about 20 families in rural areas, constituting "parallel" governing structures to "official" government institutions.

Catia TV

The seminal leader in community media is Catia TV in Caracas, the first legal community television broadcaster in the country. Catia TV's slogan "Don't Watch TV, Make TV!" is inscribed on the outside walls of its broadcast studios and demonstrated daily by collaborative teams of 4–7 community producers organized in ECPAIs (Independent Community Audiovisual Production Teams). Each ECPAI decides topics, formats, aesthetics, and content for broadcast programs, "emphasizing stories from the barrio, contradictions and changes, or not" (Vasquez, personal communication, June 2008). Catia TV lives popular education and democratic participation, articulating its television production and programming with assemblies, events, and communication guerrillas: muralists, storytellers, oral historians, artisanal creators, and puppeteers. Catia acts "as an organizing tool, where communities build their own audiovisual discourse ..." (Catia TVe Collective, 2006). Collaboratively teaching and learning creates dozens of ECPAIs, "having knowledge of communication; having a critical analysis surrounding the conditions and social context in which an individual or group must live; identifying the cultural and ideological values that effect the group's or collective's vision; developing an understanding of reality and how they act; associating learning with the collective construction of knowledge; and identifying and analyzing [their] own practices" (Catia TVe Collective, 2006).

> Catia TVe seeks community participation in the making of audiovisual productions reflecting community struggles and demonstrating how to build networks within the community ... [the] objective is to build a media that the people want, with democratic participation based on dialogue ... Because Catia TVe is a television station connected to the working class ... every Catia TVe participant has a minimum political consciousness and social responsibility ... Catia TVe shares a space for communication with organized groups that come from various communities in Caracas, as a way of protesting. (Catia TVe Collective, 2006)

Catia TV's idea is to organize collective work for community interest. Working in teams also favors the organized distribution of work and conscious analysis of how to produce material (Moen, 2009), both activities at odds with TNMC division of cultural labor based on corporate hierarchy and the alienation and dispossession of media creators from their work. Media content produced by ECPAI's never has to comply with some editorial line as in TNMC structures that determine who, what, and how media content can be produced and distributed. For Catia TV, and other community media, the right to broadcast forms part of the emerging rights of the Venezuelan working classes to organize themselves, to decide the production of goods and services, and consciously, collectively determine their own social and cultural norms (Vasquez, personal communication, June 2008).

Afro TV

Catia is not an isolated example. In Balo Vento on the east coast of Venezuela, Afro TV illustrates the cultural and social potential for community media led by community activists and linked to a politically awakening community. About 15% of Venezuela is Afro-Venezuela, the historic consequence of Spanish slavery and cocoa plantations in the east. Balo Vento had long been neglected by central government, relegated to continued exploitation by remaining small cocoa growers. Following ratification of the new Constitution that establishes Venezuela as a multi-ethnic, pluriculture society, the government established a subcommission of African descendants in the National Assembly. Education, health, and housing missions were extended to Balo Vento, along with the opportunity for public, independent, community media.

Afro TV was the early regional media project launched by local community activists. Their mission includes recovering their African past, expressing their cultural and artistic present, and organizing public dialogue on contemporary issues important to Balo Vento, such as land reform, development, and workers' control of cocoa production. In 2008, Afro TV was broadcasting 4–5 hours daily and on the Internet. Early programs included *Cimmarones*, stories of slave rebellion, and *Que Es Eso*, featuring local characters telling their life stories (Perdemo, personal communication, June 2008). Afro TV, while modest in operation, nonetheless illustrates the relationship between media access and community cultural experiences, the dialectical development of becoming new human beings through participation in creating one's own existence.

There are currently more than 100,000 community activists working at hundreds of community radio and television stations with hundreds of additional broadcasters in various stages of preparation. Community media have been a national priority for MINCI since 2008, when it unveiled a plan for funding, training, and licensing community media with national broadcast capabilities. By 2009, community media reached 56% of the population.

Community "stations now belong to the people" who should "control the strategic means of production" of communication in Venezuela (Viloria, personal communication, June 2008). At all levels, from officials to teenage producers, socialism for the twenty-first century is articulated as a process for creating new social relations, beginning with ownership and control over industry, including media that contribute to a new social consciousness and new social being across classes.

Radio everywhere

Community radio illustrates the protagonist-initiated development of political self-awareness and power: democratic ownership → participatory programming → social responsibility and cooperation. At Radio 23 de Enero (broadcasting at 3,000 watts in Caracas), community council journalists and producers from some 50 collectives broadcast weekly programs of music, opinion, health, public affairs, and news. For decades, community groups in the 23 de Enero neighborhood have worked on health care, education, sports, housing, security, and political organizing. Community participation is part of the culture; the local radio station has been broadcasting for years; community councils and media studios are only the latest manifestations of collaborative participation (Llopis, 2013).

Community assemblies culminated in deciding to start Radio Rebelde in 2003 (Dangl, 2010). Neighborhood producers host shows on local history, natural medicine, and the environment. Venezuelan music and culture are emphasized. Regular classes teach newcomers how to start their own programs. The station is run democratically, collectively, through assemblies of program producers.

Also in Caracas, teens, grandparents, DJs, and investigative journalists collectively share the broadcast schedule at Radio Primero Negro, a station with a long history of community organizing. More than 60 programs are aired weekly by "students, housewives, unemployed, and members of community organizations" (Lugo, personal communication, June 2008). The station's community activists conduct regular surveys and conversations

with neighborhood residents to assure programs meet the needs and interests of all, and to recruit more station participants, offering training and
technical expertise. Rebelde and Primero reach over a million residents of
Caracas – not your typical "community" broadcaster in the United States.

Radio Minero, in Tumeremo, is operated by working miners and their
community, producing their own news and programs. In Zulia, Maracaibo,
the indigenous community broadcasts over Radio Yupa in their native language, with stories and topics drawn from their historic culture and
everyday concerns. Radio Negro Primero, Radio Perola, TV Rubio, and
others existed prior to the Bolivarian national project. Others, like Radio
Un Nuevo Dia, Radio Tiuna, and Radio/TV Macarao arose as part of
MINCI's campaign for media access. Each thrives as licensed media with
community participation and support, and to varying degrees, each
continues to demand more from the government.

Democratic Media in Production and Distribution

Community radio and TV now air inspiring stories by novices facing
microphones for the first time and feeling the power of communication,
directly experiencing the meaning of democracy and community. Local
stations have leaders, directors, and specialists on cultural, political, and
indigenous, community issues, creating a "communication force" for
revolutionary change (Viloria, personal communication, June 2008).

Participatory journalism and democratic production at ViVe, Ávila, Catia
TV, Radio El Negro Primero, and other public and community media outlets
reflect changing social relations. University and professionally trained journalists work alongside community correspondents and participatory journalists, constructing and distributing news and news reports that are accurate,
timely, but much more democratic in framing and sourcing because they are
not bound by the advertising needs or editorial dictates of a market-driven
media. New norms of objectivity with partisanship serve the information and
educational needs of the majority striving for democratic control over their
lives. The goal of twenty-first century socialism as promulgated in word and
deed in Venezuela exists – not to provide government largess and patronizing
welfare benefits, but for nothing less than to place the working class and its
allies as historical agents in the process of restructuring social relations,
including replacing the artificial norms of professional journalism, which
pretend to separate facts from context.

Community and public media for twenty-first century socialism alter the practices and functions of media in line with human needs, so that a participatory, socially conscious media contribute to a new cultural hegemony of a creative, socialist humanity – against the hegemony of consumerism and neoliberalism – for a culture of cooperation, class solidarity, and dedication to creating social justice and solidarity. In this mix, entertainment becomes more varied and journalism of necessity becomes more vibrant, more alive, identifying facts, sources, and truths related to the real experience and conditions of the working class population (Lugo, personal communication, June 2008).

Participation in media has the ability to transform. "Community media visibilizes our faces, our voices, so we collectively know what we are doing is connected to humanity. We become protagonists ... we make for ourselves the task of learning ideas and tools that are available for the political actor" (Viloria, personal communication, June 2008). Democratic participation often generates a learning process that allows us to break with "psychological barriers that prevent us from developing our human capabilities, at the same time that it creates conditions for exercising them" (Piñeiro Harnecker, 2009, pp. 510–511), as represented by Catia TV's teenage producers. Using the National Assembly's initiative for "Legislator Pueblo," community media workers delivered a draft petition for a law on Communications for People's Power (Embassy, 2012). The community media draft proposes more equitable distribution of the radio spectrum, national coordination of news and information, and increased funding.

In 2012, MINCI organized a national media network, the national system of popular, alternative, and community communication (SiBCI), prioritizing the participation of community radio in the exchange and distribution of news and information (Carlson, 2013a; Villegas, 2013) – furthering community media's role in transforming reality and producing working class cultural references for twenty-first century socialist values. Changing the political economy of media contributes a new cultural hegemony. In the words of MINCI director Andrés Izarra, "We are advancing towards the construction of popular power, and one of the principal objectives of these alternative media sources is to produce content which will allow us to advance towards the construction of new values" (Boothroyd, 2012). MINCI takes this seriously. In December 2013, representatives of over 300 community media discussed and affirmed programs for training community media producers and expanding public access to the radio and TV spectrum. Their decisions became part of the 2014 policy agenda for MINCI implementation and funding.

A New Political Economy for a New Cultural Leadership

The trajectory of public broadcasting, community media, and participatory public media access portends a new social function for media. Legalized, funded, and supported by the Bolivarian socialist government in power, these independent community media are entertaining, even as they are striving for a new humanity. With working class-generated narratives reflecting the collaborative creativity and shared experiences of those who aspire to write their own future history, these media broadcast messages, stories, and images of collective action, participatory democracy, and communities building social justice, self-government, and working class leadership. In sum, a revolutionary leadership has used its government power against the capitalist state, expanding sites for additional democratic participation by the Venezuelan working and middle classes, women, youth, Afro-Venezuelans, indigenous populations, and others previously underserved and excluded, politically, socially, and economically. The Bolivarian government for twenty-first century socialism has been using its legislative, executive, and rhetorical power to provide Venezuelan national resources to advance working class leadership and democratic social relations.

Citizens with access to their own media are consciously working to meet the needs of the global community, including the "full development of the creative potentialities" of all humans (Mészáros, 2000, p. 817). In other words, Venezuelan community media embody the "ownership → production practices → social use" formula suggested earlier. The relations between access and practice inform the PSUV, President Maduro, MINCI, SiBCI, and leading community media workers and community activists organized in ANMCLA and RVM (Red Venezolana de Medios Communitarios – Venezuealan Network of Community Media).

Most of the 1,200 community media entail a "partisan public sphere," in the sense that the working classes are not just debating or patronizing government initiatives, but using media to articulate their own collective political and social interests through music, stories, interviews, arguments, and campaigns for a new society. Public and community media in Venezuela aspire to social ownership of all media, under the direct control of citizens, workers, and community councils (without interference by the state or commercial media institutional control). Community media are part of an organic development of a culture of collaborative, participatory production by and for the people themselves (as illustrated in Catia TV's ECPAI teams, Ávila and ViVe communal documentaries, and community radio programming across the nation).

This is as "an exquisite contradiction. The state is used to initiate new practices requiring direct working class control outside and above the state. The state did not impose, or implement. The government did not bribe or provide a gift, or even provide a service to the public. Rather, the government initiates a policy and provides funds [from the nationalized social wealth], while the communal councils and workers' councils implement, direct, create and decide how to use media to communicate their own messages and ideas" (Viloria, personal communication, June 2008). The national system of popular, alternative, and community communication (SiBCI), the community media network formed in 2013, expands media social ownership and diversity. Community media dramatically increase opportunities for public debate and public participation. With media in the hands of the people – workers, peasants, indigenous groups, and organized communities – the socialist project assembles new leaders for a cultural hegemony of human solidarity, social justice, and actual, existing democracy. In one sense, as more citizens become participants, the population transforms into its own cultural and political leadership. Riffing on Catia TV's slogan, they watch the TV they make.

Only the right to communicate guarantees full democracy and thus "the best democratic policy requires better communication" (Márquez, 2007, p. 26). One might say Venezuela is implementing American philosopher John Dewey's (1927) vision for democratic communication by improving "the methods and conditions for debate, discussion, and persuasion" (p. 208). Community media, and their national public media counterparts, also prepare the working class majority for the coming confrontation with capitalism (within Venezuela and from the United States) by experiencing and communicating new norms of democratic production and programming with collective ownership and participatory practices dedicated to improving the human condition.

References

Algan, E. (2003). Privatization of radio and media hegemony in Turkey. In L. Artz & Y. Kamalipour, (Eds.), *The globalization of corporate media hegemony* (pp. 169–192). Albany, NY: New York University Press.

ANMCLA (2012). Asociación Nacional de Medios Comunitarios, Alternativos y Libres de La Bolivariana Venezuela (National Association of Alternative Media). Retrieved from http:medioscomunitarios.org/pag/index.php?id=48

Artz, B. L. (1993). Communication and power: Popular radio in Nicaragua. *Journal of Radio Studies*, 2(1), 205–227.

Artz, L. (2006b). TeleSUR (Television of the South): Discarding contraflow for horizontal communication. *International Journal of Media and Cultural Politics*, 2(2), 225–232.

Artz, L. (2012). 21st century socialism: Making a state for revolution. *Triple C: Cognition, Communication, Co-operation*, 10(2), 537–554.

August, A. (2013). *Cuba and its neighbours: Democracy in motion*. New York: Zeb Books.

Ávila TV se remoza con lanzamiento de su nueva programación (Ávila TV is rejuvenated with launch of its new programming) (2013, January 21). Venezoalana de Televisión. Retrieved November 15, 2013, from http://www.vtv.gob.ve/articulos/2013/01/21/avila-tv-se-renueva-con-lanzamiento-de-su-nueva-programacion-1047.html

Azzellini, D. (2013). The communal state: Communal councils, communes, and workplace democracy. *NACLA Report on the Americas*, 46(2), 25–30.

Boothroyd, R. (2012, April 14). National alternative media network launched in Venezuela. Venezuelanalysis. Retrieved from http://venezuelanalysis.com/news/6924

Bourdieu, P. (1998). *On television*. New York: New Press.

Brecht, B. (1983). Radio as a means of communication: A talk on the function of radio. (Orignially published 1932). In A. Mattelard & S. Siegelaub (Eds.), *Communication and the class struggle: Liberation, socialism. Vol. 2* (pp. 169–171). New York: International General.

Carlson, C. (2013, March 3). Venezuela launches new integrated media system. Venezuelanalysis. Retrieved December 15, 2013, from http://venezuelanalysis.com/news/8007

Cassel, L. (2009, June 11). Ávila TV in Venezuela: Revolutionizing television. Upside Down World. Retrieved from http://upsidedownworld.org/main/venezuela-archives-35/1904-avila-tv-in-venezuela-revolutionizing-television

Ciccariello-Maher, G. (2007, May 29). Zero hour for Venezuela's RCTV. Venezuelanalysis. Retrieved May 12, 2014, from http://venezuelanalysis.com/analysis/2415

Coronel, S. S. (2001). The media, the market, and democracy: The case of the Philippines. *The Public*, 8(2), 109–126.

Dangl, B. (2010). *Dancing with dynamite: Social movements and states in Latin America*. Oakland, CA: AK Press.

Derné, S. D. (2008). *Globalization on the ground: New media and the transformation of culture, class, and gender in India*. Thousand Oaks, CA: Sage.

Dewey, J. (1927). *The public and its problems*. New York: Henry Holt.

Dorfman, A. (1983). *The empire's old clothes: What the Lone Ranger, Babar, and other innocent heroes do to our minds.* New York: Pantheon.

Ellner, S. (2010). Hugo Chávez's first decade in office: Breakthroughs and shortcomings. *Latin American Perspectives, 37*(1), 77–96.

Embassy of the Bolvarian Republic of Venezuela in the US (2012, January 6). Community media in Venezuela gets funding from telecoms authority. Retrieved from http://venezuela-us.org/2012/01/06/community-media-in-venezuela-gets-funding-from-telecoms-authority/print/

Fernandes, S. (2010). *Who can stop the drums? Urban social movements in Chávez's Venezuela.* Greensboro, NC: Duke University Press.

Fox, E. (1988). *Media and politics in Latin America: The struggle for democracy. Communication and human values.* Beverly Hills, CA: Sage.

Fox, E., & Waisbord, S. (2002). *Latin politics, global media.* Austin, TX: University of Texas Press.

Francia, N. (2002). *Abril rojo – el rescate de Chávez: Crónicas, análisis, documentos, entrevistas.* Caracas: Imprenta Nacional.

Golinger, E. (2004, September 25). A case study of media concentration and power. *Venezuealanalysis.* Retrieved January 15, 2012, from http://Venezuelanalysis.com/analysis/710

Golinger, E. (2006). *The Chávez code: Cracking US intervention in Venezuela.* New York: Olive Branch Press.

Gramsci, A. (1971). *Selections from the prison notebooks.* Q. Hoare & G. N. Smith, Trans. New York: International Publishers.

Hendy, D. (2013). *Public service broadcasting.* New York: Palgrave Macmillan.

Herrera Miller, K. M., & Ramos Martín, J. (2013). Comunicación, red y lucha social: hacia la reactivación de las radios mineras de Bolivia (Communication, networking and social struggle: Toward the reactivation of miners' radio in Bolivia). *Quórum Académico, 10*(1), 11–28.

Iacobelli, D., & Grioni, R. (2004, February 16). If communication is a social and an individual right, people must be able to practice it. *Venezuelanalysis.* Retrieved from http://venezuelanalysis.com/analysis/357

Ives, P. (2004). *Language and hegemony in Gramsci.* Ann Arbor, MI: Pluto Press.

Jakubowicz, K. (2007). *Rude awakening: Social and media change in Central and Eastern Europe.* Cresskill, NJ: Hampton Press.

Kalb, D. (2011). Introduction. Headlines of nation, subtexts of class: Working-class populism and the return of the repressed in neoliberal Europe. In D. Kalb & G. Halmai (Eds.), *Headlines of nation, subtexts of class: Working-class populism and the return of the repressed in neoliberal Europe* (pp. 1–36). New York: Berghahn Books.

Kitzberger, P. (2010). *The media activism of Latin America's leftist governments: Does ideology matter?* GIGA working papers, No. 151. Retrieved May 12, 2014, from http://www.econstor.eu/bitstream/10419/47769/1/64764181X.pdf

Llopis, E. (2013, October 10). The revolution has brought substantial improvements to working class neighbourhoods. Venezuelanalysis. Retrieved from http://venezuelanalysis.com/analysis/10083

López Vigil, J. I. (1998, February). Community radios: Freedom of antenna! *Revista Envio, 199*. Retrieved from http://www.envio.org.ni/articulo/1319

Lupien, P. (2013). The media in Venezuela and Bolivia attacking the "bad left" from below. *Latin American Perspectives, 40*(3), 226–246.

Márquez, A. (2007). El discurso político , la opinión pública y los medios de comunicación social en Venezuela (Political discourse, public opinion and social media in Venezuela). *Quórum Académico, 4*(2), 11–31.

Márquez, H. (2004, July 5). Soap opera propaganda in Venezuela. *Antiwar.com*. Retrieved March 15, 2013, from http://www.antiwar.com/ips/marquez.php?articleid=2934

Martinez, C., Fox, M., & Farrell, J. (Eds.). (2010). *Venezuela speaks! Voices from the grassroots*. Chicago: PM Press.

McChesney, R. W. (1995). *Telecommunications, mass media, and democracy: The battle for the control of U.S. broadcasting, 1928–1935*. New York: Oxford University Press.

McIlroy, J., & Wynter, C. (2006, February 15). Venezuela: 'Another television is possible'. *Green Left Weekly*. Retrieved March 30, 2014, from https://www.greenleft.org.au/node/34653

Mészáros, I. (2000). *Beyond capital: A theory of transition*. New York: Monthly Review Press.

Moen, D. G. (2009). Public access to alternative/critical analysis: Community media in Venezuela. *Hitotsubashi Journal of Social Studies, 41*(1). Retrieved December 15, 2013, from http://dgmoen.net/blog/public-access-to-alternativecritical-analysis-community-media-in-venezuela/

Ndlela, N. (2007). Broadcasting reforms in Southern Africa: Continuity and change in the era of globalisation. *Westminster Papers in Communication and Culture, 4*(3), 67–87.

Parra, L. N. (2009). Hacia la instauración de una nueva política comunicacional del estado Venezolano (Towards the establishment of a new political communication of the Venezuelan state). *Razon y Palabra, 68*. Retrieved from http://www.razonypalabra.org.mx/Parra.pdf

Piñeiro Harnecker, C. (2009). Workplace democracy and solidarity development: An empirical study of Venezuelan cooperatives. In K. Daly, D. Schugurensky, & K. Lopes (Eds.), *Learning democracy by doing: Alternative practices in citizenship, learning, and participatory democracy* (pp. 510–524). Toronto: Ontario Institute for Studies in Education, University of Toronto.

Presidente Maduro vamos a hacer realidad el sueño de una nueva televisión (President Maduro: Let's make the dream of new television a reality). (2013, August 23). Venezualan de Televisión. Retrieved December 21, 2013, from http://www.vtv.gob.ve/articulos/2013/08/23/presidente-maduro-vamos-a-hacer-realidad-el-sueno-de-una-nueva-television-2274.html

Robertson, E. (2011, October 29). Venezuela passes new leasing law proposed by popular initiative. Venezuelanalysis. Retrieved May 12, 2014, from http://venezuelanalysis.com/news/6588

Robinson, W. I. (2004). *A theory of global capitalism: Production, class, and state in a transnational world*. Baltimore, MD: Johns Hopkins University Press.

Sklair, L. (2001). *The transnational capitalist class*. New York: Wiley.

Thussu, D. K. (2005). The transnationalization of television: The Indian experience. In J. Chalaby (Ed.), *Transnational television worldwide: Towards a new media order* (pp. 156–172). London: I.B. Tauris.

Venezuela en Noticias (2012, January 8). Community media in Venezuela get funding from telecoms authority. Venezuelanalysis. Retrieved May 12, 2014, from https://venezuelanalysis.com/news/6731

Villegas: Con el SiBCI se acaba la competencia entre los medios del Estado (+Video). (2013, February 3). *Venezolano de Televisión*. Retrieved from http://www.vtv.gob.ve/articulos/2013/03/02/gobierno-bolivariano-presenta-el-nuevo-sibci-3861.html

Wilpert, G. (2007). *Changing Venezuela by taking power: The history and policies of the Chávez government*. London: Verso.

Wu, S. (2010). Can East Asia produce its own "Al-Jazeera"? Assessing the potential of Channel NewsAsia as a global media contra-flow. Unpublished thesis. Department of Communication, Simon Fraser University, Vancouver, CA. Retrieved March 2, 2013, from http://summit.sfu.ca/item/9960

Wynter, C. (2010, May 23). Venezuela: Creating a new, radical media. *Green Left Weekly*. Retrieved January 21, 2014, from http://www.greenleft.org.au/node/44207

Yesil, B. (2013). Media, market, and the state in Turkey. Presentation. Union for Democratic Communications National Conference. November, 2013. San Francisco, CA.

Zhao, Y. (2003). "Transnational capital, the Chinese state, and China's communication industries in a fractured society. *The Public, 10*(40), 53–74.

Zhao, Y. (2008). *Communication in China: Political economy, power, and conflict*. Lanham, MD: Rowman & Littlefield.

Further Reading

Lebowitz, M. (2006). *Build it now: Socialism for the twenty-first century*. New York: Monthly Review Press.

Wilpert, G. (2007). *Changing Venezuela by taking power: The history and policies of the Chávez government*. London: Verso.

Conclusion
The Reality of Power

Media content that truly represents the popular, that unleashes creativity and unearths narratives for human cooperation and progress, cannot be consistently expressed through transnational media corporation (TNMC) programming or format; at most, such narratives can be occasionally smuggled in. Democratic media requires upending capitalist control over production and distribution, including securing decent working conditions, higher wages, and equitable access to media production.

Media entertainment provides pleasant distractions that carry its ideology of consumerism and self-interest, but neither the ideology nor its social relations are sufficient for human fulfillment. Despite the spread of transnational media operations, democratic social relations and public media access are possible. The future is not guaranteed to the transnational capitalist class. This is not fantasy, nor some idealistic journey into the realm of possibility. The Venezuelan community media experience is historical reality, part of the material result of an unfolding revolution, part of now.

Components and intimations of popular democratic media appear across Latin America in Bolivia, Ecuador, Nicaragua, and even Argentina as working class social movements flex their power and express the social interests of humanity. In dialectical terms, the social consciousness of workers and their allies arrives before, simultaneously, or in interaction with available social structures. The material dialectic of personal and social change is based on the consciousness informed by participation, experience, and possibility (Piñeiro Harnecker, 2009). Media workers, women, youth, indigenous people, and large sections of the working class,

Global Entertainment Media: A Critical Introduction, First Edition. Lee Artz.
© 2015 John Wiley & Sons, Inc. Published 2015 by John Wiley & Sons, Inc.

middle class, and unemployed are propelled by workers and social movements to imagine and create new social practices – in violation of the norms of class society that dictate power and control from bureaucratic institutions.

New media practices champion writing our own stories, producing our own programs, relying on working class sources, recognizing the integrity and value of working class experiences and knowledge, serving our communities and cultures, and connecting with other communities (Lugo, personal communication, June 2008). These practices uncover real human potential and inspire further creative endeavors, as illustrated daily on ViVe and Ávila TV, and on Catia, Perola, and AfroTV. Communally produced news and culture are thriving across Latin America as social movements create space for democratic communication and media access. Importantly, these multiple, but shared experiences have the potential to lead participants to new understandings, including the recognition that access to communication and power can only be secured ultimately by constructing democratic social relations throughout society – not just in one plant or at one station. Individual self-realization requires the collective societal realization of twenty-first century socialism.

In Venezuela, revolutionary voices are no longer compelled to cry out from the grass roots. Revolutionary voices now broadcast from the highest hilltops of the urban centers. Because resolute leaders in the Bolivarian movement, from the president and the National Assembly to community councils, are using national resources for democratic social interests, working class voices have the power of communication, the power of action, the power of decision and control over production. In the process of democratic media production, social relations and social consciousness are being transformed.

In the transnational capitalist world, social conflict occurs daily. Class confrontation is ongoing. Civil war is not unlikely. From Venezuela, Bolivia, Ecuador, and Nicaragua, to China, Greece, and Spain, class polarization is increasing. Radical populist media are early manifestations of an awakening citizenry. Capitalism has reached an impasse. Capitalist classes in nations around the world have signed on to the transnational, neoliberal project and are intent on the further exploitation of labor at the expense of social welfare and environmental sustainability.

To the extent that community media in Venezuela provide a participatory forum for articulating socialist and humanist frames for winning social justice and protecting humanity and the earth, working classes there communicate new cultural and political possibilities. Participatory democratic media as modeled in Venezuela transcend simplistic notions of populism as working class communities self-consciously organize their own independent institutions and media capable of changing the world.

New Media, New Society

The role of media in forging a new society is quite distinct. "When a radio promotes citizens' participation and defends their interests; when it responds to the tastes of the majority and uses humor and hope as basic proposals; when it truly informs; when it helps resolve the thousand and one problems of daily life; when all ideas are debated on its programs and all opinions respected; when cultural diversity is stimulated rather than commercial homogeneity; when women are protagonists of communication and not simply decorative voice or publicity tool; when no dictatorship is tolerated; not even musical dictatorships imposed by disc jockeys; when all words flow without discrimination or censorship" – that is media for democracy (López Vigil, 1998). That is media for a new social justice cultural hegemony.

Just as media content by TNMCs communicates constructed meanings through the codes and conventions of entertainment genres and news frames, community-run working class media communicate their own constructions for understanding the world, promoting ways of being that encourage collective, social development for social justice, gender and ethnic equality, non-commercial entertainment, and other anti-consumerist views and behaviors. It is not just that ideas win consent for social change, but the language, symbols, and meanings expressed by working class programmers organize new norms for democratic social relations and the production of a new social order.

Participation in community media contributes to social development. Democratic communication is not merely technical or even distributional – it provides media space for dialogue, debate, argument, and interaction among citizens long denied access to the production of politics and culture. Democratic communication can demonstrate an instance of cultural hegemony for human solidarity and cooperation. In practice, democratic community media must be a public space where workers and citizens can consent to and dissent from official and majority voices.

Although community media in Venezuela are exceptional for their vitality and social impact, community media across Latin America have similar elements. As in Venezuela, many are reserves of indigenous resistance and experience, nourishing and transmitting languages and cultures. In Ecuador, "microphones transmit Spanish and Quechua, Mixteco and Guarani, Miskito and Quiché, all the languages of our land Abya Yala" (López Vigil, 1998). In Guatemala, 26 different languages are spoken and behind each language is a culture, "a determined way of understanding the world and an original way in which human beings relate to nature and each other" (López Vigil, 2007) – democratic community media cultivate and share these cultural experiences with the nation through translation and broadcast. Many community radio stations have collected the legends and myths of diverse cultures, their way of cultivation, genealogy, traditional medicine, and other customs, recording them from the mouths of grandparents and returning the wisdom to the people through programs containing the people's testimonies. Culture is also music. Community stations share regional and indigenous music, broadcasting open-air song festivals live.

Almost everywhere, from Venezuela and Nicaragua to Ecuador and Bolivia, audience participation in programming and content is the norm. Community journalists and correspondents are the lifeline of news and information on local and national events. The regional pan-Latin American teleSUR TV and SiBCI in Venezuela are the most developed networks due to the Bolivarian system of direct democracy and citizen participation, but other countries have nascent networks (e.g., CORADEP in Nicaragua; Artz, 1993) that have been or could become more effective as working classes and indigenous groups achieve political power.

If I Can't Dance, I Don't Want Your Revolution

Transnational capitalist cultural hegemony wins mass support for an unequal social order through consumerism, individualism, market values, hierarchical authority, and entertainment spectacles. Self-gratified, apolitical consumers are desired. In contrast, a cultural hegemony based on creative social development, social justice and collective, cooperative social relations depends on active participation. Passive spectatorship and political apathy will not lead to a new, more humanist culture.

Capitalist cultural hegemony saturates society (through the schools, media, churches, family) because for most people it corresponds to the reality of their social experience. Individual consumption is the organizing principle diffused into every area of daily life through which dominant culture perpetuates its capitalist morality that pits each against all. Capitalist cultural hegemony mystifies power relations and social issues and encourages a sense of fatalism and passivity towards political action. In this way, people contribute to the continued dominance of transnational capitalism by internalizing consumerist values and the social assumptions of the market as their own. Transnational entertainment media play an instrumental role in the perpetuation of this consumerist cultural hegemony. Transnational power survives and reproduces its required social relations partly through hybrid local expressions in the language, culture, ideology, and hierarchical work relations of everyday life. Without obvious alternatives, subordinate groups lack their own worldview and the cultural hegemony of consumerism appears normal and natural. We do what we know. As long as it works.

As social contradictions disrupt everyday life, options for other social relations and other explanations arise. As experience trashes old meanings, new understandings and possibilities emerge. In the 1990s, neoliberalism crushed the social pact among Venezuelan classes, smacking the working class in the face with a sudden realization that capitalism could not provide equality, justice, or even a semblance of opportunity. Through a series of confrontations, Venezuelan capitalists were displaced from government power and the Bolivarian alternative captured a mass following. Led by Hugo Chávez, the political power of social movements expanded, penetrating the false world of established appearances and leading an entirely new universe of socialist ideas and human values. The subordinate classes themselves, organized independently, have taken the initiative in a new hegemonic process, "creating a new consciousness embodied in everyday social processes, in thought and action, a thoroughgoing cultural revolution that sets out to transform all dimensions of everyday life" (Moen, 2009).

As part of the struggle for ideological hegemony in everyday life – a precondition for socialist transformation – democratic media must engage in ongoing dialog and debate with the full participation of the working class, indigenous, peasants, women, youth, and other citizens in communities across the country. Murals, posters, graffiti, street radio, puppeteers, newspapers, and guerrilla theater complement radio and television broadcasts. Through cooperative interactions, labor, community, and media activists are able to develop a collective consciousness, a "moral self-transformation, evidenced by greater self-confidence and feelings of control" (Piñeiro Harnecker, 2009, p. 512), transcending the narrow self-interest of entertainment media narratives as a sense of community emerges. The dynamics of a new way of being human are products of participants' experience with a genuinely democratic practice.

Media for a more human, democratic social order challenges audiences everywhere to think critically, consider alternatives, become media producers – all requiring active involvement. Passivity is for couch potatoes, not citizens. The essence of humanity is social interaction, productive activity. Changing the world is not a spectator sport. Social transformation cannot be given and cannot be broadcast or downloaded. It is not a gift, but a right, an action. Democracy is a right that must be *actively* unleashed and "the participatory nature of democracy is increasingly linked to the ways that communication occurs" (Martín-Barbero, 1991, p. 21). Without participation a democratic cultural hegemony cannot be built. Or, as Gil Scott-Heron so eloquently proclaimed, "The revolution will not be televised." It will be made, not watched.

The big question that democratic media for social change faces is how to attract, please, and join listeners and viewers in a new way of being – a way of being a participant in life. Of course, changing culture is not solely the responsibility of media. New social relations are required in production, education, housing, and political decision-making. Contributing to social transformation, democratic media expand participation, encouraging audiences to become producers. Radio Negro Primero, Radio Perola, Radio Macarao, Catia TV, and other community media give examples of how to "function through a constant process of assemblies, meetings, and consultation" with community members who are also programmers and technician (Fernandes, 2010, p. 183).

The best programming by community and public media in Venezuela reflects the creativity, skills, and passion of participants, in forms and styles pleasing to a society creating a new political economy and a new democratic cultural hegemony. This is not a given. Often the seriousness of political struggle and social change overwhelms leaders who undervalue social interaction. Hugo Chávez's mass appeal was primarily due to his ability to popularize politics in the vernacular of Venezuelan culture, indigenous, Christian, and working class. Democratic media will need to learn the same skills. "Making good radio has a lot to do with art. [Democratic media] need programming that's technically and aesthetically well polished, with good music, good sound effects, poetic, harmonious, attractive, pleasing, captivating" (López Vigil, 1993). Community media need content with humor, heat, argument, sensuality, practicality, drama, sentiment, music, and briskness. No ads. No MTV. No WWE. Just energetically creative content promoting the human over the mundane.

Aram Aharonian (personal communication, June 2008), director of TeleSUR, adds that social development media need "content factories" where programmers can learn and share formats, reports, features, stories, dramas, interviews, noncommercial music and more. In short, to replace the titillating spectacles of TNMC entertainment, a cultural hegemony of democracy and citizen participation needs interactive, entertaining programming – but programming that gives working class citizens the microphone and camera as they learn to express their own experiences and visions creatively. Democratizing radio to democratize society must be enjoyable. As American radical Emma Goldman once said, "If I can't dance, I don't want to be part of your revolution."

The practices and programs of ViVe, Ávila, and Catia TV differ from TNMC production and content in their participatory construction, their community origin and creation, their promotion of social development, cooperation, and social justice, and their intentional challenge to atomized consumerism and market values. And, yet community media is entertaining. On community radio and television "there are talks shows, educational programs, cultural shows, sports segments, local history programs, children's shows, cooking shows, and a variety of music programs, including salsa, bolero, hip-hop, rock, and *llanero* (country) music. Community newspapers have editorial pieces and discussion sections" with lively debates among contributors (Fernandes, 2010, p. 171). Ávila is hip. Catia is edgy. Radio Negro Primero is contemporary. Afro TV links past with now and future. Community media rising from social struggle is vibrant and fun. The Bolivarian revolution has dancers.

Girding media transformation, elements of a cultural hegemony of solidarity and cooperation can be discerned in Venezuela's economic policies and international relations. Venezuela established PetroCaribe with 16 nations (which receive lenient payment terms for Venezuelan oil purchased at 40% of the price), underwritten by the Latin American public television network teleSUR, expanded mass public transportation with rail and trolley systems, converted major industries like steel, aluminum, electricity, and concrete to public property with worker's co-management, prioritized social spending for health, education, housing, and public works. These initiatives are remarkable for their involvement and promotion of cooperatives, communal councils, labor unions, workers' councils, and social missions (Ellner, 2010). The emergence of a vibrant, energetic, nationally self-organized movement for communes suggests that a significant number of citizens and workers have already developed a new human consciousness, turning rhetoric, policies, and laws into direct action by organized communities working for socialist relations (Azzellini, 2013; Correo, 2013).

Central to the common sense of a liberating cultural hegemony is conscious action that transcends the local to reach collective decision-making on national priorities. Although political analysis of the Venezuelan revolution is far beyond the scope of this book, it seems that a national, internally democratic and participatory party of the working classes will ultimately be needed to lead the social transformation of and by citizen protagonists. To the extent that community and public media (now nationally organized in SiBCI) set public agendas, communication by and for the Venezuelan working classes may prompt ever-increasing public debate and action, a key element of a new cultural hegemonic project. Of course, in Venezuela and elsewhere, breaking with the cultural norms and commonsense experiences of self-gratification, political atomization, and deference to elite authority is not easy. Even with opportunities for media access and participatory democracy, many, many citizens have difficulty working cooperatively and elevating their world views beyond their own stiflingly narrow, but comforting consuming world. It takes time, but collective "decision-making in an egalitarian environment encourages individuals to view the interests of others in the participatory community as their own" because "community participation facilitates the development of collective consciousness" (Piñeiro Harnecker, 2009, pp. 515, 519). In other words, participatory debate and discussion can do much to overcome individualism and improve our social concern for others. Increased participation can also contribute to how media can better communicate social and economic democracy as a worthy cultural and political goal. The Bolivarian revolution in Venezuela, and its transformation of media, is a living example of democratic participation that can inspire other efforts challenging TNMC entertainment media.

Under intense pressure from mass social movements, Venezuela, Bolivia, Ecuador, Argentina, and even Uruguay have legislation regulations requiring community and public media access and stations. Exemplars for social change, Venezuelan citizens have taken to the streets and factories *and* have been directly involved in constituent assemblies, constitutional reform, social mission administration, and community and worker council initiatives for direct democracy in education, housing, production, and media. In Venezuela, citizens are making cultural hegemony, not watching history go by.

The example of ViVe and Ávila TV in Venezuela, the instances of programming from Catia TV and community radio in Caracas, and what we know of Nicaraguan radio in the 1980s and Bolivian miners' radio (Beltrán & Reyes, 1993; Gumucio-Dagron, 2005; Herrera Miller & Ramos Martín, 2013) indicate that workers, peasants, women, youth, and indigenous and ethnic groups can create and enjoy their own entertaining music, fiction, and cultural activities. One can only imagine the potential of democratic media access by working and middle classes in the United States and Europe where technology and education are more advanced and available.

Transnational entertainment media only appears natural because of its ubiquity and pervasive presence in the daily lives of millions. Like the loss of fresh water in a flood, media creations that inspire humanity have been drowned in a relentless river of consumerist entertainment. As transnational capital intrudes further into our daily existence, our need for alternative social and cultural ways of being will become more pressing. In the collective struggle of humanity to find and make more democratic social relations, citizens will realize that we need to determine information and entertainment that best serves social justice and encourages healthy creativity. The examples from Venezuela, Bolivia, and other democratic openings can direct and inspire. However, we have no need to reproduce their content for our own democratic media. As the awakened Chilean woman said, we will be making our own media, our own reality.

References

Artz, B. L. (1993). Communication and power: Popular radio in Nicaragua. *Journal of Radio Studies, 2*(1), 205–227.

Azzellini, D. (2013). The communal state: Communal councils, communes, and workplace democracy. *NACLA Report on the Americas, 46*(2), 25–30.

Beltrán, L. R., & Reyes, J. L. (1993). Radio popular en Bolivia: La lucha de obreros y campesinos para democratizar la comunicación (Popular radio in Bolivia: The struggle of workers and peasants to democratize communication). *Diálogos de la Comunicación, 35*, 14–31.

Correo del Orinoco. (2013, November 22). Building communities isn't just about defending the revolution, it's about moving forward. Venezuelanalysis. Retrieved December 15, 2013, from http://venezuelanalysis.com/analysis/10186

Ellner, S. (2010). Hugo Chávez's first decade in office: Breakthroughs and shortcomings. *Latin American Perspectives, 37*(1), 77–96.

Fernandes, S. (2010). *Who can stop the drums? Urban social movements in Chávez's Venezuela.* Greensboro, NC: Duke University Press.

Gumucio-Dagron, A. (2005). Miners' radio stations: A unique communication experience from Bolivia. In O. Hemer & T. Tufte (Eds.), *Media and global change: Rethinking communication for development* (pp. 317–324). Göteborg, Sweden: Göteborg University.

Herrera Miller, K. M., & Ramos Martín, J. (2013). Comunicación, red y lucha social: hacia la reactivación de las radios mineras de Bolivia (Communication, networking and social struggle: Toward the reactivation of miners' radio in Bolivia). *Quórum Académico, 10*(1), 11–28.

López Vigil, J. I. (1993, April). Community media in neoliberal times. *Revista Envio, 139.* Retrieved from http://www.envio.org.ni/articulo/1678

López Vigil, J. I. (1998, February). Community radios: Freedom of antenna! *Revista Envio, 199.* Retrieved from http://www.envio.org.ni/articulo/1319

López Vigil, J. I. (2007, November). Latin American radio: Six contributions to development. *Revista Envio, 316.* Retrieved from http://www.envio.org.ni/articulo/3689

Martín-Barbero, J. (1991). El tejido comunicativo de la democracia: Por una nueva perspectiva (The communication fabric of democracy: For a new perspective). *Telos, 27,* 13–22.

Moen, D. G. (2009). Public access to alternative/critical analysis: Community media in Venezuela. *Hitotsubashi Journal of Social Studies, 41*(1). Retrieved December 15, 2013, from http://dgmoen.net/blog/public-access-to-alternativecritical-analysis-community-media-in-venezuela/

Piñeiro Harnecker, C. (2009). Workplace democracy and solidarity development: An empirical study of Venezuelan cooperatives. In K. Daly, D. Schugurensky, & K. Lopes (Eds.), *Learning democracy by doing: Alternative practices in citizenship, learning, and participatory democracy* (pp. 510–524). Toronto: Ontario Institute for Studies in Education, University of Toronto.

Further Reading

Harnecker, M. (2014). *A world to build: New paths toward twenty-first century socialism.* New York: Monthly Review Press.

Index

Page numbers in **bold** refer to tables